Ronald Reagan

Few politicians in recent American history are as well known as Ronald Reagan, the fortieth U.S. president. An iconic leader, Reagan shifted the direction of American politics toward a newly vigorous conservatism. Although he began his career as a New Deal liberal, by the end of the 1950s, Reagan had embraced conservative views. His presidency saw the longest peacetime prosperity in American history, as well as the fall of the Berlin Wall and the end of the Cold War, but also skyrocketing deficits and the Iran-Contra scandal. In the twenty-first century, Reagan's legacy is both pervasive and contested, with supporters and detractors often divided along partisan lines. Yet Reagan's own actions did not always fit into partisan boxes.

In a clear-eyed and insightful narrative, James H. Broussard cuts through the mythology of both sides to produce a nuanced portrait of Reagan in his historical context. Supported by primary sources and a robust companion website, this concise biography is an ideal introduction to this fascinating president and the issues that shaped America in the late twentieth century.

James H. Broussard is Professor of History at Lebanon Valley College in Pennsylvania.

Routledge Historical Americans

Series Editor: Paul Finkelman

Routledge Historical Americans is a series of short, vibrant biographies that illuminate the lives of Americans who have had an impact on the world. Each book includes a short overview of the person's life and puts that person into historical context through essential primary documents, written both by the subjects and about them. A series website supports the books, containing extra images and documents, links to further research, and where possible, multimedia sources on the subjects. Perfect for including in any course on American History, the books in the Routledge Historical Americans series show the impact everyday people can have on the course of history.

Woody Guthrie: Writing America's Songs
Ronald D. Cohen

Frederick Douglass: Reformer and Statesman
L. Diane Barnes

Thurgood Marshall: Race, Rights, and the Struggle for a More Perfect Union
Charles L. Zelden

Harry S. Truman: The Coming of the Cold War
Nicole L. Anslover

John Winthrop: Founding the City upon a Hill
Michael Parker

John F. Kennedy: The Spirit of Cold War Liberalism
Jason K. Duncan

Bill Clinton: Building a Bridge to the New Millennium
David H. Bennett

Ronald Reagan: Champion of Conservative America
James H. Broussard

Laura Ingalls Wilder: American Writer on the Prairie
Sallie Ketcham

RONALD REAGAN
CHAMPION OF CONSERVATIVE AMERICA

JAMES H. BROUSSARD

To Bill Lynch —
a fellow Reaganite.
Jim Broussard

Routledge
Taylor & Francis Group

NEW YORK AND LONDON

www.routledge.com/cw/HistoricalAmericans

First published 2015
by Routledge
711 Third Avenue, New York, NY 10017

And by Routledge
2 Park Square, Milton Park, Abingdon, Oxon OX14 4RN

Routledge is an imprint of the Taylor & Francis Group, an informa business

Library of Congress Cataloging-in-Publication Data
Broussard, James H., 1941–
    Ronald Reagan : champion of conservative America / James H. Broussard.
        pages cm. — (Routledge historical Americans)
    Includes bibliographical references and index.
    1. Reagan, Ronald.   2. Presidents—United States—Biography.   3. United
States—Politics and government—1981–1989.   I. Title.
    E877.B76 2014
    973.927092—dc23
    [B]
    2014010253

ISBN: 978-0-415-52194-9 (hbk)
ISBN: 978-0-415-52195-6 (pbk)
ISBN: 978-0-203-08156-3 (ebk)

Typeset in Minion and Scala Sans
by Apex CoVantage, LLC

Printed and bound in the United States of America
by Edwards Brothers Malloy on sustainbly sourced paper.

Contents

Note on Reagan's Public Speeches

Quotations from Reagan's speeches as president are from *Public Papers of the Presidents of the United States: Ronald Reagan* (Washington, DC: U.S. Government Printing Office, 15 vols., 1982–1991). Unless otherwise noted, quotations from nonpresidential speeches are from Ronald Reagan, *Greatest Speeches of Ronald Reagan* (West Palm Beach, FL: NewsMax.com, 2001).

ACKNOWLEDGMENTS

I want to thank Paul Finkelman, editor of this series, for suggesting that I undertake this short biography of Ronald Reagan. During the process of writing and publication, it has been a pleasure to work with him and with Kimberly Guinta and Genevieve Aoki of Routledge.

A number of people read the chapters as they came forth: my colleagues John Hinshaw and Noel Hubler; also Michael Bowman, John Fund, Lorraine Kuchmy, and Grover Norquist. I received especially valuable suggestions and corrections from Earl Baker, John Belohlavek, Kenneth Carr, Charlie Gerow, Larry Hart, Paul Kengor, and Paul Finkelman.

The staffs of the Lebanon Valley College Library and the Eureka College Library helped me track down research materials, and John Morris of the Ronald W. Reagan Society at Eureka College devoted several hours to interesting and detailed discussions.

I am especially grateful to Lebanon Valley College for a research grant to defray travel expenses and a course release toward the end of the writing process that allowed me to finish the manuscript in good time.

Despite all the advice and assistance mentioned above, I claim sole personal credit for any remaining mistakes of fact and infelicities of style.

Finally, my most important debt is to my wife, Margaret, for putting up with nearly three years of constant talk about Reagan.

PART **I**

RONALD REAGAN

CHAPTER 1

A PLACE TO GO BACK TO

Dixon, Illinois, is the only town in America with a statue of Abraham Lincoln as a young soldier. It was here at Fort Dixon that Lincoln and other volunteers assembled in 1832 to fight the Black Hawk War. A quarter-century later, Lincoln was back in Dixon, speaking for the infant Republican Party and its first presidential candidate, John Fremont. Just four years later Dixon gave its votes to Lincoln himself, sending him to Washington to save the Union.

It was only fitting, then, that Ronald Reagan, whom Republicans rank with Lincoln as the two great names in their party's history, should grow up in this town so closely identified with the first Republican president. Like many adults, he later said that "everyone needs a place to go back to."[1] For him, Dixon would be that place.

But Reagan's history, like that of almost all Americans, begins not here but across the water. His father's ancestors came from County Tipperary, where, like many Irish Catholic families, they toiled for generations in extreme poverty, working the land of wealthy barons. After the great Potato Famine of the 1840s that killed a million Irish, the president's great-grandfather, Michael, took his family across the ocean and settled in northern Illinois as a farmer of modest means.

Michael's son John eventually left farming to work in the little town of Fulton, where Ronald Reagan's father, Jack, was born in 1883. Leaving school after sixth grade, Jack went to work in a dry goods store. Shoes were his specialty in the store and alcohol outside it, and when he met and courted a fellow employee, Nelle Wilson, her father did not approve. Nevertheless, the two were married in 1904 in the local Catholic church.

Like Jack Reagan's grandfather, Nelle's had come to the New World in the mid-1800s. A Scottish Protestant, he too wound up in Illinois, married a local woman, and settled down as a farmer. His son Thomas married an immigrant Englishwoman and in 1883 produced a daughter, Nelle Wilson. The family was strictly and enthusiastically religious and frowned on alcohol, hence Thomas Wilson's dislike of Jack Reagan as a suitable match for his daughter—but marry they did.

The new couple moved from Fulton to Tampico in 1906, both aged 23. Tampico was a town of barely 1,000 people and a single block of paved streets, an isolated oasis of houses in a vast desert of cornfields. Both Jack and Nelle had spent their early lives on farms and felt comfortably at home here for eight years, although their first apartment, like most in town, had no running water or indoor plumbing.

Jack, ambitious and optimistic, worked at the biggest place in town, Pitney's General Store. He also served on the town council and was an officer in his church and the local fire company. When his wife was not making the family's clothes or carrying water and coal up three flights of stairs to cook their meals, she found time to write poetry. She liked drama, he liked to dance, and as the historian Edmund Morris put it, they were "Tampico's reigning theatrical couple."[2]

Here Ronald Reagan was born on February 6, 1911, in the apartment above his father's store, two and a half years after his older brother Neil. Jack Reagan thought the new baby looked like a "fat little Dutchman," and the child grew up wanting to be called "Dutch" because "Ronald" seemed too sissified. A few months after his birth the family moved up, renting a house with a view of the park with its Civil War cannon and little pyramid of cannon balls.

It was a nice house, and in 1913 Jack even bought a Model T car, but this was only a temporary taste of prosperity and the beginning of a peripatetic existence that continued through Dutch Reagan's entire childhood. Tampico soon proved too confining to encompass Jack's dreams of shoe-salesman stardom, and when the boy was only two, the family moved to Chicago. It took his father nearly two years of poor sales and an arrest for public drunkenness to realize that working in a huge department store in a huge city was not to his liking.

This was the first of the Reagans' low points. They lived in a cold-water apartment with coin-operated gas and were so poor that they literally ate cat food. Unable to afford a standard cut of meat, Nelle sent the boys to the butcher's on weekends for a soupbone and a pound of liver for a nonexistent "family cat." People thought liver was good only for pet food, but the Reagans would cook it as their Sunday dinner and then live off the soupbone, with a few vegetables added, for the rest of the week.

After Jack's arrest and firing, it was off to Galesburg and another department store for a few years until he lost that job, again for drinking. Then the family moved down the road to Monmouth for a year, where Dutch showed early promise in school, being promoted ahead of his class. His mother's love for acting echoed in him as well, and the youngster began to join her in recitations at church. But his father, always imagining more success in the next town, took the family back to Tampico when Dutch was eight. Mr. Pitney needed help at the old store.

Tampico at least was familiar, and Dutch continued to prosper as an "A" student in the fifth grade and led the "West Side Gang" in childhood tussles. The Reagans were still poor, but so were many others in the little town. Dutch's best friend said that "when our shoes wore out we put cardboard in the bottoms and when we got holes in our stockings we painted in shoe polish to cover 'em up."[3] The bicycle the Reagan boys shared was one of the few in town and even it was secondhand.

The full measure of Tampico's isolation from the outside world can be seen in the excitement of nine-year-old Dutch and his friends on first hearing Pittsburgh's radio station KDKA on a primitive crystal set. "We passed the headphones around," he remembered, "and heard this orchestra playing, coming out of the air! . . . That was a miracle."[4]

Shortly before Dutch Reagan's tenth birthday, the opportunity for success that his father had always sought finally arrived. Mr. Pitney was opening a fancy new store, the Fashion Boot Shop, in nearby Dixon, Illinois, and offered Jack a partnership, to be paid for out of his sales commissions. The wandering family had finally come to rest, and Dixon was Dutch's home until he left for college.

A century before the Reagans arrived, this area had been the raw frontier, but by the 1850s the Rock River was dammed to provide power for local mills. In the following decades, growth was slow but steady as farms filled up the countryside and the town became both their market and their source of supply. A hundred miles west of Chicago, Dixon had about 8,000 people in 1920. Although the town sat amid a circle of dairy farms, nearly half of its people worked in manufacturing. Served by two railroad lines, Dixon's factories turned out shoes, cement, tractors, wire, and animal feed for the agricultural Midwest.

It was a typical small city of medium-sized frame houses, and the modest downtown had a single movie theater, the standard drugstore with obligatory soda fountain, and a memorial to the honored dead of World War I. Like many rural places, it hosted Chautauqua lectures in the summer with their mixture of education, inspiration, and entertainment. For those more interested in outdoor recreation there was Lowell Park.

There were few African-American families in Dixon, and as usual in 1920s America they were not allowed on the golf course, at the hotel, or in the local barber and beauty shops. Still, this was not the rigid and ruthless segregation of the South; churches, schools, and the movie theater were integrated, and the Reagans were not the only white family whose children thought it perfectly normal to play with black friends and bring them home for meals.

Throughout his life, Ronald Reagan always spoke with pride of his father's opposition to any form of bigotry. As a Catholic himself, Jack Reagan had no use for the Ku Klux Klan, which targeted both blacks and Catholics in the 1920s. When one of the most famous early movies, *Birth of a Nation*, came to Dixon, he refused to let the boys attend because it glorified the Klan "against the colored folks and I'm damned if anyone in this family will go see it."[5] On another occasion when he stopped at a hotel on a sales trip, the desk clerk assured him that no Jews were allowed in. Jack walked right outside and slept in his car instead.

As an adult, Ronald Reagan displayed not the slightest shred of racial prejudice. His father's example and his formative years in a place where the few black families seemed to fit naturally into the life of the town, helped to shape this aspect of Reagan's character. At the same time, the almost invisible black presence in Dixon kept him from fully realizing what it meant to live everyday life as a second-class citizen.

Like most northern whites in nearly all-white communities, Reagan presumably never thought, for instance, of the hurdles a black family would experience when traveling. Unwelcome at nearly all motels and restaurants on their route, black travelers were constantly reminded that they were the bottom rail of American society. Reagan never commented in his adult life about the exclusion of African Americans even in Dixon itself from such places as the barber shop and the hotel. Probably it never entered his mind while he was growing up. Even in college, a classmate believed that Dutch was "not conscious of race at all."[6] His biographer Edmund Morris concluded that "a youth unaware of evil must also be unaware of evil's effects."[7]

So while he came to manhood without prejudice, he was also without a full emotional realization of the simply ordinary, taken-for-granted, casual racism that made its constant impact on the daily life of blacks even in the North, not to speak of the much cruder, more powerful, and more brutal discrimination in the South, where most African Americans lived. In this, Reagan was perfectly typical of most white people in the nearly all-white rural areas of the North.

Arriving in Dixon in December 1920, the Reagans rented a two-story house on South Hennepin Avenue, preserved today as "Ronald Reagan's

Boyhood Home." But Jack's hope of prosperity at the Fashion Boot Shop soon began to fade, and in 1923 the family had to relocate to a smaller house where the boys slept on an enclosed porch. Even this was not the end of the line; there were three more moves before 1928. Dutch always had to wear Neil's hand-me-down clothes and shoes and only got his "own" clothes when he left for college.

As a normal young boy of the 1920s, he loved movies, especially westerns. Like Granny of the *Beverly Hillbillies*, his favorite actors were Tom Mix and William S. Hart. Dutch also liked to read, and soon after the move to Dixon, ten-year-old Dutch got his own card at the town library and quickly put it to good use, averaging two books a week. Probably few boys that age ever go through 100 books a year.

Thus began a lifelong habit; his son Ron said decades later that the adult Reagan never felt right without something to read. Most of young Dutch's books were the usual preteen selections: adventure stories, science fiction, westerns, tales of the Indians and of medieval knights. He later said that his avid reading "left an abiding belief in the triumph of good over evil."[8]

One book in particular made a deep impression. Just as he turned eleven, he happened upon *That Printer of Udell's*, now an obscure title but then part of the widely read juvenile novels of Christian author Harold Bell Wright. It is the story of Dick Falkner, a son of poverty whose father had been an alcoholic. Penniless but ambitious, Dick arrives a stranger in a new town. He hires on with the local printer, finds that he has a talent for eloquence, joins the Disciples of Christ church, and resolves to help the city's deserving poor.

Scorning the idea of a bureaucratic "poverty program," he convinces a group of the benevolent rich to fund a shelter-for-work plan. Private citizens, not government, meet the need. Soon Dick's likeability and power as a speaker get him elected to Congress, and as the book ends he is just stepping out into that wider world. When Dutch finished the story he told his mother, "I want to be like that man."[9]

What a temptation for the psychohistorians, especially as Dick, like the adult Reagan, was partial to brown suits. Yet one must recognize that of the thousands of boys who read the same book, only one became Ronald Reagan. Still, the story made a powerful impression, and he remembered it well many decades later. Rather than shaping who he would become, it probably simply reflected who he already was—or wished he were.

One other event at age eleven made an even stronger impression. There is no better way to describe it than in his own words: "I came home to find my father flat on his back on the front porch. . . . He was drunk, dead to the world. . . . I wanted to let myself in the house and go to bed and pretend he wasn't there. . . . I felt myself fill with grief for my father at the same time I was feeling sorry for myself."[10] The boy reached down, grabbed his father's overcoat, and "managed to drag him inside and get him to bed." Another time some years later, Jack staggered home without the family car and could not remember where he had left it. Dutch, then a young man, had to roam the streets of Dixon until he found the automobile in an intersection, the motor still running.

Jack Reagan struggled with alcohol all of his adult life. He was not an abusive man, and his drunkenness came in sporadic binges rather than an ongoing daily haze, but it had cost him at least two jobs and produced many a nighttime argument with Nelle. Like many wives of alcoholics, she taught her sons not to blame their father, that his behavior was a sickness. Dutch apparently never talked about Jack's drunken episodes until he revealed them in his 1960s autobiography, *Where's The Rest of Me?*

The constant uprootings of his first ten years and the impact of his father's condition may have shaped one of the most pronounced features of Reagan's personality. From childhood on, he was a very private person. This might seem odd in one so gregarious and so fond of the spotlight—the life-guard, the radio personality, the actor, and the avid politician. It is a common trait in those who have to move often as children—those whose parents are in the military, for instance—and in the children of alcoholics. Both of these circumstances were present in Reagan's early years.

Growing up in the time before Dixon, he made friends easily but then had to leave them behind in the family's next move—a pattern repeated five times in nine years. Even when the Reagans settled down in Dixon, the growing boy seemed quieter than most. While his brother played with other boys, Dutch played with lead Civil War soldiers and read his two books a week. Later, Neil hung around the pool hall; Dutch took elocution lessons from his mother. He also took up competitive swimming and was good at it. One biographer has commented that swimming is even lonelier than long-distance running and, noting "Reagan's cool, unhurried progress through crises of politics and personnel," concluded that "he sees the world as a swimmer sees it."[11]

Year by year, Neil grew closer to his gregarious father, while Dutch, like his mother, found comfort in the church. The Disciples of Christ stressed education, individual responsibility, and racial equality, and they abhorred liquor; the saloon-busting Carrie Nation was one of the flock. They also believed that baptism should be a voluntary act, postponed until the age of reason. Dutch was brought into the church by full immersion in 1920 and heard the pastor intone, "Arise, and walk in newness of faith."

Nelle was the choir director, taught adult Sunday school, and led the women's missionary society. She prayed often, "like she knew God personally," one person said, "like she had had lots of dealings with Him before."[12]

Even when she had to take in a roomer and do sewing to make ends meet at home, Nelle insisted that the family tithe to the church.

Soon she began involving Dutch in church dramatic skits and by age fifteen he was leading prayer meetings himself. He had always been innately polite, and he developed a gracious, easy manner with adults—not something one finds in every teenaged boy. His mother taught him that disappointments and defeats in life were part of God's plan.

There is much else in the doctrine of the Disciples of Christ that, slowly absorbed by the young Dutch, became part of his adult personality. The assumption that America was a blessed land, set apart by God for a special mission in human history, the optimistic belief in progress, the emphasis on private charity to heal the world's ills—all these found a place in his rhetoric and public actions. He once told the pastor of his Dixon days that "all the hours in the old church . . . and all of Nelle's faith have come together in a kind of inheritance without which I'd be lost and helpless."[13]

By the time high school came around, Dutch had filled out physically and was a muscular, attractive young man with a mellow voice and a quiet confidence. Of the two high schools in town, the Northside was more upscale and academic; the Southside was rougher and drew its students chiefly from Dixon's factory families. Though neither parent had gone beyond elementary school, both insisted that the boys get a good education in hopes of attending college. Jack moved to the Northside so Dutch could go to that school, although it meant a smaller house and a long walk to work at the Fashion Boot Shop.

The high school years began to give hints about the future direction of Reagan's adult life. Despite poor vision—he had to wear embarrassingly thick glasses even to see the blackboard—he did reasonably well in class thanks to a photographic memory. But, as often happens with high school students, classrooms were not the center of Dutch Reagan's teenage life. In particular, sports drew him in.

Kept out of baseball by his poor eyesight, he played basketball, excelled as a swimmer, and especially threw himself into football. He suffered a frustrating two years on the bench while better players marched down the field, but Dutch memorized the plays and won the coach's praise for "grinding it out" in practice. Finally, in his junior year the day came when the coach ran down the starting lineup, read off the list until he got to right guard, and called out: "Reagan." Not the most glamorous position to play, but he was on the varsity, had grown to his adult height of six feet, and had become a Big Man on Campus.

No wonder classes seemed secondary. Dutch also found time for a number of student clubs and would have joined the Boy Scouts but was too poor to afford the uniform. His fellow students elected him president, and he was the art director of the yearbook, which he organized like a movie script, progressing from scene to scene. He even added drawings of himself along the way as director of the show. Was this a hint of his Hollywood future or simply a coincidental touch of egotistical "senioritis"?

Dutch found acting quite to his taste and wound up leading the Drama Club; this was the one thing that could seriously compete with sports for his attention. Encouraged by his English teacher, he developed a particular interest in literature and the theater. The teacher thought him the best actor in the club, able to handle a wide range of roles. Being up front on the stage, learning to project emotion through the parts he played, absorbing the approval of an audience—Dutch enjoyed it all.

Even more did he enjoy a budding relationship with Margaret Cleaver, the daughter of Reverend Ben Cleaver, pastor of Dixon's Disciples of Christ church where Dutch and his mother could be found every Sunday. Petite, pretty, and cultured, she was the best student at Northside High. When Dutch was president of the student body, Margaret was senior class president, and they both acted in the Drama Club and worked together on the school yearbook. From the beginning, Dutch was smitten, but she kept things merely friendly until they knew each other well. By the time of the senior banquet, everyone knew the two were officially a couple.

Despite their growing closeness, Margaret said that she never did fully understand her boyfriend. She found him charming, polite, almost painfully kind, but there was some inner part of him that seemed always out of reach. Significantly, the biggest argument they had was over Jack's drunken behavior; she was quite upset when Dutch repeated his mother's explanation that alcoholism was a sickness, not a moral failing.

While he was finding a talent for acting, making the grade in football, and growing closer to his girlfriend, Dutch was spending his summers in the job that brought him his first public recognition—lifeguarding. In 1926 Dutch signed on as a summer lifeguard at Dixon's Lowell Park. For $18 a week and all the soft drinks and food he could eat, he worked twelve hours a day, seven days a week, for the next seven summers. Lowell Park was a half-square-mile stretch of forest straddling the Rock River, a deep and swift stream dangerously attractive to swimmers. Drownings were not unknown. At his father's suggestion, he began making a notch on a log every time he had to dive in to save a floundering swimmer, and eventually the total reached 77. Quite a few of the rescues were written up in the local newspaper, marking Reagan's first appearance as a celebrity.

It was a considerable responsibility for a teenager, keeping watch over a constantly changing crowd in the water, and the job helped Dutch develop an ability to work independently. (Coincidentally, one of the lives he guarded was that of little Dwayne Andreas, who grew up to become, fifty years later, Mikhail Gorbachev's closest American friend.) Like football and the Drama Club, being a lifeguard fed his need to be the object of attention. It was fun, he said, "because I was the only one up there. . . . It was like a stage. Everyone had to look at me."[14] And, of course, there was the intense satisfaction of doing heroic things; he did save people's lives. The ultimate compliment came from his boss: "we had a good lifeguard; there was no bodies at the bottom."[15]

As he graduated high school, Dutch was a happy young man. He knew he was a good football player, an even better swimmer, and a talented actor. He was an elected student leader and had a steady girlfriend. Almost as an afterthought, he managed a B average in his classes with little effort. What he wrote under his picture in the yearbook summed it up: "life is just one grand sweet song, so start the music."

How does one assess these years from birth through high school? Is the human personality firmly fixed by experiences early in life? In its most general sense, history is a series of case studies in human behavior: why did people do what they did, and what were the consequences of their actions? In short, history is about psychoanalyzing dead people. From this assumption grew the field of psychohistory, asserting that studying a person's childhood can yield hints about the values, beliefs, and actions of the adult. And so might it be with Ronald Reagan: in the career of the adult one might see the life of the child writ large. Hence, his biographers have examined the future president's early years for clues to the development of his adult personality and beliefs.

Growing up as Reagan did—if not in poverty, then certainly in very straitened circumstances—certainly might have had an impact on his future habits of thought and action. It is well established that children of alcoholics usually carry some clear marks of that ordeal into their adult lives. The deeply religious attitude of Nelle Reagan and her determination to impress on her son the moral values of her own faith can also be seen in his adult years. Even the small-town environment, with nature lying just beyond the last row of houses, and the willingness of neighbors to help the needy, might affect how the boy grown to manhood sees his world.

Still, one should not be tempted to see the Ronald Reagan of history as inflexibly formed by his early circumstances. Typical of this is one biographer's belief that Reagan's small-town upbringing explains "the simple moral and conservative approach he brought to public life," a personality "determinedly conservative; mistrusting of change."[16] The difficulty with this analysis is that Reagan did not become a conservative until he was forty years old and had put Dixon far behind him.

From his teenage years right through college and almost until the end of his career in movies, he was a New Deal Democrat who idolized Franklin

Roosevelt. He was an example of what conservatives today mock as a "Hollywood liberal" from the "Left Coast." As with everyone, Reagan's early years no doubt did help to shape his adult personality, but one must look elsewhere for the source of his political conservatism as a governor and president.

It is significant that Dutch and his brother, Neil, lived the same life from birth to college but emerged with different impressions of those years. Dutch had placid, almost fond, memories of his family's hard economic times, "the days when I learned the real riches of rags." He said that "we were poor, but we didn't know we were poor" because so many other families were, too.[17] Neil, two years older, rendered a more blunt verdict: "we were poor, and I *mean* poor."[18] Two boys, same family, same years—but two different responses to that common experience.

Going out into the world after high school, they had different expectations as well. Only one in fifty American high school graduates went off to college that fall, but the Reagans wanted their boys to be in that select group. Neil disappointed his parents by going straight to a job at the local cement plant, but Dutch set his sights on Eureka College, one hundred miles away, largely because his girlfriend Margaret was headed there. They drove off together in September 1928, bound for his next adventure.

Eureka was even then an old college, founded by antislavery members of the Disciples of Christ church in 1855. It was only the third college in America to admit female students equally with men and tried to help as many poor students as possible by keeping tuition low. With its red brick buildings, plentiful ivy, and sweeping green lawns, Eureka might have had a faculty of only twenty, but it looked every bit a genuine college.

It had always been a small place in a small town. Eureka, Illinois, had no traffic light and only a few hundred families in 1928, although it claimed to be the pumpkin capital of the world. The college itself enrolled two hundred students and was almost proud of being perpetually poor. The most recent history of the institution, looking back from the more prosperous 1980s, speaks of recurrent financial problems throughout the first century of existence. Still, there were things to make students and alumni smile—winning teams in football and basketball, a thriving "Greek" social life, and a fall picnic on Flunk Hill when students skipped classes, listened to radical speakers, and generally ate too much.

The connection to the Disciples of Christ meant strict rules for students— no smoking, drinking, or dancing, and daily chapel service, all of which President Bert Wilson enforced to the letter. With its small-town location, church affiliation, and stern leadership, Eureka floated placidly in an educational backwater, almost untouched by the stronger currents of the "Roaring Twenties." Raccoon coats, bobbed hair, "petting parties," and a cynical secularism might have been the order of the day in higher education elsewhere, but not at Eureka.

It was to this highly disciplined, financially challenged school that Dutch Reagan arrived in the fall of 1928. He had become quite a handsome, thoroughly confident young man, although his conservative clothes and horn-rimmed glasses made him look somewhat the "nerd." Toting his belongings in a large steamer trunk, he had $400 in his pocket for the year's expenses, had already pledged Tau Kappa Epsilon, and would live at the "frat house" for all four years.

The college had an open-admissions policy for any high school graduate, but his challenge was to pay the bill. He got a half-tuition athletic scholarship and earned free meals by washing dishes at the fraternity house, but he still had to pay for his room, the other half of his tuition, and miscellaneous expenses. To his regular dishwashing job Dutch added working at the college steam plant and coaching the swim team, and he spent each summer at his regular lifeguard job in Dixon. Even so, he wound up flat broke at graduation. It was a hard existence but not an unusual one, especially once the full financial brutality of the Great Depression hit the college, the students, and their families.

Just as the young Dutch arrived on campus, peaceful Eureka found itself swept by a genuine rebellion. President Wilson had pushed students too far with his strict regulations and angered the faculty with cuts in several programs. The college's dire financial straits were true enough, but Wilson's effort to face reality sparked an emotional backlash. With some faculty encouragement, a majority of the student body petitioned the trustees, demanding the president's removal.

Shortly before classes adjourned for Thanksgiving, the chapel bell summoned everyone to a midnight rally. Hardly on the scene long enough to unpack his trunk, Dutch was chosen to represent the freshman class at the big meeting. Just as when he was on the stage or saving swimmers from the Rock River, he was in the limelight that night, and he loved it. In a rousing speech he urged the students to go on strike.

Strike they did, boycotting classes after Thanksgiving break. A week later the president was gone, and Dutch Reagan had made his mark on campus. Decades later he still marveled at the sensations of that evening. He had discovered "that an audience has a feel to it, . . . that the audience and I were together. . . . It was heady wine."[19]

Everyone got something from the week of upheaval. Wilson went on to a better job, the trustees tightened their oversight, the faculty escaped major cuts, the students enjoyed an extra-long holiday—and Dutch had his first standing ovation. The college survived and in future decades grew and prospered. The Eureka that Reagan frequently revisited later in life was far stronger than the struggling school he attended.

The new freshman found that Eureka reminded him of Dixon itself. The college's hard times only reflected those of his own experience, and "bound us all together, much as a poverty-stricken family is bound."[20] The Disciples of Christ influence would have been comfortably familiar to a young man so closely bound up with his mother's increasing activities in the hometown church. The student body, too, might have been transplanted from Dixon—children of rural and small-town Midwestern families, almost all white, and few—except Margaret Cleaver—very sophisticated.

Dutch and Margaret continued their budding high school romance; everyone knew that she was his "steady girl" from their first day on campus. Like other impecunious student couples, they had cheap dates eating ice cream at the drug store or wandering through the cemetery, and they talked about postgraduate dreams and politics—he being, like his father, a devout liberal Democrat in this redoubt of rural Republicanism.

Dutch hoped to be a radio announcer, but, despite her fondness for him, Margaret doubted that he would ever amount to much. His grades were barely adequate, while she was at the head of her class and talked of going overseas and studying other cultures. Around campus she was called "Young Miss Brains," while his nickname was merely "Mr. Congeniality."

They did both excel at one thing: the theater. Dutch joined her in the Dramatic Club and got most of the male leads. He had a certain bearing, a presence that attracted attention, and he carried himself in a way "that made him seem at once proud and humble." His voice was mellow and easily modulated, projecting confidence and "the humility and passion of a true believer."[21] These were great advantages in the Dramatic Club, as they were later to be in Hollywood and politics.

As in Dixon High, college class work was not a high priority for Dutch. Football was his true calling, and it was a stunning disappointment when he missed the varsity squad. "It was tough," he said, "to go . . . from first string end to the end of the bench,"[22] although he did at least shine as a swimmer. Finally, as a junior, he won his spot on the first team. In fact, Dutch threw himself into all sports that year, snaring a varsity letter in track as well as football and actually coaching the swim team.

Besides dramatics, sports, and his on-campus jobs, Dutch found still more ways to take his attention away from his actual classes. He was president of the Booster Club and editor of the yearbook, and his lingering acclaim from the "student strike" speech as a freshman won him election as a student senator and then as senior class president. With his success on the stage, on the gridiron, and in student politics, it was a satisfying time for one who craved applause and wanted life to be "one sweet song."

Dutch left a stack of creative writing papers in which one historian finds "an ardent, if dreamy young man."[23] Many were sports stories and a few dealt with drinking problems like Jack Reagan's. The longest, "Moral Victory: A Football Story" features a player who, fed up with wearing himself out in a losing game, quits the team in angry frustration but eventually calls himself back to do his duty.

They reflect Dutch's dual personality—outgoing but reserved—and show "a tall, genial, good-looking boy" going about his business, "unconcerned with the agitation of others." Most of the stories also illustrate the protagonist's "intense delight at being looked at," as Dutch himself had felt perched atop the lifeguard stand on Rock River.[24]

Each summer in his college years, Dutch resumed his lifeguard role at Lowell Park, where the younger swimmers increasingly regarded him as a local hero. The row of notches on the "official log," each one marking a swimmer saved, grew longer by the season, and it was taken for granted in Dixon that he would someday win renown as a champion swimmer. A side benefit of the job, and of occasional caddying at the country club, was that Dutch got to know several wealthy Chicago families who spent their summer in the area, among them Philip Wrigley, the chewing-gum king, and Charles Walgreen, the drug-store tycoon. From time to time he asked their advice about postcollege opportunities.

As their senior year drew to a close, he and Margaret seemed closer than ever. After Dutch made his last speech as senior class president, Reverend Cleaver gave the final commencement blessing, and all the students stood in a circle holding a rope of ivy. Then they broke it, signaling their departure into the wider world. The two sweethearts kept their strand intact, the traditional Eureka symbol that they would remain a couple after graduation.

But would they? Margaret was eager for broader possibilities than farm country could provide; her father had always taught her that women, while not neglecting home and hearth, should think boldly about careers as well. Even in college, she had spent a year at the University of Illinois while Dutch was happy in Eureka's more sheltered academic world. A year after graduation, she was off to France, far beyond her boyfriend's rural horizons.

Dutch himself was not sure what to do. He boasted to his fraternity brothers that he would be making $5,000 a year within five years, but that seemed a brash dream. College expenses and his family's pinched finances had left him broke; he could not even afford a senior ring. Success in high school and college endeavors had built his confidence that he could achieve great things out in the world, but what things? His real hope was to be an actor, but that seemed too foolish to mention.

Meantime, there was his family to think of. While the son had flourished at college, the same years had not been so kind to his family. Jack Reagan's dream of full partnership in a successful upscale shoe store never came to pass. He became so discouraged that he left the Fashion Boot Shop and for two years worked out of Springfield, almost two hundred miles away, as a traveling sales-man. Even this ended on Christmas Eve, 1931, when Jack was fired.

Like millions of others, he had fallen victim to the Great Depression and was unemployed throughout the next year. Although Nelle continued work-ing at a dress shop while Dutch was in college, the family was financially squeezed even before Jack's job vanished. They moved out of their house to an apartment, and then to a smaller apartment, and finally had to sublet all but a single room in which they slept, ate, and cooked on a hotplate. To help them out, neighbors often brought meals over, and some of Dutch's lifeguard earn-ings went simply to buy food for the family. A fortunate turn in the family's economic position came in 1933. As a lifetime enthusiastic Democrat, Jack had worked hard for Al Smith in 1928 and for Franklin Roosevelt's 1932 presidential campaign, spending many an hour at the Dixon Democratic headquarters. Dutch showed his own colors on the lifeguard stand by flaunting an FDR pin on his swimming suit. In November 1932, President Herbert Hoover carried Lee County, but Roosevelt swept Illinois and the country, much to the delight of the Reagans, both father and son.

Dutch loved the new president's "fireside chats" over the radio, but more to the point, Jack snared a patronage appointment with the Federal Emer-gency Relief Administration. Considering Ronald Reagan's future fulmina-tions against federal bureaucrats, it is ironic that it was this very stroke of luck that lifted the Reagan family out of the mass of the unemployed and rescued them from even more debilitating poverty. Another political plum came the family's way when Neil Reagan was made district representative for the Federal Reemployment Bureau.

Having graduated college with no job in prospect, Dutch spent one final summer as a lifeguard, making his last few rescues from the river's unpre-dictable currents. His great desire was still to become an actor, as he remem-bered his triumph over competitors from haughty Ivy League schools in a prestigious collegiate drama contest.

No door seemed to open toward the theater, so the young man turned to radio as an alternate way to perform for an audience. In September 1932, Dutch hitchhiked all the way to Chicago, the regional radio capital. Compe-tition for the few available jobs was fierce, and all the major networks turned him away without even an interview. "Go out in the sticks . . . and try some of the smaller stations," he was told.[25]

It was good advice. Defeated but still determined, he drove to the nearest substantial town: Davenport, Iowa. He was about to be turned down there, too, until the manager asked him to broadcast an imaginary football game. Reagan produced a convincing recreation of a Eureka College contest, and when he finished, he heard the magic words: "be here Saturday." Dutch had his foot in the door. It might have opened barely a crack—he was hired to do only the last four local games of the season—but soon enough it would swing wide and lead him into bigger things than he had ever imagined.

The station's call letters, WOC, referred to the World of Chiropractic, whose millionaire owner, in addition to the radio station, a medical center, and the Davenport newspaper, had interests around the world and a nice collection of human spines. Dutch did his temporary work well enough to be taken on permanently at $100 a month. After sending his mother $20 and his brother, Neil, $10 for college, he had barely enough left for a room and meals.

Still, he enjoyed the job immensely and when WOC merged with its larger partner WHO in Des Moines next year, he was hired as the chief sports announcer for $2,400—good pay for the times. Iowa's major city and state capital was far bigger than anywhere Reagan had lived before—it had dozens of movie theaters and hotels to Dixon's one of each, and 140,000 people to Dixon's 8,000—but he seemed to fit right in with his pleasing blend of confidence and friendly modesty. For a boy who still dreamed of being an actor, here was a much larger stage upon which to prepare for his craft. Soon he became a favorite of the owner, interviewing important local people and visitors between sports events.

Dutch made many longtime friends at the station, especially a fellow announcer and future conservative congressman, H. R. Gross, with whom he had endless political discussions. Gross never budged from his views, and Reagan remained a New Deal Democrat, but the two formed a bond that lasted into the 1970s, by which time the California governor and the Iowa congressman shared the same conservative ideology.

The rise of radio was one of the most powerful forces breaking down the cultural isolation of rural America in the 1920s and 1930s. As the boxy receivers found a place in more living rooms and parlors, the news, entertainment, and advertising beamed from big cities reached a growing audience on farms and in small towns. "Real-time" sports news, made possible by a partnership of telegraph and radio, was an especially welcome garnish to the often drab flatness of rural existence. The play-by-play from a big-league baseball game went out over the wire to radio stations in far-distant places. There, the man at the mike would expand a terse "Smith flies out to right" into a tense, emotion-packed few minutes of colorful description for the listeners in radioland.

Dutch Reagan was a master at this semi-fictional embellishment of telegraphic reports from Chicago Cubs games. He recreated the scene so vividly that the radio audience could well imagine him really broadcasting from Wrigley Field. From a fifty-square-foot studio at WHO, the powerful 50,000-watt NBC affiliate in Des Moines, Reagan's voice reached throughout the Midwest in the mid-1930s, bringing entertainment to farm-belt families stricken by the Great Depression.

His most famous radio incident showed his knowledge of baseball, ability to think quickly, and coolness under pressure. He was broadcasting a Cubs game, embellishing the cryptic notes passed to him by the telegrapher, when the instrument went dead. With nothing to announce, Reagan had to think up something for the batter to do that would not show in the record books. Foul balls would work, so he strung out the telegraph's silent minutes by describing in imaginary detail the batter's repeated foul tips, stalling until the machine finally came back to life after six nervous minutes.

As a major regional clear-channel station, WHO offered much more than just sports. It carried popular comedy shows like "Fibber McGee and Molly," "Lum and Abner," and "The Great Gildersleeve," as well as interviews with the leading names in sports, film, and popular culture. Reagan himself did many of these one-on-one conversations with such personalities as James Cagney and Leslie Howard of Hollywood, the revivalist Aimee Semple McPherson, and world champion boxer Max Baer.

Within little more than a year, Dutch Reagan had become a "man about town" in Des Moines, frequently pictured in the newspapers and attracting a retinue of fans. One of his several local girlfriends said that "he was a born politician, courting important people, wanting goodwill,"[26] which he had in abundance. Beyond the city, he was almost a celebrity to his Midwestern listening audience, such a valuable "property" that the station raised him to $3,900 a year (equivalent to nearly $60,000 today). He was all of twenty-three years old.

By 1934 Dutch had gone from newcomer with a shaky future at the station to having his own show twice a day. The owner liked him, the listeners liked him, and he liked what he did. With his job apparently secure and his salary rising along with his status, he was in a fine position to marry Margaret Cleaver and settle down in Des Moines. But, to his dismay, she was no longer his. Margaret had gone abroad seeking the wider world and had met a young man far more cosmopolitan than Dutch. She fell in love with him and dropped her high school and college beau.

Although he said that Margaret's decision "shattered" him, Dutch had already begun dating other women in Des Moines. As his radio reputation grew, so did his ability to attract congenial female companions. He was a regular at some of the best nightclubs and was the center of an ever-larger social circle.

He also discovered Camp Dodge, where the 14th U.S. Cavalry Regiment was stationed outside of town. Ever since his boyhood fascination with cowboy movies, Dutch had liked horses. He learned that as a reserve officer in the regiment, he could ride without the expense of actually owning a mount. By faking his eye exam, taking correspondence courses, and attending the occasional on-post class, he earned a reserve commission and then rode to his heart's content.

After two more years of growing radio fame and local popularity, Dutch might have settled in permanently to his comfortable niche in the upper element of Des Moines's "younger set." For his family back in Dixon, he was able to send home much-needed monthly checks and had even gotten his brother a radio job. Yet all this was not enough. He still regarded radio simply as preparation for becoming an actor. This craving had grown stronger as he interviewed, one by one, the stream of movie stars passing through Des Moines. At last he devised a way in 1936 to have a taste of Hollywood without giving up his comfortable radio life.

The Chicago Cubs took spring training on Catalina Island, just offshore from Los Angeles, and Dutch convinced the station that his popular broadcast of Cubs' games would be even better if he got to know the players. The twenty-five-year-old Dutch thoroughly enjoyed being around men he had regarded as sports heroes, and they, in turn, respected him as a fellow athlete and not some "microphone nerd" who knew nothing of baseball. When the players made their evening rounds of Hollywood clubs, they took Dutch, who basked in their company, along with them.

His reports from Catalina enlarged his already sizeable local reputation, and the station rewarded him with his own evening show, "The World of Sports with Dutch Reagan." When his Cubs did well in the 1936 season, they invited him to their big celebration dinner in Chicago as "one of the boys." It was taken for granted that Dutch would follow them west again for next year's spring training.

Meanwhile, his lust for a film career received an additional boost when he did a radio interview with Joy Hodges, a Des Moines local who had achieved some success in Hollywood. Dutch asked her how it felt to be a star, and she said, "well, Mr. Reagan, you may know one day."[27] With this perhaps offhand encouragement, he went to Los Angeles in 1937 determined to do more than pal around with his baseball buddies.

As soon as Dutch reached town, he found Hodges and told her he wanted to have a screen test. She looked him over, ordered him to take off his thick glasses and never put them on again, and lined up a test. Her agent thought Dutch had a "likeable, clean-cut" look but typed him as "good buddy" material, not likely to become a leading man. Still, Warner Brothers agreed to give Reagan a chance.

The major studios together did hundreds of movies and even more "short subjects" each year and needed a constant supply of new actors. Dutch got a quick screen test and was looked over from top to bottom: "Are those your own shoulders? Is that your voice?"[28] It resembled a horse auction; they did everything but pry his jaw open to check his teeth. Dutch had to return to Des Moines before learning the results of his test, normally a fatal mistake, but while he was heading eastward on the train, Jack Warner himself saw the screen test and liked the new find's wholesome aura. That settled the issue.

On his first day back at work, just as Dutch was leaving for lunch, a telegram arrived from his agent: Warner was offering a seven-year contract at $200 a week; "what shall I do?" Reagan, hardly able to absorb the good news, telegraphed back: "sign before they change their minds."[29] The salary figure was very substantial. A new car cost $850, a new house $4,000, and gasoline was 10 cents a gallon; Reagan's $10,000 was equal to about $150,000 in today's dollars. He had more than doubled his graduation boast of a $5,000 salary within five years.

As befit a Midwestern radio celebrity, Reagan's farewell party included the mayor of Des Moines and other leading citizens. He was trading a solid future at WHO to join the lowest rank of aspiring actors, bound to a contract that tied him up for seven years but let the studio fire him at any time after six months. His salary could rise to $30,000 in four years ($450,000 today), but that of course assumed that he would do well enough to become one of Warner's stars. Obviously, most new actors never approached that level. He was facing long odds.

He faced moral dangers, too, or so the family's friends in Dixon thought. But Nelle was sure that she could trust young Dutch anywhere, even in "such a wicked place as Hollywood."[30] For a year he had been sending home $120 each month from his radio salary, and he promised to bring his parents out to join him in California once he settled in. With contract in hand, Dutch Reagan bought a new Nash convertible and one of his trademark brown suits. Then he drove six hundred miles a day to Hollywood, arriving exhausted but excited on June 1, 1937.

NOTES

1. Ronald Reagan, *Where's the Rest of Me?* (New York: Dell Publishing Co., 1963), 22.
2. Edmund Morris, *Dutch: A Memoir of Ronald Reagan* (New York: Random House, 1999), 19.
3. Anne Edwards, *Early Reagan: The Rise to Power* (New York: William Morrow, 1987), 42.
4. Reagan quoted in Morris, *Dutch*, 37.
5. Reagan, *Where's the Rest of Me?*, 13.
6. Franklin Burghardt quoted in Morris, *Dutch*, 89.
7. Morris, *ibid.*
8. Reagan quoted in Lou Cannon, *Reagan* (New York: Putnam, 1982), 19.
9. Reagan quoted in Morris, *Dutch*, 42.
10. Reagan in *Where's the Rest of Me?*, 12.
11. Morris, *Dutch*, 62.
12. Edwards, *Early Reagan*, 105.
13. Reagan quoted in Stephen Vaughn, "The Moral Inheritance of a President: Reagan and the Dixon Disciples of Christ," *Presidential Studies*, v. 25, no. 1 (Winter, 1995), 106.

14. Edwards, *Early Reagan*, 64.
15. *Ibid.*
16. Bill Boyarsky, *The Rise of Ronald Reagan* (New York: Random House, 1968), 28.
17. Reagan quoted in Cannon, *Reagan*, 22.
18. Neil Reagan, "Private Dimensions and Public Images: The Early Political Campaigns of Ronald Reagan," Oral History Program, University of California Los Angeles, 43.
19. Reagan in *Where's the Rest of Me?*, 36–37.
20. *Ibid.*, 33.
21. Edwards, *Early Reagan*, 105–106.
22. Reagan in *Where's the Rest of Me?*, 32.
23. Morris, *Dutch*, 94.
24. *Ibid.*, 102.
25. Quoted in Reagan, *Where's the Rest of Me?*, 56.
26. Quoted in Edwards, Early Reagan, 142.
27. Quoted in Edwards, *Early Reagan*, 151.
28. Quoted in Reagan, *Where's the Rest of Me?*, 86.
29. Reagan, *ibid.*, 88.
30. Nelle quoted in Bob Colacello, *Ronnie and Nancy: Their Path to the White House, 1911–1980* (New York: Warner Books, 2004), 71.

CHAPTER 2

HOLLYWOOD LIBERAL

Hollywood in the 1930s created an artificial life on film so that audiences could, for a few hours, escape the grim reality of the Depression. Even the place itself was artificial, a wasteland turned green and livable by water drawn from 230 miles away in the world's longest aqueduct. Tens of thousands like Dutch Reagan came in 1937, many drawn by the same dream of becoming an actor. He at any rate had a contract, which most never got, and within a few days of arriving he was actually in a movie.

First he had to go through the "studio makeover mill." They changed his hairstyle and gave him tailor-made shirts to alter the look of his wide shoulders and short neck. At least he got to keep his name. The studios often changed names: Leonard Slye into Roy Rogers and Marion Morrison into John Wayne. But the name-changers thought "Ronald Reagan" sounded "about right," so the nickname he had borne from early childhood was dropped. In the future he was "Dutch" only to his oldest friends.

It took some time to get used to his new surroundings. In 1932 Reagan had found Des Moines a strikingly big city compared to Dixon, but Los Angeles was on an entirely different, more intimidating scale. Ten times bigger than Des Moines, 150 times bigger than Dixon, it was the nation's fifth largest city, having more than doubled its population in a decade.

The Warner Brothers studio was more reminiscent of home, a virtually self-contained community of a few thousand people: actors and extras, those who attended them, and those who ruled them, ending at the top with Jack Warner himself. Hollywood had been the realm of the "studio system" for more than a decade. The five largest, including Warner Brothers, had achieved what economists call "vertical integration." They produced movies with actors bound by contract, controlled distribution of the finished films, and owned many of the theaters showing the films. With control of a movie's life cycle from script writing to public screening, the studios increased profits by making theaters accept "block booking," which combined one good "A" film with several low-budget "B" movies.

Jack Warner governed his studio lot and all who worked therein. Seeking a distinctive brand for his films, he emphasized powerful dramas of crime, poverty, and other social problems. A Republican himself, he supported Franklin Roosevelt in 1932 (as Reagan did) and hired many actors and writers of left-wing political views so long as they professed to be patriotic Americans.

He governed, however, as a monarch, not an egalitarian, and his mania was keeping costs low. The Warner commissary served only one meal a day, old scripts were tweaked to produce new movies, and retakes were anathema. Warner tied his producers to strict budgets but was glad to pay top dollar to stars who drew large audiences and made ticket sales soar.

As a newcomer to Hollywood, Reagan marveled at the lovely weather, enjoyed the fancy restaurants, saw the great stars close up, and made his first movies. His rise from "a complete unknown in a crowded field of unknowns," as one writer puts it, was aided by several strokes of luck.[1] His agent recognized Reagan's potential and did everything possible to propel his career forward, while Jack Warner liked him from the start and thought he might have future star quality. In his second movie Reagan was cast with gossip columnist Louella Parsons, and she, also hailing from Dixon, gave him favorable mention in her influential columns.

None of this would have mattered unless Reagan had been able to act, and it took several films during his first year to prove that to the studio. In his freshman effort, *Love is On the Air*, he was cast as a radio announcer and had little trouble essentially playing himself, but the trick was to rise above that elementary level. It was rare for an actor who started at the lower level to win promotion into the A ranks.

Reagan was fortunate in his first year, playing the lead in a few B movies but also a supporting role in several A films. None were grand triumphs of acting skill, but several made money, pleasing Jack Warner to no end. In one, *Cowboy From Brooklyn*, Reagan found another friend and powerful patron, Pat O'Brien, leader of the studio's "Irish Mafia."

This group included Humphrey Bogart, James Cagney, and Errol Flynn and had an exclusive table in the commissary, a more relaxed and definitely less intellectual version of New York's famous Algonquin Round Table. O'Brien appreciated that the young Reagan looked up to him, never complained, and—perhaps most important—never tried to steal a scene. In return he granted the newcomer admission to the Irish table, where Reagan got to know some of Hollywood's great names.

He also had the pleasure of being reunited with his parents. When Warner Brothers renewed his option at the end of his first six months, Reagan put Jack and Nelle up in a small apartment and later bought them a house—the only one they ever owned. He became closer to his father than ever; they were both Democrats and "drys" in a community run by Republicans and populated with drinkers and carousers. Reagan also continued his father's firm dislike of ethnic bigotry. As a sign of his rising status in Hollywood, he joined the Lakeside Country Club, but, learning that Jack Warner was rejected because he was Jewish, Reagan resigned his membership on the spot.

In a community of hedonists, as Hollywood was reputed to be, people like Reagan who took their religion seriously were uncommon. He was never preachy, never paraded his faith, but he went to the Beverly Christian church regularly with his mother. Meanwhile, Nelle made her faith the center of her activities in Hollywood. Most days were spent doing missionary work, visiting tuberculosis patients at the local sanitarium, and at Christmastime wrapping hundreds of presents for the poor.

Dutch Reagan's peripatetic childhood and his father's alcoholism had made it difficult to cultivate close friends and had drawn him inward. Hollywood had the same effect on the adult Reagan for a different reason. Movies were shot in a few weeks of frantic effort, after which the group of actors—close-knit for that short time—dispersed to a variety of new projects. There was little time to forge tight bonds. While everyone saw Reagan as an open and friendly person, they all sensed that he kept something of himself inside and unrevealed.

He began to make some friends, but unfortunately tried the patience of many. Like the annoying mailman Cliff Clavin in the *Cheers* sitcom, Reagan would fill the endless downtime on the set by unleashing a constant patter of obscure information on his bored comrades. One recalled that "Ron had the dope on just about everything—economic and sports statistics, the output of sugar beets, Lenin's grandfather's occupation," and even three millennia of Chinese history.[2] So it went, day after tiresome day, until his victims finally resorted to sitting apart from the chatterbox at lunch to have at least that single hour in silence.

By the end of his first year, Reagan was an experienced B-movie actor, no longer so fascinated by Hollywood and less willing to endure with quiet good humor the irritations of the job. He began to resent the virtual indentured servitude in which actors were ensnared by studio contracts. Warner had the right to control an actor's life for seven years, but could cut him loose at the end of every six months and impose unpaid suspensions on anyone who turned down a movie role.

When Reagan's contract was up for its first yearly renewal, he insisted on a thorough and critical examination. His surprised agent told him that it was useless to complain; this was the way Hollywood worked. Taking up the challenge, the new boy in town replied, "well, a way has to be figured out to turn that around."[3] It would not be the last time Ronald Reagan refused to accept the world as it was. He was going to change it. For such an avid liberal as he, the "way" was to balance Warner's economic power with the collective power of a union. The Screen Actors Guild had been formed in 1933, and after a few years' struggle it won the right to bargain as a "closed shop," meaning that every actor had to join, like it or not. Reagan, like many workers then and since, at first resented being forced to join a union to hold his job, but the more he thought about the studio's great power over actors on and off the set, the more he came to realize what SAG might be able to do.

Meantime, Jack Warner continued to hope that his new "find" would rise into the first rank of actors and late in 1938 finally tried him out as the co-star in an A movie, *Brother Rat*. There Reagan met Jane Wyman, who immediately set her sights on the handsome young actor, and soon they became an "item" in Louella Parsons's gossip columns.

Wyman, six years younger than Reagan, had endured a sobering childhood and grew up distrusting people, especially men. At age seventeen she came to Hollywood and snared a few roles in B movies. She was in her second unhappy marriage when she worked with Reagan on *Brother Rat* and was "drawn to him at once. . . . He was such a sunny person."[4] She quickly filed for divorce, and soon the two were dating steadily, although their personalities were quite different. The divorcee "who trusted no one" and the bachelor "who trusted everyone" is how one writer put it.[5]

After *Brother Rat*, Reagan got his first movie series, four films starring as a young, courageous federal Treasury agent, "Brass" Bancroft, battling criminals and spies. Bancroft was the embodiment of the old hymn's injunction: "where duty calls, or danger, be never wanting there." This was a new theme in the studio's movies beginning with *G-Men* in 1935, showing law enforcement and the military as heroes and playing on the rising fear of Nazism as Europe careened toward a new world war.

The Brass Bancroft movies lifted Reagan from the aspiring newcomer to what one might call an "entry-level star." As in so many films, he essentially played himself—a handsome, confident, athletic, young man with a sense of duty. Bancroft was an appealing character, especially to young boys like Jerry Parr, who was so enchanted that he vowed to join the Secret Service when he grew up. This he did, and four decades later, on a cold March day in Washington, he saved the life of Ronald Reagan.

The Bancroft movies were not great films, but they made money—Jack Warner's great desideratum. He continued to put Reagan in a few better movies between the regular low-budget, quickly produced Bs. What they lacked in quality many of these made up in popularity. By 1941 only the long-established star Errol Flynn outdid Reagan in the volume of fan mail.

In one of the "quickie Bs," Reagan played a social worker to Leo Gorcey's "Bowery Boys," who picked on him and hazed him relentlessly on the set. For once, the usually long-suffering Reagan had enough of the pestering and told Gorcey to stop or he would "slap hell out of them." They stopped. The Bowery Boys were not the last people to learn that one could push Ronald Reagan only so far, that there was steel beneath the smile.

When the last film of 1939 was done and Wyman's divorce was final, Reagan proposed, and they married in January 1940, with Louella Parsons hosting their wedding reception. She kept the two young actors under her protection and used her radio show and newspaper column to foster their careers. Reagan's mother was more reserved. "I hope my Ronald has made the right choice," she mused, for she had hoped that "he would fall in love with some sweet girl who is not in the movies."[6]

Barely three years out of Des Moines, Reagan had finally "arrived" in Hollywood. He had a comfortable salary (more than half a million in today's dollars), an adoring wife, and even a fine collection of pipes. His new agent, Lew Wasserman, was a master at promoting clients and got lucrative contracts for both Reagan and Wyman. The local media fawned upon them as "the ideal couple" because they seemed a living refutation of all the scandalous stories about Hollywood's loose morals. Wyman played this role to the hilt, saying they were "just two kids trying to get the breaks in pictures" and that she was "terribly proud" of her husband.[7]

The year 1940 started well, with the newlyweds appearing in *Brother Rat and a Baby*, a sequel to the film in which they had met. It was nothing much as a movie, but it introduced Reagan to Justin Dart, who was dating one of the actresses. Dart had been married to the daughter of Charles Walgreen, for whom Dutch had caddied when the drug-store king vacationed in Dixon, and he owned a sizeable part of the business.

As a Republican millionaire, Dart enjoyed arguing politics with the liberal Reagan, and the two became close friends. In later decades when they were finally on the same side of the ideological divide, Dart's financial backing and political connections were quite helpful. In fact, Dart seemed to be the first person actually able to shake Reagan's intense pro–New Deal sympathies in their frequent debates about economic issues.

After *Brother Rat* and the last of the Bancroft movies came Reagan's first chance at greatness in *Knute Rockne: All-American*. With help from his aggressive agent and his "Irish table" patron, Pat O'Brien, Reagan was cast as George Gipp to O'Brien's Rockne. Gipp had been one of Dutch's childhood football heroes—a star on the gridiron felled by an untimely death—and it was a thrill to play him, if only for ten minutes of screen time. Those ten minutes made Reagan a sensation both in Hollywood and to movie audiences nationwide; his deathbed injunction to "win one for the Gipper" is one of the most memorable lines in any film.

Another success quickly followed—*Santa Fe Trail*, in which Reagan played George Armstrong Custer from his West Point days to the capture of the abolitionist John Brown. In a production that made antislavery sentiment seem fanatical, Reagan's character was the only one who sympathized with fearful blacks and warned his Southern fellow officers that slavery was pushing America toward the abyss. The part of Custer fit well with the hostility toward racism that Reagan had inherited from his father.

Doing the movie also showed how a capricious fate could turn film careers from hope to obscurity. Another actor had originally been picked to play Custer. When Reagan won the part instead, he was in the dressing room when a prop man walked in, snatched the losing actor's clothes off the rack, and tossed them away, putting Reagan's up in their place. Here was a stark reminder of how expendable an actor was and how fragile his future.

One of the high points of Reagan's entire Hollywood experience came a year later when his hometown, Dixon, prepared to celebrate "Louella Parsons Day." Reagan had star billing in *International Squadron*, a film about the Battle of Britain, which was scheduled to open in Dixon coinciding with the Parsons event. Jack Warner put his two Dixonites, Parsons and Reagan, on the train with a few other stars, determined to make the local event a national publicity bonanza for Warner Brothers.

When the train pulled into Dixon, it was met by 50,000 people and the largest parade in the town's history. Though it was officially "Louella Parsons Day," most of the banners said, "Welcome Home, Dutch!" and that was whom the multitude had come to see. Several people he had rescued in his lifeguard days even came to thank him. The Hollywood group was put up at Hazelwood, the Walgreen mansion, a home so palatial that even the guest cottage had nineteen bedrooms. Telling endless stories of his Dixon days, Reagan far outshone Parsons as the center of attention.

The premier of *International Squadron* was at the same theater where young Dutch had been mesmerized by so many films. As a boy, he had imagined himself the hero of the movies he watched; now he could see himself on the same screen. Nothing made him feel so successful as this triumphal return to Dixon. Yearning for the limelight is a common human hope that had long held Reagan in its grip. As a lifeguard high above the beach, a freshman calling for a student strike, or a radio personality in a vast Midwestern market, he had basked in the glow of an audience.

The popularity of *International Squadron* and some good reviews for his last few movies moved Reagan up to the level of "potential star quality" in the Warner list, which led directly to *King's Row*. In this very dark A-list film, he co-stars as Drake McHugh, a wealthy philanderer attracted to a doctor's daughter. The surgeon dislikes McHugh intensely and, while treating him for an injury, amputates both his legs in a grotesque act of revenge. McHugh groggily revives, looks down and screams, "where's the rest of me?" After days of preparing psychologically, Reagan did the scene perfectly in one take. Critics praised it as his best work, and the famous line became the title of his first autobiography.

The upward course of events was broken by one tragedy. Jack Reagan's bad heart finally gave out, and on May 18, 1941, he died. Despite the father's failing health, the son was shocked by the event. Sunk deep in sadness, he rushed back from a publicity tour in the East. At the funeral, he confessed that "my soul was just desolate. . . . Desolate. And empty." Then he heard his father's voice saying, "I'm OK, and where I am it's very nice. Please don't be unhappy." At that, Reagan's soul revived; "the emptiness was all gone."[8]

By the end of 1941, still glowing from his performance in *King's Row*, Reagan was enjoying life with Jane Wyman. They went to the best restaurants with the best people. His wife looked up to him, felt protected by his easy self-confidence, and was for a time content with household details while he decided all the important things, except having children. Wyman wanted a baby, but Reagan told her that newlyweds should wait a year. "She agreed I was right as usual and she was wrong," he said. "So we had a baby."[9] Maureen was born January 4, 1941.

The one continuity tying this existence to his pre-Hollywood years was Reagan's constant need to talk—or rather, to argue—politics. It was most pronounced during long waits on the set, but even at dinners and pool parties he kept at it. "The trouble with you guys," Reagan said to his Republican brother, Neil, is that "anybody who voted for Roosevelt is a Communist."[10] Neil would agree just to watch his brother go into another liberal rant. This began to wear on Reagan's wife, who complained that politics was "all he talks about, how he's going to save the world."[11]

In fact, they were ill matched as a couple for the long run. She was used to going into debt to buy anything she wanted; he insisted on locking away half of their joint income in a savings account. Show-business life would have been difficult for any couple because weeks of intense effort learning a role and filming left both husband and wife tense and exhausted from work, with little time for a personal life. In between films were aimless weeks of idleness, needing to be filled with outside activities that often pulled Reagan and Wyman in different directions.

She took up this downtime with almost compulsive housekeeping, shopping, sports, reading, and union activity, while he became ever more absorbed with the state of world affairs—especially the war in Europe.

Every day Reagan would peruse the *Washington Post*, the *Wall Street Journal*, the *Christian Science Monitor*, and even the deadly dull *Congressional Record*. On the set or at parties his frequent spouting of opinion and miscellaneous information earned a little more respect now that it dealt with the overriding vital issue of the day.

In the process, Reagan talked increasingly with Justin Dart, already a powerhouse Republican fundraiser, and through him got to know other conservatives. He also spent more time with two Republican actors, Dick Powell and George Murphy, the future senator. Powell's wife was amused to watch "Ronnie, a staunch Democrat, trying to convert" her husband, while he "argued just as hard to turn Ronnie Republican."[12] Powell even told Reagan that if he would switch parties and run for Congress as a Republican, funding would be forthcoming for his campaign. The still-ardent New Dealer shrugged off that heretical suggestion.

Reagan did find one of his wife's interests very much to his liking. In 1941, Wyman was asked to serve on the Screen Actors Guild board, but she offered her husband as a better choice. Supposedly she said, "he might even become president of SAG one day—or maybe America."[13] As he began to take an active part in union affairs, Reagan quickly became adept at political maneuvering and tough negotiation.

Meantime, like his boss Jack Warner, Reagan applauded the demands of his idol in the White House, Franklin Roosevelt, for military preparedness, as Hitler's blitzkrieg shattered one European country after another. Neither Reagan nor Warner, however, liked the unwelcome attention Hollywood was receiving from anti-Roosevelt isolationists.

In the late 1930s Congress created what became known as the House Un-American Activities Committee to expose "subversives." By 1940 its liberal chairman had been supplanted by a Texas Democrat, Martin Dies, who turned the committee's main target from fascists to Communists—or, more broadly, to "interventionists," who wanted the United States to give all possible aid to Hitler's opponents.

Isolationists accused Warner Brothers of making "war propaganda" movies—including Reagan's *International Squadron* and the Brass Bancroft films. Warner shot back that he was indeed anti-Nazi, "but no one can charge me with being anti-American."[14] As a good liberal and eager Roosevelt supporter, Reagan fully shared Warner's sentiments. Decades later, as president, he was equally determined to rebuild the nation's military strength in the face of another totalitarian regime.

However, the prewar Reagan had an even more personal worry than isolationist grumbling at the movie industry. If war came, he, as a reserve officer, would be a prime candidate for active duty. With a new family and a film career that seemed headed for the heights, he would hardly welcome an interruption for military service. The studio, too, did not like the idea of losing the man who just might be its next major movie star.

When Reagan received his first induction notice in February 1941, Warner secured him a series of deferments for more than a year. In the meantime, the studio put him in as many movies as possible, one of which, *Desperate Journey*, fit right in with Warner's desire for anti-Nazi propaganda. It follows several Allied flyers shot down over Germany and their eventual successful escape. Despite fitting the public mood well, *Desperate Journey* had very mixed reviews. In a striking preview of Reagan's presidential years, most of the intellectual critics hooted at his performance, but the "lowbrow" audiences loved it.

Finally, the studio could put off Reagan's call to service no longer, and he reported for active duty in April 1942. On Warner's suggestion, the army created the First Motion Picture Unit, transferred Reagan to it, and set up shop in the former Hal Roach Studios—naturally called "Fort Roach"—a few miles from the Reagan residence. His poor eyesight would have kept him out of a combat role in any case.

In an article for one of the movie magazines, Reagan showed how he thought of himself—or rather, how he wanted others to think of him—as he put on a uniform after four years in Hollywood. He liked "to swim, hike, and sleep," to eat "steak smothered with onions," and to relax in his new home. He drove a "so-so convertible coupe" and read *Tom Sawyer*, H. G. Wells, and Pearl Buck. He carried a good luck charm. All in all, he said, "Mr. Norm is my alias."[15]

The job of his military unit was making training films to turn raw civilians into skilled airmen and propaganda movies to keep civilian morale high. It turned out almost one hundred movies a year, of which the most famous is *Memphis Belle*, the story of a B-17 bomber's missions over Europe. Reagan starred in one of the most successful films, *Rear Gunner*, designed to increase Air Force enlistments. He made many similar "shorts" over the next two years, occasionally on screen but usually narrating. Some were propaganda movies shown in theaters, while others were training films on such topics as *Recognition of the Japanese Zero Fighter*. The historian Garry Wills believes that in these films Reagan was "as passionate a communicator of the war's importance as was the President himself."[16]

Warner eventually convinced the army to let him use Lt. Reagan in a commercial film, in return for which he donated the profits to Army Relief. It was another peak performance for Reagan; *This Is The Army* sold far more tickets than *King's Row*, and he was now, at age thirty-two, the leading draw in all of Hollywood, ahead even of Cagney and Crosby, Gable and Grant. It was a brief moment at the top, and then back to training films and a three-year wait before he could get a part in even a B-level commercial movie.

Reagan himself believed that his single most useful task at Fort Roach was in a top-secret project. High-level bombing was notoriously inaccurate and very few bombs fell within even three miles of their target. To correct this, the Army Air Force built a huge mockup of Japanese cities. An overhead camera panned slowly along, showing precisely what a pilot would see from different heights, and B-29 crews watched the simulated bombing runs before they took to the air. Reagan narrated most of these target-identification films and was proud of his part in the effort to bomb Japan into surrender: "My voice said 'Bombs away!'"[17]

When not making films, Reagan's other military duty was to show up at war bond drives, give "pep talks" to troops headed to the Pacific, and speak before countless civilian groups. Once again, he was the center of attention, and it was excellent training for future political campaigns. As a radio personality and as an actor, Reagan had spoken to large unseen audiences, but only indirectly through the microphone or the camera. Now he was speaking directly and in person, able to observe the effect of his words and of the mood that they conveyed.

Always emotionally patriotic, Reagan was powerfully moved by his association with troops heading toward danger and civilians who did their own part for the cause. He recalled that once when a singer began *The Battle Hymn of the Republic*, "a strange and wonderful thing happened. All over . . . men started coming to their feet and, when she finished, seventeen thousand soldiers were standing, singing with her."[18]

Jack Warner did his best to keep Reagan, with many years of potential stardom ahead, constantly in the public eye. The picture of this virile lieutenant, uniformed and confident, appeared often on magazine covers, usually with a proud flag in the background. It was the same smiling pose, minus uniform, that would be his trademark image as president. The studio also presented Wyman to the movie-going public as the "dutiful war wife."

This portrayal of the Reagans, he as a patriotic soldier and she loyally bearing the burden at home, was important to their futures. The promising careers of several other actors were damaged by a reputation for wartime shirking because they had avoided the draft, and this handicap would have been even more crippling for a postwar political candidate. Ironically, it was precisely Reagan's military service that sent his movie career into a slow decline. His performance in *King's Row* (which hit theaters early in 1942) would have given him the lead in *Casablanca* later that year, but the army barred him from making commercial movies. The starring role, and all the recognition that it earned, went to Humphrey Bogart instead.

Even though he worked in Hollywood and could go home nearly every evening, the war years had their difficulties. The studio paid him nothing while he served, so Wyman's income had to support the family. They were hardly poor—she had two servants—but money was definitely tighter. Besides her busy film schedule, she was mother to a young daughter and had to look in frequently on Nelle. Home duties doubled when the Reagans adopted a newborn son, Michael, in 1945.

While her husband was "off at war," Wyman was stuck playing in various comedies, none of which tested her ability. Her break finally came when Warner lent her to Paramount Pictures for *Lost Weekend*, which won Best Picture of 1945, but success brought its own problems. As her career began to flourish while her husband's was in limbo, she had little time to sit home with her military man in the evenings. At loose ends after his daily duties at Fort Roach, Reagan joined the Hollywood Democratic Committee, which supported Roosevelt's successful reelection in 1944. Once more they were heading in different directions.

During his tour of duty, Reagan, although an officer, ignored the rigid hierarchy of the military, mingling democratically with men of every rank or none. He also kept up his habit of telling everyone who would listen how nobly heroic Franklin Roosevelt was; one of his fellow "actors in uniform" predicted that "if that son of a bitch doesn't stop making speeches, he'll end up in the White House."[19]

In September 1945, Reagan was finally mustered out of the army. Among his last duties was to review footage of the gruesome scenes in the liberated Nazi concentration camps. He never forgot the horror. Later, he made both of his sons watch the film at age fourteen to sear into their own memories, as the film had into his, the all-too-real evidence of the Holocaust.

Reagan was more fortunate than most in the military; he had been stationed locally and could often go home to see wife and children. He was even able, to some degree, to keep his name before theater audiences by acting in or narrating wartime films. But like nearly all who wore the uniform, for him the war years were a detour from his former occupation. He returned to a career grown stale and in danger from newer, fresher faces. He was never to recover his prewar standing as a rising star.

But if the war closed one door, it opened another. Reagan had become interested in politics and public affairs, and some of his wartime colleagues began to think of him as a future politician. For him, as for FDR, the war illuminated one of those bright lines that appear in the human experience to distinguish good from evil. On this occasion his fellow liberals fully shared Reagan's outrage at Nazi tyranny. Four decades later, the same moral condemnation of Soviet tyranny brought only mockery and criticism from liberals who had long since become his political opponents.

Reagan resumed the lush contract that guaranteed him $3,500 a week whether he worked or not. At age thirty-four, he was financially well off and looked forward to family life and career success, and Jack Warner's advice was to "relax until we find a good property for you." They never did. Reagan made fifteen postwar films, some of them complete duds and none approaching *Knute Rockne* or *King's Row* in quality. Meantime, Jane Wyman had done *Lost Weekend* and was working on *The Yearling*, destined to be another success. She was by now just "Wyman" in the trade magazines, while he was still "*Ronald* Reagan," as though there were other Reagans to distinguish him from. Clearly she was on her way to stardom as he had been in 1941, but with no war to interrupt her upward course.

To the world they seemed a happy couple in the postwar months, but there was increasing tension at home. When working, Wyman was utterly absorbed in her character and hardly noticed husband or children. Reagan, by contrast, had always been able to "put on" his character each morning and become himself again at day's end. As he left the service, he thought about his role in postwar America. Being an actor was no longer enough; he would "try to bring about the regeneration of the world."[20] Husband and wife were clearly treading different paths.

Having no movie to make, Reagan said he "blindly" started joining "every organization I could find that would guarantee to save the world."[21] He was especially active in two: the Hollywood Independent Citizens Committee of Arts, Sciences, and Professions (HICCASP) and the American Veterans Committee, one of the few veterans' groups that expressed no racial or religious prejudice. Reagan served on the board of the AVC, although it was suspected of being a Communist front group. He admitted that there were "some 'Commies' aboard" but defended the AVC as a patriotic organization. It advocated United Nations control of atomic energy, federal full-employment economic policies, and repeal of the Taft-Hartley Act, which labor leaders despised.

Reagan gave many speeches for HICCASP and AVC because, he said, "it fed my ego. . . . I loved it."[22] His first, in December 1945, only four years and a day after the Pearl Harbor attack, praised Japanese-American veterans. America, he said, "stands unique in the world—a country not founded on race, but on a way and an ideal," a nation strong "not in spite of, but because of our polyglot background."[23] He was to carry these sentiments forward into his presidency, where, unlike some Republicans, he supported a liberal immigration policy.

Continuing his crusade into 1946, Reagan warned of the danger of nuclear war, called for greater international cooperation, and made an angry radio broadcast blasting the Ku Klux Klan as "an organized systematic campaign of fascist violence" by "the kind of crackpots that became Reich Fuehrer." The Communist Party praised his program, but California's Un-American Activities Committee accused Reagan and his allies of "fomenting racial prejudice."[24]

He even put his name on a statement in the local Communist newspaper criticizing Chiang Kai-shek's Nationalist government in China as it fought desperately to hold off Mao Tse-tung's advancing army. It was no wonder that, to his chagrin, he was "being called a Red in certain Hollywood circles."[25] The local FBI office began watching him as a suspected Communist sympathizer.

Reagan spoke out not only for the AVC but also for HICCASP, which included the full range of Hollywood's left-of-center politics, from moderate liberals like James Roosevelt to Communist Party members like Dalton Trumbo and John Howard Lawson. By the middle of 1946, tired of criticism that HICCASP was harboring Communists, the liberal majority proposed a resolution to declare Communism undesirable for the United States. The radicals erupted in outrage. One declared that the Soviet constitution was more democratic than the American; another said if there was war between the United States and Russia, he would fight for Russia.

To Reagan's stunned surprise, when he spoke for the resolution, he was denounced as "capitalist scum" and a fascist—he, who had served in a war against fascism and who had himself denounced real fascists only months before. It was his first taste of the hatred facing liberals who were not, like Lawson and Trumbo, eager tools of Soviet postwar policy. When Reagan mildly suggested that the full membership vote on the resolution, Communists sneered that the members were not "politically intelligent enough" to be trusted with the right to vote. It was quite an eye-opener for a naïve New Dealer. He and many other liberals soon quit the organization, and Trumbo, Lawson, and their fellow Communists were left with a much-diminished organization, now openly branded by people like Eleanor Roosevelt as a Communist front.

The incident was typical of many across the country in the early postwar years, as democratic liberals began to pull away from those further to the left who had been their allies in the fight against Hitler's dictatorship but who found Stalin's quite acceptable. For Reagan personally, it represented the first realization that "too many of the patches on the progressive coat were of a color I didn't personally care for."[26]

Today, when the full horror of Stalin's rule in the Soviet Union is common knowledge, it might be hard to imagine why so many people in Hollywood would gravitate to such an ideology. But in the early 1930s, with the United States mired in the Great Depression, the Soviet Union had great attraction for some Americans, and Marxism promised a bright economic future, while capitalism seemed to be failing. Furthermore, Communist parties fought the rise of Nazism in Europe, and when the Spanish Civil War broke out in 1936, Russia provided the only real help to the hard-pressed Republican government against Francisco Franco's fascists.

At home, Communists worked in the fast-growing labor union movement and in the Southern struggle for African-American civil rights. In the climate of the times, it was easy for many in Hollywood to see the Communists as the "good guys" in a world beset by Nazis, fascists, racists, and anti-union corporations. During World War II, the U.S. propaganda machine praised Stalin as a faithful ally against the Nazi enemy and glorified the Soviet people and the Red Army.

When the war ended, however, Stalin ordered Communists in the United States and elsewhere to end the "Popular Front" alliance with liberals and to resume ideological combat against capitalism and democracy. Reagan and most of his fellow liberals were startled and disheartened by the sudden savagery of their wartime comrades. To draw a clear line between the democratic left and the totalitarians, people like Eleanor Roosevelt, Hubert Humphrey, Walter Reuther, and Reinhold Niebuhr founded Americans for Democratic Action in January 1947. Reagan helped organize the California branch and the next year was elected to the national board. He said that "the ADA offers the only voice for real liberals."[27]

So worried was Reagan about Communist influence in his industry that he began passing information to the FBI. It is perhaps odd that a man the agency so recently suspected of Communist leanings would become "confidential informant T-10." Meanwhile another SAG member, informant T-9, was keeping the FBI up to date on Reagan himself. It was a case of the watcher watched: *quis custodiet ipsos custodes?*

In mid-1947 an interview entitled "Mr. Reagan Airs His Views" ran in major newspapers. He repeated his oft-declared claim that "tyranny is tyranny, and whether it comes from right, left, or center, it's evil." Liberals, he said, were the Communists' worst enemy because "the Reds know that if we can make America a decent living place for all our people their cause is lost here." Individual freedom should be the nation's highest aim. He opposed outlawing the Communist party because "tomorrow it may be the Democratic or the Republican Party that gets the ax."[28]

By 1948 liberals of the ADA stripe supported President Harry Truman's "Fair Deal" politics at home and resistance to Soviet power abroad. A minority on the left continued their cooperation with the Communist Party and became "fellow travelers." One actress explained why she and others in Hollywood had embraced the radical cause. They "read right through Marx, Engels, and Lenin," she said, "and it was kind of fun,"[29] an opinion possibly not shared, Reagan thought, by the millions forced to live under the ideology of Marx, Engels, and Lenin.

A second major event pushing Reagan away from his former dalliance with the far left was the rise of labor strife in the movie industry. The International Alliance of Theatrical Stage Employees (IATSE) fell under gangster control in the 1930s, and while Reagan was in the Army, a radical union organizer, Herbert Sorrell, built a rival empire, the Conference of Studio Unions. The local Communist Party became "very much interested" in Sorrell, hoping that the CSU would be a "progressive center" in Hollywood for "Party policy and Party people."[30] In 1946 the two unions fought each other in a strike that lasted several years. IATSE complained of Communist influence in the CSU, which in turn said the other group was controlled by hoodlums.

The leadership of SAG had no wish to be drawn in, so the actors continued to work. Reagan, out of the Army and back on the SAG board, was deeply worried. Sorrell admitted taking money from Communists, and a group of Party members within the Guild supported CSU's strike. In response, Reagan and other SAG leaders became distinctly hostile and drew closer to the AFL union, IATSE. Reagan led the resistance, warning that Communists wanted to control Hollywood "for a grand world-wide propaganda base." American movies monopolized theaters around the world, and "it would have been a magnificent coup for our enemies."[31]

The Guild held a mass meeting in October 1946, to decide whether to honor or ignore the CSU strike. Reagan chaired the event, much to the distress of gossip columnist Hedda Hopper, who had sized him up as "quiet, unassuming, and not the two-fisted fighter we needed." Afterward, she admitted, "I was never more wrong,"[32] the first of many who were to underestimate Reagan's political ability. He was booed and denounced by the Communist-led minority, but a huge majority of SAG's 3,000 members voted to endorse his call for neutrality and to cross the CSU picket line. It was his first great triumph of public speaking since the "student strike" oration at Eureka College. Afterward, a fellow actor told him, "you have an obligation to do something for this country."[33]

Reagan then led a SAG delegation to the national AFL convention in Chicago, where the display of arrogant bullying, threats of violence, and personal empire building at the heart of America's largest labor organization shocked him. He came away with a much altered opinion of the union movement of which he himself was a local leader, another small crack in his formerly rock-solid allegiance to New Deal liberalism.

He was even more disturbed by brutal tactics in Hollywood itself. The CSU turned out hundreds to picket Warner Brothers, and Sorrell threatened that "there may be men hurt, there may be men killed."[34] Reagan and the other actors had to be bused to work, and he personally was threatened with disfigurement by acid. This convinced him all the more that Communist-inspired violence was a growing danger to the Hollywood community.

The CSU strike and the violence continued into 1947; nonstrikers had their arms broken and their homes firebombed. The political lines became ever starker, as the CSU attracted more support from Communists and other leftists, while SAG and Reagan, now its president, drew closer to the studios. In the larger picture, this was but one episode in a wave of strikes and labor violence that spread across the country in the late 1940s.

Everywhere, Democrats like Reagan who had joined with those further left to battle Hitler abroad and conservatives at home, drifted away from their former allies and began to share the concerns of their one-time political opponents. While some of Reagan's fellow actors turned on him and cursed him for not supporting the CSU, most of the SAG membership stood where he did. In 1948 he was triumphantly reelected SAG president.

For Reagan, the most controversial event of the postwar years involved the decision of the House Un-American Activities Committee to conduct hearings into the apparent expansion of Communist influence in Hollywood. Their particular fear was that writers were turning out scripts aimed at cleverly undermining public confidence in America's democratic, free-market system. It seems amazing today that anyone seriously thought that a few faint propaganda themes stuck into a few films might turn millions of gullible moviegoers into "fellow travelers." But the Communist Party itself—including devout members like Lawson and Trumbo—believed exactly that, so it cannot be very surprising that the studios, liberal actors like Reagan, and many congressmen also believed it.

In October 1947 Reagan was among nearly four dozen movie figures called to testify before the committee. One of its new Republican members, Richard Nixon, especially wanted Reagan on the list. He said his fellow Californian was "a liberal and as such would not be accused of simply being a red-baiting reactionary."[35] Hundreds of Hollywood's prominent liberals believed that the HUAC subpoenas were a threat to civil liberties and formed the Committee for the First Amendment to launch a public protest. Reagan was not among them, although he remained active in Americans for Democratic Action, which also opposed the hearings.

The hearings began with studio heads testifying about Communist infiltration. Then it was Reagan's turn, and he struck a very different note.[36] When asked if the "clique" had tried to dominate SAG, he allowed that they had, but " I guess . . . that our side was attempting to dominate, too, because we were fighting just as hard to put over our views." Asked how Hollywood should rid itself of Communist influence, again he disappointed the congressmen. Reagan said, "the best thing to do is to make democracy work ... insuring everyone a vote and keeping everyone informed." Jefferson had the right idea: "if all the American people know all of the facts they will never make a mistake."

One of the committee's goals was to have the Communist party banned, but Reagan again dissented; no party should be outlawed "on the basis of its political ideology." He did admit that if "an organization is an agent of ... a foreign power, ... then that is another matter." Of course it is well known that the American party was financed and controlled from Moscow, so it actually did fit the definition of "an agent of ... a foreign power."

Reagan left the hearings believing that he had done well. He had told the truth: there was a tiny group of Communists in SAG, but a coalition of liberals and conservatives had beaten them. He had also drawn a clear line between loathing Communism as a tyrannical ideology and compromising "any of our democratic principles" out of fear. Reagan had mixed feelings about the whole episode. He was proud that "we stopped the Communists cold in Hollywood" but disliked the "witch hunt" in which "many fine people were accused wrongly of being Communists simply because they were liberals."[37] In this he agreed with the overwhelming majority of his fellow New Dealers, many of whom praised Reagan's testimony. The ADA, the *New York Times*, and the *Washington Post* all thought he was one of the heroes of the hearing.

When the "unfriendly witnesses" were called, they denounced the congressmen as Nazis and generally mocked the entire proceedings. Nearly all those tagged as unfriendly by the Committee actually *were* members of the Communist party, but in the words of one sympathizer, they were mostly "belligerent buffoons" and "well-intentioned boobs" rather than dangerous plotters.[38]

Ten were cited for contempt of Congress and served prison time. The studios fired the "Hollywood Ten" and created an unofficial blacklist of Communists and "fellow travelers," which included a vast number of people and lasted more than a decade. To achieve a united front within the industry, appease the general public, and head off more federal regulation, the owners wanted all three major guilds—actors, writers, and directors—to endorse the blacklist.

As SAG president, Reagan had some tough questions for the studio bosses. What were their standards for branding someone a Communist? What would happen to non-Communists who might have belonged to a "Communist-front" group (like Reagan himself)? He warned that trampling on liberty in this one instance, although induced by very understandable fears, might lead to broader threats to everyone's freedom.

In December 1947, he asked the Guild to declare that, while it would cooperate with the lawful authorities, it would refuse to adopt "Communist tactics" by acting as "lawmaker, judge and jury" against any accused person. His own guild thought Reagan too soft and killed his resolution; he lamented that "some . . . believed I was red as Moscow."[39]

Unable to carry his fellow actors with him, Reagan finally gave up and fought no more against the Hollywood blacklist. He even came around to the idea of outlawing the Communist Party, a reversal of what he told HUAC a few months earlier. He apparently was not enthusiastic about it but, to preserve peace in Hollywood, he believed that SAG should reach some middle ground with the much tougher position of the studios. And he was, all the while, continuing his sporadic meeting with FBI agents, keeping them informed on the debates within his guild.

His awkward position, between the conservatives he had always argued with and new opponents on the far left, showed up even in his private life. He and Wyman spent much of their social time with millionaires like Justin Dart, the drugstore magnate, and Leonard Firestone, the tire king, both of whom later became part of his informal "Kitchen Cabinet" in politics. At this time, however, they still saw Reagan as a misguided liberal whose outspoken beliefs touched off "spirited discussions."

People to his left, meanwhile, thought he was insufficiently radical. One of them complained that "he would buttonhole you at a party and talk liberalism at you. You'd look for an escape." Another dismissed him as "an airhead."[40] More importantly, his own wife was becoming ever more irritated with his constant talking. She said, "Don't ask Ronnie what time it is because he will tell you how a watch is made."[41]

Reagan's incessant need to hold forth was not the only reason that things went rapidly downhill for the couple in 1947. The year had actually begun well; Wyman was nominated for an Oscar, Reagan was elected president of the Screen Actors Guild, and they both started working on new movies. This, however, seemed only to pull them further apart. He spent his days on location and his evenings negotiating with the studios, while she was totally absorbed in her film, *Johnny Belinda*. Neither spent much time with the children or with each other.

Soon after her film closed production, Wyman told Reagan that their marriage was finished. He could scarcely believe it. Despite the gradually accumulating evidence of his wife's dissatisfaction, Reagan was utterly unprepared for the break. Hollywood generally sympathized with him, but this was little comfort to a man who had thought his marriage, like that of his parents, would be strong enough to endure the rough patches. The official divorce came in June 1948. Wyman went on to a long acting career but had no better luck with husbands after Reagan. She married her fourth in 1952, divorced him in 1955, married him again in 1961, and divorced yet again in 1964, remaining single for the rest of her life.

As for Reagan, the final reality of divorce hit him hard. Usually the cheery optimist, he became a forlorn figure and for a while almost withdrew from the world. He said he felt "dead inside for several years." Looking back later, Reagan thought, "perhaps I should have let someone else save the world and have saved my own home."[42]

NOTES

1. Marc Eliot, *Reagan: The Hollywood Years* (New York: Harmony Books, 2008), 8.
2. Quoted in Edwards, *Early Reagan*, 171–172.
3. *Ibid.*, 178.
4. Wyman quoted *ibid.*, 188.
5. Eliot, *Reagan: The Hollywood Years*, 84.
6. Quoted in Morris, *Dutch*, 164.
7. Wyman in Doug McClelland, *Hollywood on Ronald Reagan: Friends and Enemies Discuss Our President, the Actor* (Winchester, MA: Faber & Faber, 1983), 24–26.
8. Quoted in Maureen Reagan, *First Father, First Daughter: A Memoir* (Boston: Little, Brown, 1989), 61.
9. Reagan quoted in Joe Morella and Edward Z. Epstein, *Jane Wyman: A Biography* (New York: Delacorte Press, 1985), 42.
10. Neil Reagan, "Private Dimensions," UCLA Oral History Program, 22.
11. Wyman quoted in Eliot, *Reagan: The Hollywood Years*, 154.
12. June Allyson, *June Allyson* (New York: G.P. Putnam, 1982), 95–96.
13. Jack Dales, "Pragmatic Leadership: Ronald Reagan as President of the Screen Actors Guild," Oral History Program, University of California Los Angeles, 20.
14. Warner testimony in Edwards, *Early Reagan*, 258.
15. Cannon, *Reagan*, 59.
16. Garry Wills, *Reagan's America: Innocents at Home* (Garden City, NY: Doubleday, 1987), 162.
17. Reagan in *Where's the Rest of Me?*, 139.
18. *Ibid.*, 131.
19. Alan Hale quoted in Morris, *Dutch*, 205.
20. Reagan in *Where's the Rest of Me?*, 161.
21. *Ibid.*, 162–163.
22. *Ibid.*
23. Quoted in Morris, *Dutch*, 228.
24. Quoted in Stephen Vaughn, *Ronald Reagan in Hollywood: Movies and Politics* (New York: Cambridge University Press, 1994), 172.
25. Quoted in Morris, *Dutch*, 230.
26. Reagan in *Where's the Rest of Me?*, 194.
27. Reagan quoted in Vaughn, *Reagan in Hollywood*, 168.
28. *Chicago Tribune,* May 18, 1947, quoted in Edwards, *Early Reagan*, 324.
29. *Los Angeles Times,* August 17, 1980 quoted in Edwards, *Early Reagan*, 351.
30. Quoted in Edwards, *Early Reagan*, 310.
31. Reagan in *Where's the Rest of Me?*, 186–187.
32. Hopper quoted in Edwards, *Early Reagan*, 312; Morella and Epstein, *Wyman*, 104.
33. Robert Stack quoted in Morris, *Dutch*, 242.
34. Sorrell quoted in Vaughn, *Reagan in Hollywood*, 139.

35. Nixon quoted in Irwin F. Gellman, *The Contender, Richard Nixon: The Congress Years, 1946–1952* (New York: Free Press, 1999), 117.
36. Reagan's testimony in Edwards, *Early Reagan*, 342–349.
37. Reagan quoted in Ross, *Hollywood Left and Right: How Movie Stars Shaped American Politics* (New York: Oxford University Press, 2011), 156.
38. Quoted in Lawrence Grobel, *The Hustons* (New York: Scribner's, 1989), 300.
39. Reagan, *Where's the Rest of Me?*, 205.
40. Quoted in Colacello, *Ronnie and Nancy*, 205.
41. Wyman quoted in Allyson, *June Allyson*, 96.
42. Reagan quoted in Cannon, *Reagan*, 64.

CHAPTER 3

THE LIBERAL BECOMES CONSERVATIVE

In the emotional doldrums after his divorce, Reagan signed on to do *The Hasty Heart*, filmed in England, in the fall of 1948. He was struck by the mood of postwar Europe, struggling economically and worried about the threat from the East. Since Hitler's defeat, the Soviet Union had taken over Eastern Europe, and many feared that the Red Army might march to the Channel. Even the future nuclear-disarmament guru, philosopher Bertrand Russell, urged an atomic war against Russia before it was too late. It was in this atmosphere that Reagan first began to contemplate the problems of the wider world. He studied British politics, and on a drive through France he read the legacy of world war: along the roadside "clusters of white crosses, each hung with a helmet," and in the fields the hulking remains of burnt-out tanks.[1] This heightened the conviction he shared with his fallen hero, FDR, that the United States must not lapse again into isolation, that it had a mission to defend liberty in the world. An English colleague on *The Hasty Heart* said that he had "never met an American who so profoundly believed in the greatness of his nation."[2]

Reagan later claimed that his time in England was among the experiences that made him begin to question his New Deal roots. First had been the wartime irritation of seeing the inefficiency and empire building of the civilian bureaucracy at Fort Roach. Next came the postwar shock of seeing many of his fellow liberals so easily manipulated by the tiny Communist minority in Hollywood.

Now in England he had firsthand experience of an actual socialist regime, a shabby existence of regulation, regimentation, and shortages. Of course, some of what he experienced was simply the inevitable aftermath of a long, debilitating war that had left Britain economically drained.

Reagan, however, assumed that it was all the result of a Labour Party government's socialist economic policies. He said, "I shed the last ideas I'd ever had about government ownership of anything."[3]

Although glad to return home, he found his movie career slipping slowly downhill. Jack Warner could not quite puzzle out how best to use his actor's talents, and Reagan actually had no films at all released in 1948, after three full years struggling to resume the upward climb that his war service had cut short. Even in 1949 he was stuck making light comedies of little audience appeal, while Wyman rose to super-stardom, listed that year as the best-liked actress in the world.

Emotionally, Reagan continued to drift aimlessly; friends and fellow actors could do nothing for his mood. As he had since childhood, he kept a part of himself wrapped deep inside and seemed a "charming but very private" person. He was often unbearably lonely, sliding from date to date, drinking too much, looking for someone who would not fail him as Margaret Cleaver and Jane Wyman had.

Then, in November of 1949, he met Nancy Davis. Nancy's mother had grown up poor but married Loyal Davis, a prominent surgeon of Chicago, where Nancy grew to adulthood. By the 1930s, they were a successful family, moving in the best circles and befriending prominent movie actors. After four years at Smith College, Nancy used her mother's influence to make a start in Hollywood. Despite the help, she was barely adequate, but a reluctant MGM put her on contract in the spring of 1949. She made several films, but neither she nor the movies proved to be hits.

She also had a political problem, being confused with a different Nancy Davis who was suspected of Communist sympathies. The studio asked Reagan, as SAG president, to straighten things out, which he quickly did, clearing her name. The two met at a dinner party where he gave one of his patented monologues; whatever the reaction of the other diners, Nancy was fascinated.

They shortly had their first date, talked for hours, and left enchanted with each other. She said, "he was everything that I wanted." She liked that "he didn't talk only about himself" but expounded on a wide range of topics—the Guild, horses, wines, the Civil War.[4] The constant random patter that had for a decade driven his colleagues to distraction and his wife out of the home had at last found a willing audience.

Since the shattering impact of his divorce, Ronald Reagan had been a "revolving door date" for a remarkable number of Hollywood women. Gossip columnists made his rotating romances their regular fare. And this was the man Nancy Davis had her eye on—a challenge, indeed. She correctly perceived that "he was in no hurry to make a commitment. He had been burned in his first marriage, and the pain went deep," not to mention his earlier rejection by Margaret Cleaver.[5]

After a few dates, they let things coast for more than a year; Reagan did not want to make another mistake of the heart. He was also hard at work again, doing four movies in 1950 and serving his third term as SAG president. Still, by the fall of that year, "Nancy and Ronnie" were a steady item, although often separated by their various movie projects. On location in Arizona, he wrote her the first of a copious flow of notes and letters that would continue for nearly half a century. For her part, Nancy devised ways to fit into his world—learning to ride, tolerating alcohol, and securing a place on the SAG board. In October 1950, according to Guild's records, "President Reagan welcomed Nancy Davis to her first Board meeting."[6]

"President Reagan." No other occupant of the White House has had the experience of being called "president" for six years before ever entering elective politics. SAG was becoming an ever-larger part of his life as he planned strategy, negotiated with the studios, and ran board meetings. In colonial days, one could tell a person's occupation by his dress—the gentleman's lace collar, the artisan's leather apron. It was the same with Reagan's slow transformation from plebeian actor to SAG executive; his former garb of slacks and sweaters gave way to suits and ties.

As one biographer summarized his transition, "the charm was retained, but the boyishness and the down-home quality were fast disappearing."[7] He was developing the skills of a politician, and perhaps the ambition too. Robert Cummings told him, "one day you should run for president." When Cummings made the same remark a few years earlier on the set of *King's Row*, Reagan had passed it off with a laugh. This time the reply was simply: "yes."[8]

Throughout the next year he became increasingly serious about Nancy, who more than ever joined in his favorite activities, even an astrologer's monthly parties. At Reagan's new 350-acre ranch in Malibu Canyon, as he built length after length of redwood fence, she would follow with paint and brush. The children, Maureen, now ten, and Michael, six, happily found the time with her more congenial than their own mother's moodiness.

The couple finally married on March 4, 1952. Coincidentally, for the first century and a half of the Republic, March 4 was the date fixed by law for the swearing-in of presidents of the United States. Reagan often said later that "my life really began when I met Nancy." She "replaced an emptiness that I'd been trying to ignore for a long time."[9] For her part, she put aside her own Hollywood ambitions and became a full-time wife; fostering and guarding her husband's future became her career. Seven months later, their daughter Patti was born.

For the Reagans, that future seemed at first quite cloudy. By the end of 1951, MGM had already decided that Nancy's audience appeal was very limited and cancelled her contract. Meantime, Reagan wrapped up his own last contract film just after the turn of the year. In fact, the entire industry faced a very uncertain prospect. Attendance had dropped by half in only a few years, the Supreme Court forced studios to give up their profitable control of theater chains, and television provided ever-fiercer competition for viewers. It seemed that Reagan, at age 40, might have to think about changing his career path.

One thing he did not change—yet—was his liberal politics. He had been remarkably active in the 1948 election, organizing the Labor League of Hollywood Voters to support anti-Communist liberals. He led a massive pro-Truman rally in Los Angeles and helped Hubert Humphrey, a man of Midwestern small-town origins like himself, to win a Senate race in Minnesota. Reagan spoke up for "low-cost housing, for civil rights, for prices people can afford to pay, and for a labor movement free of the Taft-Hartley Law," claiming that "higher prices have not been caused by higher wages, but by bigger and bigger profits."[10] It sounded remarkably like what his own liberal critics would say forty years later.

In the 1950 election, Reagan supported Congresswoman Helen Gahagan Douglas, whose opponent for the U.S. Senate, Richard Nixon, accused her of being "soft on Communism." It is a measure of the actor's still fervent New Deal beliefs that some in the Douglas campaign saw him as such a "far-out liberal" that his support might actually cost her votes. Democrats tried to recruit Reagan himself for Congress in 1946 and again in 1950 to replace Douglas because he was "a stellar attraction on his own" and a good speaker.[11]

Some might see a hint of his future turn to the political right in his eager work for the Crusade for Freedom. When the Soviet "Iron Curtain" fell across Eastern Europe after 1945, Radio Free Europe was created to beam uncensored news to the Soviet satellites. The Crusade for Freedom raised funds and rallied domestic support for RFE, with help from President Truman, future president Dwight Eisenhower, and Hollywood stars including Reagan. His most visible contribution was narrating *The Big Truth*, a movie "short" for the Crusade's 1951 fund drive.

In it, he appealed for donations to RFE, which "daily pierces the iron curtain with the truth, answering the lies of the Kremlin and bringing a message of hope to millions." It was "your chance, and mine, to fight Communism."[12] Strong sentiments, but conservatives had no monopoly on anti-Communism; many a liberal was proud to express a firm resolve to resist Communism at home and abroad. President Truman and many leaders of organized labor, for instance, were fully as supportive as Reagan of the Crusade's fundraising efforts.

In November 1952, Reagan finally broke his lifelong Democratic allegiance (and that of his parents) to support Republican Dwight Eisenhower for president. The next year he became campaign chairman for Los Angeles's moderate Republican mayor, Fletcher Bowron, but he firmly turned down suggestions that he run for the U.S. Senate himself and personally remained a Democrat for another ten years.

What increasingly came to define Reagan in this time was not his occasional political activity or his fading appeal as an actor, but his work as a union leader. As president of the Screen Actors Guild for half a dozen years, his job was to represent members' welfare in their dealings with the studio bosses, and by all reports he was a very tough negotiator.

He also tried to improve race relations in Hollywood. The NAACP had long complained that African Americans were caricatured in movies and relegated to menial jobs in the studio workforce. According to one historian of Hollywood, "before Reagan's presidency, SAG had treated black grievances with a politeness that bordered on indifference."[13] Even with his support, the NAACP was able to make only very modest progress in movie casting and work assignments, but at least Reagan tried.

Another of his endeavors was more successful: his work with the Motion Picture Industry Council to polish Hollywood's public image. The MPIC was largely the creation of anti-Communist liberals, and Reagan served one term as chairman. This provided his first education in public relations, and he spoke often to service clubs and business groups, denying that Hollywood was a den of immorality and Communism.

Reagan blamed much of Hollywood's bad image on negative reporting, his first complaint about the "media bias" that was to recur often as a candidate and officeholder. Many reporters had no journalistic ethics, he said. The movie industry did not produce reprobates; "they were that way before they came here."[14] As for the Communists, he claimed that the patriotic majority in the film industry had thoroughly defeated them simply by letting democracy work. The MPIC even used some of Reagan's own films to show Hollywood's wholesome image, which of course helped enlarge his own reputation among the general public.

Part of his presidential duty was also to protect reputations that had been scorched by the "Red Scare." In the heated atmosphere of McCarthy and the Hollywood blacklist, many were falsely accused of Communist sympathies, which bothered Reagan considerably. In his capacity as SAG president, he often looked into such cases (as he had with Nancy Davis) and helped to clear the names of quite a few innocent victims.

According to SAG's longtime secretary, it "became almost a career for Reagan, . . . in correcting this."[15] However, he also insisted that anyone who had actually been in the Party but had since recanted "should be willing to stand up and be counted, admit 'I was wrong' and give all the information he has to the government agencies who are combating the Red plotters."[16] In short, they should name names.

The most controversial thing Reagan did as SAG president brought upon him the wrath of the Justice Department and the IRS and the suspicions of liberal critics even to this day. In the early 1950s, television had become a serious challenger to the film studios for the same audience of viewers and also competed for the same pool of acting talent.

Long-standing SAG rules forbade talent agencies to make movies; it was a conflict of interest to be an actress's agent and her employer. The rule did not cover television, which was brand new, and the Music Corporation of America wanted to make sure that it never would. MCA, run by Lew Wasserman, Reagan's own agent, had a near-monopoly on representing Hollywood actors. It also began to produce TV shows, and that raised the issue of the agent/producer conflict.

MCA had grand plans for dominating television. Representing the actors, the company would control the talent available to TV; making the shows, it would control the work available to the actors. The key was getting SAG to waive its conflict-of-interest rule for television, which it did in July 1952. SAG's board decided that giving MCA what it wanted would mean a vast number of new jobs for actors, who were having trouble finding work as Hollywood's movie production slumped.

As guild president, Reagan strongly supported the action. Two years later, MCA helped him land the opportunity that renewed his faltering career: host, occasional star, and eventual producer of *General Electric Theater* on television. Some people wondered, then and later, whether this plum was a delayed payoff for Reagan's help in obtaining the SAG waiver. During John Kennedy's presidency, after Reagan had become a Republican critic of "big government," the president's brother, Attorney General Robert Kennedy, launched a Justice Department investigation of the MCA deal.

The government examined his tax returns, called numerous witnesses, and grilled Reagan himself, but found no evidence of a payoff. Nevertheless, as one writer has said, "the waiver *looked* like they must have bribed some-one,"[17] and Reagan's enemies never gave up their suspicions. Actually, while Reagan certainly endorsed the MCA request, he had no vote on the board. The guild's professional staff negotiated the waiver, and the board members approved it. A recent historian concludes, "If Ronald Reagan had never been born, the guild would still have granted the waiver to MCA," and "neither the Justice Department, nor historians, nor journalists have ever been able to come up with any solid evidence" of a shady deal.[18]

After several years out of office, Reagan's last service as SAG president, in 1959, left another lingering question about his conduct. The guild brought him back for his negotiating skills in a major battle over pension and health benefits as well as "residual" payments for old movies shown on TV. After an angry six-month strike, pressure from worried members forced SAG to compromise. At one point, Reagan became so frustrated that he shouted at a waverer, "damn it . . . you are a lousy, damn strike-breaker!"—the same curse that would be hurled at him in turn when he broke the illegal Air Traffic Controllers strike in 1981.[19]

Reagan finally got the studios to create a pension fund and health insurance for actors and pay residuals on all films made after 1959. In return the guild abandoned any claim to residuals on pre-1960 movies, and some SAG members thought this gave up too much for little benefit. Although the guild's professional staff scoffed at this claim, bitter critics on the left still believed as "an article of faith that Reagan crumbled in the clutch" and practiced "sweetheart unionism" to please the studios.[20]

Professionally, the early fifties were not kind to him. Having been in Hollywood for nearly twenty years, he was a bit "shopworn," no longer the fresh-faced, eager young man of the dashing "Brass Bancroft" films. The studios had to pay ever-higher salaries to the really major stars, and with movie attendance sharply down, "actors of Reagan's modest box-office potential were an endangered species," as one biographer put it.[21]

He did make half a dozen movies from 1951 to 1953, but after that Reagan had nothing in progress. Nancy had one movie each in 1952 and 1953, but neither of them appeared in anything approaching a hit. Meanwhile, they were spending a worrisome amount of money. Besides the usual requirements of a growing family with a large house, the ranch, with its horses and staff, was an expensive proposition.

Reagan was hardly broke; he earned something from speaking engagements and the occasional guest spot on television. Still, the margin was too thin for comfort, and he was forced to think beyond the bounds of the theater. His agency, MCA, suggested a Las Vegas act in February 1954—emcee, some jokes, and a bit of song-and-dance—for the same money Reagan was making per picture in these declining years. He was doubtful, but money was money. He insisted on taking suitcases full of books with him, though, to continue his habit of constant reading, which surprised the nightclub owner who had "never seen an entertainer bring books to Las Vegas before."[22] As Reagan had feared, the act was not a memorable performance; he considered it his professional nadir.

Then the trajectory of Reagan's life began to rise again, not to peak until he left a triumphant presidency more than three decades later. His new opportunity was the product of three necessities. General Electric wanted a major TV show where it could highlight its wares, MCA wanted to break down the resistance of Hollywood stars to television, and Reagan wanted a steady—and preferably, large—income.

The result was *General Electric Theater*, beginning in September 1954. It was a half hour in Sunday evening prime time with Reagan as regular host and occasional star. *GE Theater* quickly rose to the top of the 9 p.m. Sunday lineup, partly because of the good plots and Reagan's ability as an emcee, and partly because so many popular actors were glad to appear on his show. For almost eight years, it was a stunning success.

Reagan would also spend a dozen weeks each year visiting GE's many plants around the country. His starting salary was $125,000 a year and eventually $150,000, plus a bonus for shows in which he was the lead actor, and "residual" payment when his shows were rerun. The total was about $1.5 million in today's dollars, but federal income taxes took back almost 60 percent of this, as Reagan frequently bemoaned. Eventually, his yearly earnings with GE reached some $2 million in modern purchasing power, putting him in the best financial position of his life.

These were good times for the family, as well. Husband and wife loved each other deeply; he "could never wait to get home. Nancy never tired of hearing him speak . . . [and] took an interest in whatever he liked most—the horses, baseball, politics."[23] They built a new house in 1955, outfitted with every imaginable GE device for better living, compliments of the company. To fill the cup of domestic satisfaction, another son was born in May 1958, named Ronald *Prescott* Reagan so that he would not have to go through life being called "junior."

These years changed Reagan's political outlook, fundamentally and forever. Ironically, his transformation from liberal actor and union president to conservative "Great Communicator" was the result of one man's plan to help his company overcome its own union troubles. What is called "Boulwarism" was the creation of Lemuel Boulware, the man in charge of GE relations with employees and the general public.

His unique strategy was to outflank the leadership of GE's unions by going "directly to the blue-collar workers, their families, and their neighbors."[24] Seeing Boulwarism close up—indeed, actually being a key part of it—was what Reagan called his "apprenticeship for public life." He was to use Boulware's methods very effectively as president, especially in mastering radio and television to reach around congressional opponents and take his plea for support right into the homes of voters.

Boulware regarded labor relations as a year-round process, using television, radio, local newspapers, and GE's own internal publications to "prepare the battlefield." The capstone of this program, Boulware believed, was finding a popular individual who could make the "grand tour" of GE plants year after year. This would give workers throughout the vast industrial empire a memorable shared experience and a reminder that, while they might toil in isolated factories, they were comrades in a common cause.

This is where Ronald Reagan, the actor, came in. His *GE Theater* contract had him spending a fourth of each year touring plants, where he would do

Boulware's "outreach" both to managers and to workers, a living symbol of General Electric as one united family. At first he made no speeches, simply walking the factory floor, chatting with employees about GE products and entertaining them with Hollywood stories.

Boulwarism had actually been at work for half a dozen years before Reagan came on board in 1954. Anyone employed by General Electric for that entire period would have received thousands of pages presenting the company's side of internal concerns and national economic and political issues. Hence, when Reagan began his tours, he was struck by the fact that employees themselves brought forth examples of bureaucracy and government red tape. It was Boulware's greatest triumph: an audience of workers already inclined to conservatism who gradually pulled the former Hollywood liberal from the mild left to the hard right.

Reagan calculated that, in eight years of plant tours, he was "on stage" speaking for 250,000 minutes—equivalent to an eighteen-month national political campaign, eight hours a day, seven days a week. When he was on tour, local newspapers frequently ran articles before and after his visit. In the later years, when Reagan's talks were more about conservatism than Hollywood stories, papers reported the ideological message as well.

His first tour began at company headquarters in Schenectady, New York, in August 1954. To help him along, and to rein him in if necessary, a company "minder" traveled with him, whose observations illustrate Reagan's evolving performance. At Erie, Pennsylvania, for instance, the corporate aide reported that "the women would come rushing up—mash notes, autographs and all that kind of thing," while the men stood by with disdain, "obviously saying something very derogatory." Then he drifted over for some "guy talk," and after ten minutes "they were all slapping him on the back saying 'That's the way, Ron.'"[25]

And so it went, place after place, week after week, for eight full years. Reagan also liked to break up the routine by seeing the local sights. One day, on a side visit to a state capitol, he ran across a group of grade-school children and gave them an impromptu talk. "It was part Jack Kennedy, part William Jennings Bryan," his aide remembered, and left the students and their teacher dazzled.[26]

Reagan had no formal speeches scheduled because the GE man did not want the trouble of writing them, but he soon learned that the Hollywood actor could do fine on his own. After one plant visit, Reagan talked to a convention of teachers whose scheduled speaker was sick. With no preparation, after a day of meetings, he shifted mental gears, and "gave a speech on education that just dropped them in the aisles," according to his minder. "He got a good ten-minute standing applause afterward." His companion realized that "everything that went into that mind stayed there. He could quote it out like a computer any time you wanted."[27] Or, as his fellow actors and his first wife had found, even when they didn't want it.

After the first year, the company was confident enough to expand the variety of Reagan's performances. A typical stopover in the middle years was the one at Henderson, North Carolina, in March of 1957. It was minutely scheduled and tightly packed: breakfast with the local media, thirty minutes with the managers, a cafeteria talk with white-collar and hourly workers, and a lunch visit with the local service clubs.

The afternoon included a tour of the Outdoor Lighting plant and a side visit to the high school, where Reagan showed GE employees and families the upcoming episode of *GE Theater*. Finally, he spent the evening at a country-club reception with plant executives, their wives, and local community leaders. From morning to night, almost nonstop—and this was only one of fifty visits on this national tour.

Throughout each day, Reagan fit his performance to his audience—to managers, product talk; with the employees, Hollywood gossip and "fellow union member" bonding; at the local receptions, a series of one-on-one chats. His corporate companion marveled at Reagan's energy. Between stops, Reagan studied company publications so that he could discuss them easily and field questions without hesitation.

He did even more reading on the cross-country train, having for many years refused to fly (his official GE contract even specified "no airplanes"). As the "Super Chief" carried him from Los Angeles to Chicago and points East for his annual tour, Reagan spent hours each day reading and taking frequent notes on index cards. These grew in number to form an eventual mountain of information—not all of it accurate—with which he peppered his speeches even into the presidency and beyond.

In the later GE years, there were fewer plant visits and more speeches to outside groups—local chambers of commerce and service clubs at first, but eventually statewide conferences or "upscale" groups in major cities. The 1957 North Carolina stopover was at this intermediate stage, a combination of company and community events. By 1958, Boulware had changed focus even more, to encompass almost entirely speeches outside GE on the "meat and potatoes" circuit, and this overtly political campaign lasted through the remainder of Reagan's years with the company.

Why the shift from in-plant morale-boosting visits, to local group talks, and finally to national audiences? Simply put, Boulware had become very worried about labor relations and the political climate. The two great national union groups, the American Federation of Labor and the Congress of Industrial Organizations, merged in 1955, so that companies like General Electric faced a more formidable united labor front.

The political world seemed more dangerous also. In 1958, "right to work" laws, allowing people to hold jobs without joining a union, were resoundingly defeated in half a dozen states. (Reagan himself opposed the Right to Work initiative on the California ballot that year.) Democrats won a landslide victory in the November elections, bringing dozens of pro-union senators and congressmen to Washington. Finally, in 1960, Eisenhower's pro-business Republican administration gave way to John F. Kennedy's "New Frontier."

In response, Boulware shifted the target of Reagan's tours from the company's workers to the voters at large. The impact of the new campaign was increased by Reagan's own wide national popularity from hosting the television show. *General Electric Theater* was the most-watched show in Sunday evening prime time for seven years straight, and Reagan himself was one of the best-paid stars on TV and "one of the most recognized men in the country."[28]

A swing through Schenectady in 1959 illustrates the new strategy of using Reagan beyond the company's own audience. For months ahead of time, the factory newspaper prepared the way with articles denouncing liberal legislation, inflation, and high taxes. By the time Reagan arrived, his speech at the YMCA was almost an anticlimax. He lamented high taxes and the federal bureaucracy and warned that economic freedom itself was in danger. It was this message, repeated endlessly before audiences small and large, that the company hoped would move public opinion in a conservative direction. It certainly moved Reagan himself.

He quickly noticed an interesting reaction: "No matter where I was, I'd find people from the audience waiting to talk to me after the speech and they'd all say, 'Hey, if you think things are bad in your business, let me tell you what is happening in my business.'"[29] He began including their examples in later speeches, and very gradually his Hollywood content diminished, and each talk became a diatribe against "big government."

One might ask, "why, then, was Reagan still a Democrat?" He finally asked himself that very question and told his wife, "all these things I've been criticizing about government being too big, well, it just dawned on me that every four years when an election comes along, I go out and support the people who are responsible for the things I've been criticizing."[30] By 1960, he realized that he should be a Republican, although it took him two more years to make the switch official.

The state of Reagan's political mind toward the end of the General Electric years is well illustrated in "Losing Freedom by Installments," a speech typical of many he gave before community audiences in pursuit of Boulware's public-outreach strategy. It shows what Reagan meant when he said that "I wasn't just making speeches—I was preaching a sermon."[31]

He began with the overriding issue of the day, the contest "between the free world and Soviet slavery," warning that Communism advanced by playing upon the West's fear of war. Of course, this sentiment was widely shared even among liberals like President Kennedy, who one year later led the world to the doorstep of destruction over Russian missiles in Cuba.

The rest of the speech showed just how far Reagan had moved in the past dozen years. He scoffed at liberal claims that "the welfare state is the best insurance against revolution," an argument he himself had made in the early postwar period. He denounced federal aid to education, farm subsidies, foreign aid, public housing, and government health insurance (or "socialized medicine" in the conservative vocabulary).

This critique of federal programs led the speaker to his ultimate quarry: high taxes. No nation, he claimed, had ever survived taxation equaling a third or more of its income, and the United States was exactly at that tipping point. The basic message of the tax-raising, big-spending liberals was that "you and I are not smart enough to spend our own money."

The whole tone of the speech was accusatory toward government and pessimistic about the future. There was little here of the later Reagan, of the optimistic, almost triumphal rhetoric of the presidential years. He called for a rising of the people to roll back the liberal tide. Otherwise, the future would be dismal, "telling our children and our children's children what it once was like in America when men were free."

The same warning, against big government at home and Communist encroachment abroad, was the theme of nearly all Reagan's rhetoric in the early 1960s. At several massive televised rallies for the Southern California School of Anti-Communism, he cautioned a youthful audience that "Communists will appeal to your rebellious nature." He padded out these sentiments, which he had held even as a postwar liberal, with newly conservative critiques of "big government," the progressive income tax, and Kennedy's "New Frontier." As one scholar says, "by the beginning of 1962, Reagan had purged himself of all former taints of liberalism."[32]

Reagan was part of a national revival of conservative ideas and political action that gathered strength after 1945. The postwar conservative movement actually began during the war, with the publication of Friedrich Hayek's *The Road to Serfdom* in 1944. Hayek's message was stern and stark: central economic planning leads to dictatorship. In its early stages—whether welfare-state capitalism or democratic socialism—government control can seem compatible with political liberty. But the appetite grows by what it feeds upon, and power lusts for yet more power. What begins as a benign attempt at efficient economic planning necessarily ends in Mussolini's fascism, Hitler's Nazism, or Stalin's Communism.

It was a fertile time for a voice like Hayek's. The federal government responded to depression in the 1930s and world war in the 1940s with a pervasive control of economic life unimaginable to earlier generations. Thousands of pages of minute regulations on business, record-high taxes, and wartime rationing had been endured out of the necessity to overcome those two great challenges. Now the Depression was a memory and Hitler was a corpse. In the years of peace after 1945, more people began to think of Washington as a dangerous "governmental octopus."

The Road to Serfdom was the opening shot in the slow rallying of a conservative skirmish line against the powers of liberalism that seemed, on every side, to command the political high ground: the presidency, Congress, Hollywood, and the academic world. There were path-breaking books like Henry Hazlitt's 1946 *Economics in One Lesson* and *God and Man at Yale* by the young college graduate William F. Buckley in 1951. There were magazines like *Human Events*, begun in 1944, *The Freeman* in 1950, and—most influential of all—*National Review* in 1955. There was the Intercollegiate Society of Individualists, which began training college students to question their professors' liberal orthodoxy in 1953, and even a new publishing house founded by Henry Regnery in 1947.

The leading conservatives of the 1950s and 1960s were men like Russell Kirk, William Buckley, and William Rusher. Theirs were the ideas that guided Reagan's slow glide from a New Deal liberal to a Goldwater conservative. Kirk's book *The Conservative Mind*, Buckley's and Rusher's magazine *National Review*, and Regnery's weekly *Human Events* were the conservative answer to the liberal *New Republic* and *The Nation*.

In his first conservative years through the mid-1960s, Reagan absorbed what these men wrote and shared their intense concern about politics and government. Later, especially in his presidential years, Reagan's thinking about America and its future came to have little in common with these traditional conservatives. They looked to Edmund Burke, the English thinker of the late eighteenth century, as their model, while the man Reagan quoted most fondly was Thomas Paine, Burke's great nemesis in that Age of Revolutions.

Paine's exuberant claim from the Revolutionary pamphlet *Common Sense*, that "we have it in our power to make the world over again!" was one of Reagan's favorites. The last thing Edmund Burke ever wanted was to remake the world. To him, the standing order of things was quite good enough. Burke looked fondly backward, not forward into the future. Stability, order, tradition—these were his watchwords and those of his mid-twentieth century disciples like Kirk, Buckley, and Rusher.

Furthermore, Reagan's personality and experience ill fit the pattern of the traditional conservatives. They were ideologues and intellectuals; Reagan was a pragmatic "common man." They were educated in the Ivy League; Reagan went to Eureka. They were of the "country club" set; Reagan had been a country-club caddy. Most of all, they were pessimistic about the course of history. They fancied themselves fighting a courageous rear-guard action against the relentless push of collectivism at home and Communism abroad. Whitaker Chambers feared that his conversion from Communist Party member to anti-Communist meant that he had gone from the winning to the losing side in the modern world. In a 1955 *National Review* editorial, Bill Buckley memorably said that the duty of conservatives was to "stand athwart history, yelling STOP."

Here the contrast with the later Reagan of the 1970s and 1980s was immense. He was the eternal optimist. In the common method of calculating time, the future might not have arrived yet, but Ronald Reagan already lived in it. The song "America the Beautiful" celebrates the "patriot dream that sees beyond the years," and if ever a man embodied that sentiment, it was Reagan.

Still, this positive outlook took some time to form. As an advocate of Boulwarism in the General Electric period, his emergent conservatism was still heavily weighted with the dark forebodings of the men whose books and magazines he read and whose ideas he absorbed. The pressure that liberals began to apply in attempting to silence him only increased his sense that America was fast sliding toward a crisis of freedom.

The most serious censorship effort involved the Tennessee Valley Authority. Among Reagan's many examples of federal programs that had ballooned far beyond their original limits was the TVA, a New Deal agency created to generate cheap electric power for rural counties. General Electric had sold the TVA millions of dollars of equipment, and in 1959 the government threatened to cancel GE's federal business if the company did not shut Reagan up. Ralph Cordiner, GE's chairman, absolutely refused, but Reagan thought the blunt threats to punish GE's business showed "how late it is if we are to save freedom."[33]

Among other incidents, the local teachers' union tried to prevent him from speaking to high school students in Minnesota. Reagan pushed ahead anyway and proudly noted that his audience "stood and cheered for five minutes. They damn well didn't want someone telling them whom they could or couldn't listen to."[34] Labor unions in general, which had seen Reagan as one of their own and had praised his leadership of the SAG strike in 1959, now turned upon him as a traitor. "Right-wing extremist" was the mildest of the labels his former union friends pasted on him.

Reagan said that when he spoke against "big government during six years of the Eisenhower administration" it was "accepted as . . . nonpartisan." Once Kennedy was president, the same speech was denounced as "a partisan political attack, an expression of right-wing extremism." He attributed this to the fact that as a "Democrat for Nixon" in 1960, he had become "a target on the priority list."[35] Although many liberals had dismissed Kennedy as far too moderate during the campaign, Reagan feared that "under the tousled boyish hair cut it is still old Karl Marx."[36]

With a Democratic regime in the White House, GE moguls had to be more careful what their spokesman said. Some of them wanted Reagan to forget the "government is out to get you" theme and simply promote the company's products, but he would not hear of it. Shortly, the show and his national tours were canceled. One might suppose that this had something to do with fears of retaliation from the Kennedys.

In fact, pure market economics largely dictated that decision. After ruling Sunday evening prime time for seven years, *GE Theater* met its match in the new Western series, *Bonanza*, whose hour-long color program with four regular stars made GE's half-hour of random guest stars in black and white seem tame and old-fashioned. Reagan was sent packing in the spring of 1962 (ironically, *Bonanza* was later his favorite television series.) A harder and more personal blow came in July when his mother, Nelle, died after suffering in her declining years from Alzheimer's disease.

For the next two years, Reagan had no steady income, although he certainly made good money from guest spots on TV and from speaking engagements that were lined up several years ahead by the time GE let him go. He also did one last movie, *The Killers*, late in 1963. Twenty-six years earlier in his very first film, he got star billing; in this, his last one, he was listed fifth. Adding injury to insult, the film flopped at the box office.

Freed from being a company spokesman, Reagan became active in a directly political way. In 1962 he raised money for Congressman John Rousselot, a member of the far-right John Birch Society, and supported Richard Nixon against Democratic governor Pat Brown. More boldly, he backed a conservative challenger to California's moderate Republican Senator, Thomas Kuchel. All three lost. Some people had wanted Reagan himself to oppose Kuchel, but that was too aggressive even for him.

Nevertheless, it was clear that Reagan's next role would be not on the sound stage but in electoral politics. He worked with a professional writer on his autobiography, *Where's the Rest of Me?* Even a casual reading shows that Reagan's aim was not to tell the full story of his life but to emphasize his leadership in SAG and in the struggle against Hollywood Communists. There is barely a mention of his nine-year marriage to Jane Wyman, and his years in radio get only ten pages, while the details of battling studio heads and Communist agitators cover a full hundred.

When Arizona Senator Barry Goldwater sought the Republican presidential nomination in 1964, conservatives rushed to join his crusade.

Reagan did everything he could to help, becoming co-chairman of the senator's California campaign and speaking all over the state to huge crowds. It was sometimes not clear whether the audience came to cheer for Goldwater or for Reagan himself.

The Reagans were alternate delegates to the national convention in San Francisco, where the Goldwater majority booed liberal Republicans and cast angry looks at journalists. As former president Eisenhower spoke, Reagan watched him intently with a look the liberal novelist Gore Vidal had often seen in rehearsals: "the understudy examines the star's performance and tries to figure how it is done. An actor prepares, I said to myself: Mr. Reagan is planning to go into politics." Vidal thought that mayor of Beverly Hills might be within his reach.[37]

After San Francisco, Reagan continued to boost Goldwater's uphill campaign against President Lyndon Johnson. His greatest service, and a life-changing moment for Reagan himself, came in late October. He spoke at a Los Angeles event and his remarks, entitled "A Time for Choosing," gripped his audience as nothing else had in that long year of speeches. Two of Goldwater's wealthy supporters thought the speech was just the thing to give the floundering campaign a charge of energy. They bought television time and unleashed Reagan on his first national political audience.

Speaking as a former Democrat, he said that "the issues confronting us cross party lines. . . . We are at war with the most dangerous enemy that has ever faced mankind in his long climb from the swamp to the stars." He told of two friends talking to a Cuban refugee from Castro's regime. Hearing the grim tale of life under Communism, one marveled, "we don't know how lucky we are." The Cuban said, "how lucky you are? I had some place to escape to." Reagan warned his audience, "in that sentence he told us the entire story. If we lose freedom here, there's no place to escape to. This is the last stand on earth."

It was not an especially eloquent address. There were sparks of eloquence in it, but for the most part it was a routine recital of conservative talking points. "We have come," Reagan said, "to a time for choosing. Either we accept the responsibility for our own destiny, or we abandon the American Revolution. . . . Already the hour is late. Government has laid its hands on health, housing, farming, industry, commerce, education."

It was a far better argument for Goldwater's issues than the candidate himself had made. He closed with a typical Reagan flourish: "You and I have a rendezvous with destiny. We can preserve for our children this, the last best hope of man on earth, or we can sentence them to take the first step into a thousand years of darkness."

The public response was astounding: a last-minute outpouring of money for Goldwater, over a million dollars in 24 hours. There was also a new conservative hero in the land. The reaction of a precinct chairman in North Carolina was typical; hearing Reagan on the radio that night, he said to himself *"that's* who we should be running for president!"[38]

That evening, Reagan had doubts about his performance; "I hope I haven't let Barry down," he worried. In the middle of the night, a phone call woke him up. It was Goldwater headquarters, reporting a massive flood of contributions unlike anything Washington had ever seen. "Of course, you probably expected this reaction all along," the caller said. Altogether, his effort, rebroadcast in many places, supposedly raised $8 million, about half of the Goldwater campaign's entire budget.[39]

"The Speech," as it came to be known, did not save Goldwater's campaign—nothing could have done that. As anyone who knew public opinion polling could have predicted, there were no hidden millions of nonvoting conservatives eager to rush to the polls for "a choice, not an echo." If anything, nonvoters—being, as a group, less wealthy, less educated, and less white than frequent voters—were more liberal and more Democratic than people who usually did vote.

Instead of attracting hordes of new voters, Goldwater did the opposite. His combative attitude, refusal to make peace with the moderates, and reckless statements about nuclear weapons drove away millions of traditional Republicans. The result was disaster. Johnson won over 61 percent of the popular vote, the highest for any candidate in American history. Goldwater was the only Republican ever to lose all but one non-Southern state. In ten states he carried not a single county.

There was never any doubt that Goldwater would lose, but the size of his defeat was catastrophic for the Republican Party and especially for conservatives. No one could have defeated Johnson, running as the "JFK Memorial President" so soon after Kennedy's assassination. Polling indicated, however, that either Rockefeller or Nixon would have lost by far less. As it was, not only did Goldwater lose by a historic margin, he dragged down dozens of Republicans running for Congress, the Senate, and state offices. The next day, conservatives in Michigan, looking to the future, created a new group—"Republicans for Ronald Reagan."[40]

California conservatives had the same thought, and Reagan, for his part, kept himself in the public eye. In the spring of 1965, while many Republicans still winced at the painful memory of the Goldwater disaster, Reagan urged a renewed commitment to the cause. Speaking to a California Young Republican convention, he conjured them to "rise up from this defeat and start the second round of our struggle to restore the republic."[41]

It sounded for all the world like the hopeful music of the choir on All Saints' Day: "When the strife is fierce, the warfare long; steals on the ear the distant triumph song; and hearts are brave again, and arms are strong." A new note of optimism was beginning to lighten the formerly somber tone of so many of Reagan's past jeremiads. A transformation was underway, from the fearful depiction of America on the brink of disaster in "A Time for Choosing" to a more confident tone that summoned the faithful to overcome all difficulties and secure the ultimate victory.

Reagan was in fact ideally suited, by training, temperament, and even geography, to relight the torch snuffed out by Goldwater's defeat. He lived in the center of California conservatism, the fast-growing Los Angeles metropolitan area, home to huge fundamentalist Protestant churches, the Christian Anti-Communism Crusade, and the largest John Birch Society membership in the nation.

In 1964 these zealots helped Goldwater win a narrow victory over Rockefeller in the California primary, but, except in fundamental beliefs, Reagan was no Barry Goldwater. In fact, he "was everything the bristly Goldwater was not: personable, self-effacing, and eternally optimistic even in the face of the Soviet menace."[42]

On the eve of his transformation from private critic to public candidate, here is what Ronald Reagan had come to believe, laid out in *Where's the Rest of Me?*, published in 1965. Liberals, he said, used to think that "the individual was, and should be forever, the master of his destiny. That is now the conservative position. The liberal used to believe in freedom under law" but now worships "stronger central government" and thinks that "control is better than freedom." He ruefully concluded that "the labels somehow have got pasted on the wrong people."[43]

Of course the liberal might reply that, often, government power is what preserves and expands freedom—for African Americans to vote in the South, for women to seek employment in any field, for workers to form a union, for consumers to buy without being cheated. Nor would Reagan himself have disagreed with any of these achievements.

His complaint was simply that, to preserve liberty, power must have clear limits and it increasingly seemed to recognize none. To him, taxing away over half of a person's income was unfair; spending ten times as much on welfare as in the depths of the Depression was absurd; telling a farmer what he could grow on his own land for his own use was insane. He often warned that "already the hour is late." To paraphrase Dunning's famous parliamentary challenge to George III, Reagan believed that "the power of government has increased, is increasing, and ought to be diminished."

Notes

1. Reagan in *Where's The Rest of Me?*, 241.
2. Richard Todd, *Caught in the Act: The Story of My Life* (London, Hutchinson, 1986), 234.
3. Reagan quoted in Morris, *Dutch*, 271.

4. Nancy Reagan, *My Turn: The Memoirs of Nancy Reagan* (New York: Random House, 1989), 95.
5. *Ibid.*, 98.
6. Board minutes quoted in Colacello, *Ronnie and Nancy*, 250.
7. Edwards, *Early Reagan*, 361.
8. *Ibid.*
9. Reagan, *An American Life*, 123.
10. Vaughn, *Ronald Reagan in Hollywood*, 158.
11. Sally Denton, *The Pink Lady: The Many Lives of Helen Gahagan Douglas* (New York: Bloomsbury Press, 2009), 136.
12. Reagan quoted in Richard H. Cummings, *Radio Free Europe's "Crusade for Freedom" Rallying Americans Behind Cold War Broadcasting, 1950-1960* (Jefferson, NC: McFarland & Co., 2009), 53.
13. Vaughn, *Ronald Reagan in Hollywood*, 176.
14. *Ibid.*, 189.
15. Jack Dales, "Pragmatic Leadership," UCLA Oral History Program, 22.
16. Reagan newspaper column, in Edwards, *Early Reagan*, 404.
17. Connie Bruck, *When Hollywood Had a King: The Reign of Lew Wasserman, Who Leveraged Talent into Power and Influence* (New York: Random House, 2003), 187.
18. David F. Prindle, *The Politics of Glamour: Ideology and Politics in the Screen Actors Guild* (Madison: University of Wisconsin Press, 1988), 81.
19. Reagan, *Where's the Rest of Me?*, 318.
20. *Ibid.*, 87.
21. Edwards, *Early Reagan*, 444.
22. Nancy Reagan, *My Turn*, 130.
23. Edwards, *Early Reagan*, 460.
24. Thomas W. Evans, *The Education of Ronald Reagan: The General Electric Years and the Untold Story of His Conversion of Conservatism* (New York: Columbia University Press, 2006), 38.
25. Earl B. Dunkel, "Ronald Reagan and the General Electric Theater, 1954-1955," Regional Oral History Office, Bancroft Library, University of California Berkeley, 10.
26. Quoted in Evans, *Education of Reagan*, 60.
27. Dunkel, "Ronald Reagan and General Electric," UC Berkeley Oral History Office, 13-15.
28. Morris, *Dutch*, 305.
29. Ronald Reagan, *An American Life* (New York: Simon & Schuster, 1990), 129.
30. *Ibid.*, 132.
31. Reagan in *An American Life*, 132-134. The speech was printed in the trade magazine *Qualified Contractor* in November 1961.
32. Ross, *Hollywood Left and Right*, 163
33. Reagan, *Where's the Rest of Me?*, 305-306.
34. *Ibid.*, 307.
35. *Ibid.*, 307, 336.
36. Reagan to Richard Nixon, in Morris, *Dutch*, 316.
37. Gore Vidal, *Homage to Daniel Shays: Collected Essays, 1952-1972* (New York: Random House, 1972), 309.
38. This incident was witnessed by the author.
39. Evans, *Education of Reagan*, 169.
40. Edwards, *Early Reagan*, 486.
41. Ross, *Hollywood Left and Right*, 173.
42. *Ibid.*
43. Reagan, *Where's the Rest of Me?*, 337.

CHAPTER **4**

GOVERNOR REAGAN

Ronald Reagan's transition to the world of politics was made easier by the absence of powerful leaders in the California Republican party. More than half a century of Republican rule had come undone in the late 1950s, and by the mid-1960s California was slipping fast toward long-term Democratic dominance. This was a shocking change for a Republican Party used to winning easily, often with no effective opposition.

After the Goldwater disaster, some Republicans concluded that the best way to revive their feeble party was to put Reagan up for governor in 1966. In many ways, he seemed the ideal candidate. He was from the Los Angeles area, home to half the state's people; he would have the Goldwater ground organization working for him; he was a former Democrat who could eat into that party's three-to-two majority of voters; and he was already a household name to millions.

Above all, he was well suited to the new age of media politics. In the Nixon-Kennedy debates of 1960, people who read about or listened to the debates thought Nixon had won, while those who watched on TV picked Kennedy. Every smart politician took notice. Because of his long movie career and his eight-year run on *GE Theater*, Reagan was already a master of TV, even as most politicians were still struggling to understand it.

In early 1965 a small group of former Goldwater men set out to groom Reagan for governor. Meantime, Neil Reagan, who had become a successful advertising executive, got his brother a two-year television contract hosting the series *Death Valley Days*. It paid the same as General Electric, but for much less work, leaving Reagan free to explore political possibilities. He spent six months traveling and speaking all over California, getting large crowds and a good response.

Understandably cautious about the life-changing possibilities of a new career in politics, Reagan held back as long as he could. Finally, the enthusiastic public response from his travels pushed him over the line in September. "And there we were," his wife said, "on a road we never intended to be on. Ever."[1] For twenty years Reagan had often been asked to run for office. Had the idea really never appealed to him? Whatever the truth of Nancy's disclaimer, he was ready now.

A few businessmen and lawyers created a "Kitchen Cabinet" that became Reagan's advisors during the campaign and his governorship. They asked the prestigious political consultants Stuart Spencer and William Roberts to handle the candidate. The Spencer-Roberts team usually worked for more moderate Republicans, and at first they were uncertain about taking Reagan on, so they took their time sizing the man up. Finally, tired of their caution, he challenged them to make up their minds. "We're not finished checking," they said. "We don't want to find out you're a Bircher or something."[2] So the next time they saw Reagan, he sported blazing red socks as if to say, "guys, would a John Bircher wear these things?" That was enough to sign them up.

Reagan announced in January 1966. Reporters questioned his support by members of the John Birch Society, but he said that whoever endorsed him "has bought my philosophy; I haven't bought his." The major issues of the campaign could be collapsed into one: "retire Pat Brown."[3] His press conference was a triumph of its type, but the media-savvy Reagan did more. He blanketed the state with a half-hour television program, introducing himself directly to voters in their living rooms. Others had tried to use television, but Reagan was the first to make it the center of his campaign. It was Day One of a new age in American politics.

Speaking without notes, Reagan denounced high taxes, high crime, high welfare spending, and high unemployment—the sad story of Pat Brown's Seven Lean Years as governor. He concluded by asking viewers the perennial question at the core of conservative ideology: how can politicians and bureaucrats "manage our lives better than we can manage them ourselves?" The event impressed even liberal reporters. One said that Reagan had "found his true calling in politics. . . . He was so enormously gifted that he seemed a president-in-waiting."[4]

The voters were impressed also. Lyn Nofziger, who would become one of Reagan's closest advisors, told Bill Roberts, "There's something out there. . . . I don't know what it is, but there's something between Reagan and the people. He's going to be elected." And he added, "someday he might even be president." Roberts, although hired to run the campaign, wondered, "what will the poor soul do if he's ever elected governor!"[5]

Worried that Reagan was too conservative and too naïve to survive a tough fall campaign against Pat Brown, some Republicans supported former San Francisco mayor George Christopher in the primary. They believed that the more moderate Christopher could defeat Brown, while Reagan, nice fellow though he was, risked being another "Goldwater embarrassment." The candidate himself had no such doubts, confident that party politics could be no worse than the union politics he had mastered in the Screen Actors Guild.

California in 1966 was a huge place, daunting to any candidate—the third largest state in area, the largest in population, and immensely varied—but Reagan had performed on an even bigger stage. For eight years with General Electric, he had in effect campaigned nationwide, speaking many times a day, judging his audience, honing his message, and carefully measuring out his energy to last the day. After this preparation, running in a single state might almost have seemed a vacation.

During these months, Nancy Reagan began her own transformation from supportive wife to active partner in her husband's political career. Stuart Spencer found her a natural politician, and the pair of them a formidable team. She had a clearer insight, he thought, "in terms of what was better for Ron," than the candidate did.[6] He was a master at expressing his own principles, while she was an abler judge of who would serve the campaign best. Spencer said, "he'd never have made it without her."[7]

With divorce still a black mark against a candidate for office, Nancy agreed with Spencer-Roberts that the campaign's "family focus" should be on Patti and Ron, with no mention of Maureen and Michael, products of her husband's failed marriage to Jane Wyman. It was an unnatural and painful situation; one can imagine how the two children felt who were thrust nameless into the shadows. Both had already had problems with their stepmother and found their father emotionally distant, and now came this new indignity, being airbrushed from the family portrait.

As many in Hollywood had noticed, the outwardly gregarious Reagan was actually a very private person. He had many acquaintances but almost no close friends. This drawing-in was very probably the lifelong inheritance of a child constantly uprooted from his young friends by a peripatetic family, as well as having to build a protective emotional wall against the shame of an alcoholic father.

But, family and personality aside, the campaign must go on, so Spencer-Roberts put a pair of college professors with Reagan, priming him on the state's issues and political landscape. They found him charismatic, widely read in political philosophy, and a man of firm convictions; "everything, for him, flows from the Constitution."[8] The candidate wrote his own speeches, as he always had, but the academics gave him specific examples to rotate into each speech.

In this campaign Reagan's rhetoric began to shift away from the old conservative jeremiad about the sad state of America and assume a more optimistic tone. The complaints about liberal misgovernment and a decadent society were still there, but now Reagan assured his audience that a solution was at hand if they would entrust their future to him. A resolute America could conquer every problem.

Of course, any campaign against an incumbent must focus on the negative, and there was much that Reagan criticized. Governor Brown had doubled state spending, welfare costs were rising rapidly, and taxes had gone up 50 percent. The crime rate was twice the national average, and race riots and campus protests produced an angry public. Reagan played upon this anger as he denounced student radicals, black rioters, and welfare cheats. But unlike other critics of 'Sixties America, he looked reassuringly beyond the angry present to unfold a vision of the triumphant future, of a state governed by 'moral truth,' not by "political hacks. . . . A dream you can believe in. . . . A dream that can come true."[9]

He made only one serious blunder in the primary campaign. At a joint appearance before the Negro Republican Assembly, Christopher virtually accused Reagan of bigotry for opposing the 1964 Civil Rights Bill as an unconstitutional use of federal power. Tired and slightly ill, Reagan denounced his opponent and stormed out, although he soon calmed down, came back, and apologized to his audience.

There was no lasting harm, but the incident did illustrate a difficulty for conservatives. Given the nation's long history of slavery and discrimination, how did someone like Reagan—who had not a bigoted bone in his body—distinguish his opposition to civil rights laws on constitutional grounds from the more racial opposition by Southern Democrats like George Wallace?

On election day, Reagan beat George Christopher more than two to one, a greater margin than Brown's over his Democratic rival, Los Angeles Mayor Sam Yorty (who quickly endorsed Reagan, bringing many other conservative Democrats with him). The happy nominee believed that he could move toward November with Democrats divided and Republicans united, but he hoped "we can keep some of the kooks quiet."[10] This from the man whom many liberals thought was himself King of the Kooks.

Reagan immediately brought Christopher's key supporters into the campaign. This was exactly the opposite of Goldwater's cold refusal two years earlier to soothe the bruises on the Republican body politic produced by his presidential nomination. Some of Reagan's own "Goldwaterite" enthusiasts were dismayed to see their hero inviting the vanquished enemy to join the feast in the victor's tent. Associating with moderates might seduce Reagan from his core beliefs. This would become a perennial concern of the Republican right wing, whose battle cry during his presidency was "Let Reagan Be Reagan!"

Pat Brown could hardly wait to get at his man; he agreed with *The New York Times* that the idea of Reagan as governor was absurd. It was the mistake of his political life. One of his staff knew better, telling the governor frankly that "this sonofabitch is going to beat the shit out of you . . . He's the guy with the white hat. You just can't make him a bad guy."[11] Ignoring this advice, Brown tried to do what he had in all his previous campaigns: turn his opponent into a demon so that voters would recoil in horror. He scoffed at Reagan's movie roles and tried to make him out as an extremist. The state Democratic chairman helped by peddling to the media a screed on "Ronald Reagan, Extremist Collaborator."

It proved impossible to do a "hatchet job" on Reagan, whose genial countenance and unthreatening rhetoric were a sufficient aegis to shelter him from the governor's attacks. Instead, as often happens in negative campaigns, polls showed that Brown himself seemed the demon. He was like the man who "digged a pit. He digged it deep; he digged it for his brother. But he fell in, was drowned therein, and died instead of t'other."

Meanwhile, the Reagan campaign, well-run and well-funded, kept its focus on the few issues that voters cared most about—taxes, welfare, crime, and campus unrest—and wrapped them into one overriding theme: Brown's incompetence and failed leadership. When the governor complained that Reagan had no political experience, the challenger happily agreed: "I am not a politician, I am an ordinary citizen. . . . If we ordinary citizens don't run government, government is going to run us."[12]

Unlike some conservatives, Reagan got along well with the press and got generally good treatment, although most reporters were politically liberal and saw him as a mental lightweight. As the campaign wore on, he did impress some of them with his skill on the stump, and his brother, Neil, described one cynical reporter's realization that Reagan was more than a smooth tongue in an empty head. When the candidate stood up to speak on a complicated topic with only a few note cards, the big-city journalist was sure that Reagan would embarrass himself. After listening to a perfectly delivered talk, every fact accurately conveyed, the reporter told Neil, "I would never have believed it if I hadn't seen it."[13] That was the usual reaction of many who underestimated Ronald Reagan. At least the reporter's error did not cost him his job, as happened to poor Pat Brown.

The contrast between Reagan and Brown almost personified the divide between past and future. The newcomer used television to reach mass audiences; the incumbent relied on traditional handshaking tours and personal appearances. When Brown finally did appear on TV, this only drove home the contrast. One journalist noticed that while the governor might stumble over a word, Reagan's delivery was smooth and capable, and "Brown never smiles; Reagan has that beautiful smile."[14]

Attacking the governor for reckless spending, high taxes, and helpless acquiescence to riots and radicals, Reagan seemed competent and assured. Belittled as a political neophyte, he turned the handicap into a weapon, lecturing Brown that America "was created by ordinary citizens, not by politicians." This was technically a misstatement, given the long political service of the Founders, but Reagan's audience knew what he meant: they were the masters in America; politicians were their servants.

In the end, the remaining undecided voters flocked to Reagan and a close race became a million-vote landslide. Brown's manager, explaining why his candidate lost so badly, laid much of the blame on their underestimation of Reagan, who was "terribly pleasant, highly articulate, and has a serious approach about politics. People like him, and we didn't understand that. We missed the human dimension of Ronald Reagan."[15]

Reagan was sworn in as governor the very minute it was legally possible—midnight on January 2, 1967—to cut short a spate of post-election judicial appointments by Pat Brown. The evening before, his Kitchen Cabinet had celebrated with a toast: "To the Governor! Who knows, one day he may be our president."[16]

He and his staff came into office suspicious of the government they would run, a sentiment born partly of ignorance. With no clear idea of what a governor actually did, the new occupant assumed that competent business and professional people would be eager to join his administration and reform state government. In this he was disappointed. Few were willing to take the substantial pay cut that government service required or to subject their financial and personal history to public scrutiny.

Those who did were often wholly innocent of the workings of state government. In the computer age they would have been "clueless newbies." One of their most dangerous deficiencies, shared by Reagan himself, was not understanding the vital need for a good working relationship with the legislature. In any government there is usually tension between the executive and legislative branches, and this was especially so in 1967 Sacramento, where the executive was inexperienced, conservative, and Republican and the legislature experienced, liberal, and Democratic.

While Reagan struggled through the initial disappointments of putting an administration together, his wife had her own difficult time adjusting to life in Sacramento. At first, the couple did not even want to be in the capital city any more than they had to. For nearly two years, they escaped back to

Los Angeles most weekends, drawn by the pleasure of associating with their old Hollywood friends instead of grubby politicians.

In the "slack years" when their movie careers were fading, they were rarely invited to posh events, much to Nancy's dismay. Now, as California's most sought-after couple, the "best people" competed to host them. Sacramento's stale political atmosphere could hardly compare. When the Reagans did settle down in the capital, they fled the fancy but decrepit governor's mansion to live in a luxurious house owned by friends and furnished with tax-deductible gifts, to much media criticism.

This distressed Nancy Reagan, and from then on, through the presidency and after, she displayed a steely alertness against hostile journalists. The governor himself was casually dismissive toward hard knocks from the media; he had seen enough critical reviews of his acting not to let them bother him. Sometimes, though, he had to restrain his wife from going after the critics head-on. "I have to bar the door every once in a while," he said, "or she'll march forth and do battle."[17]

As the most "public" person in his state, any governor is on display to legislators, journalists, and the voters. Despite this constant requirement of his office, Reagan remained remarkably private during his eight years in Sacramento. His staff found him a pleasure to work for, always courteous, rarely demanding, but formal and emotionally distant.

With legislators, this aloofness was a serious problem. Politicos are notoriously gregarious; even those who clash in debate will drink together in the evening. The Sacramento crowd wondered why Reagan would never "pal around" with them instead of contentedly going home to his wife. His staff tried to get the governor together with groups of legislators, but he resisted any "merely social" connection. Even in small parties the Reagans occasionally held at home, "legislators were always let know . . . that about 9:30 or ten o'clock they were expected to go home, please."[18]

Reagan found the entire experience of his first months in office depressing. As all successful candidates discover, the job is more difficult than it looks. In Reagan's case this deflation of expectations was compounded by the fact that the Democrats who ran the legislature were determined to keep him from accomplishing his goals. The Assembly Speaker, Jesse Unruh, in particular hoped that Reagan would fail so that he himself could become governor in 1970.

Still, the newcomer gradually put together a new administration staffed by conservative, free-market people, competent but not necessarily politically experienced. Everyone in a top position got a one-page summary of Reagan's ideas to guide them: reduce costs and bureaucracy, seek creative solutions, and rely on the private sector where possible. Good management, not ideological crusading, was the key.

Reagan had been a team player on the football field, at Warner Brothers, and at GE, and he ran his administration on the same principle. Decisions were made only in the cabinet, where each member could have his say; there was no backstairs access to the governor. While Reagan presided at cabinet meetings, they were actually run by his chief of staff, who worked through the day's agenda issue by issue. He presented each to the governor in a single-page memo listing the issue, the facts of the case, the arguments on each side, and a recommended decision.

This worked well for routine items, and on difficult matters the governor got a more thorough briefing. After more or less discussion, Reagan would decide the issue and move on to the next item. He made policy decisions and left details for his staff or cabinet members to handle. A thorough academic analysis concluded that Reagan's management practices "enabled an inexperienced executive to run a large organization effectively and to run it in a way consonant with his philosophy."[19]

Reagan intensely disliked choosing among subordinates when disagreements occurred and especially shied from the responsibility of dismissing anyone. In the campaign, his Kitchen Cabinet handled these duties that the candidate avoided. In the gubernatorial years Nancy Reagan took on that "bad cop" burden herself so that her husband could remain the genial "good cop" to his loyal crew. She was, one observer said, "the most formidable personality of the Reagan administration."[20]

The administration's first great challenge was the budget. In his campaign, Reagan had virtually promised to limit the growth of state government, and he looked forward to making large cuts in spending. Yet the budget deficit Brown had left him was over $400 million, far bigger than Reagan had imagined; it was almost as though his predecessor had deliberately spent the state into a fiscal crisis to embarrass him.

State law required a balanced budget by June 30, and Reagan's first thought was a 10 percent cut in spending. The animal on the state flag, he said, was a noble bear, "not a cow to be milked," but a reduction that large was simply naïve. Such a thrown-together budget could never pass the Democratic legislature. His press secretary, Lyn Nofziger, confessed, "we were not only amateurs, we were novice amateurs."[21]

In the end, with liberal legislators of both parties unwilling to make draconian cuts, Reagan had to abandon his pledge to cut taxes. Instead, he proposed a tax increase—and not simply *an* increase, but the largest by any state ever until that time. When the Democratic majority finished padding the budget, the new taxes totaled more than $1 billion.

The past year's campaign had shown Reagan a master of the emerging Television Age, and he proved it again in the tax-hike fight. Fearing serious resistance from conservative legislators, he went over their heads by filming short television spots for local broadcasts across the state. He told voters that Brown had "looted" California and "drained its financial resources in a manner unique in our history" and that while raising taxes was always a last resort, that painful time was at hand.[22]

Although Democrats were eager for more spending, Speaker Unruh refused to provide Democratic votes until Republican members were on record supporting a tax increase that most of them despised. Twisting their arms required the governor's active involvement, and Reagan was unlimbered like the great gun at a medieval siege, to batter down the last wall of resistance. Now came carrot-and-stick time for legislators. One got his spending bill approved, two got friends appointed judges, and one resister was threatened with a veto of every bill he would ever propose.

One politico said, "it was the first time the Reagan administration showed any . . . wheeler-dealer ability."[23] And the wheeling and dealing by this conservative champion was not to cut spending or red tape or taxes, but to raise far more revenue than liberal Pat Brown had ever contemplated. It was a humbling moment for a man who had fully expected to come into office reducing spending and taxes.

In the post-Reagan era, any Republican governor who signed such a budget would be denounced by conservatives and have little chance of a national political future. Reagan suffered little criticism and no reprisals. In the end, people accepted his explanation that the deed had to be done, and he got his tax increase and a record-high budget without a dent in his popularity. He remained the one great hope of conservative Republicans in California and elsewhere, who focused on his rhetoric rather than his actions. When he said that he was "just as frightened of government now that I am a part of it," that was enough.[24]

As soon as the budget battle was over, Reagan faced another difficult choice, this time on abortion. In the 1960s, before "pro-life" and "pro-choice" became labels, abortion was a shadow issue. Catholics opposed it, others were mostly unconcerned, and it rarely appeared on the political agenda. In all of California there were barely 500 legal abortions in 1967. Opinion was quietly shifting, though; the respected Field Poll showed almost three-fourths of Californians favoring a more permissive abortion law.

Taking advantage of this trend, a liberal Democrat introduced the cleverly named Therapeutic Abortion Bill. It would legalize abortions in cases of rape, incest, or to protect the physical or mental health of the mother. Reagan supported the bill at first but was confused by sharply conflicting advice. Even on his own staff, Catholics were opposed, Protestants in favor. In the legislature, most Republicans voted for the bill, most Democrats— more of whom were Catholic—against, and after much debate it passed.

The governor stalled and fidgeted but ultimately signed the bill with serious misgivings.

Looking back later, he deeply regretted his decision, stunned that doctors had stretched the "mental health" provision to allow abortion for almost any reason at all. The 500 legal abortions in his first year as governor, became 500 every two days—or 100,000 each year in California—by 1975. In 1980 the number was 200,000. This "slaughter of the innocents," as opponents regarded it, pushed Reagan firmly into the pro-life camp for the rest of his life. However, abortion was never among the issues he cared most about; he mentioned it only once in the hundreds of radio talks he gave between leaving the governorship and becoming president.

Reagan's signature on this bill, combined with the appointment of many moderate Republicans and even Democrats to office, was to some of his supporters even more disappointing than the budget battle. Could their hero really have done these things? Reagan understood their disappointment; in fact, he shared it, but his tough negotiations with the studios as SAG president had taught him that one cannot always have everything on the wish list.

He said the disgruntled conservatives "would rather see someone go down in glorious defeat, jump off the cliff with flag flying, than . . . promote your philosophy and get it a step at a time." They seemed to hope that "someplace out of the sunrise a man on a white horse is going to wave a wand and . . . change everything all at once."[25] Ironically, Reagan's own rhetoric had led many to believe that he *was* precisely that man and would *do* precisely that thing. Still, his standing with the public, and even with Republicans outside the "hard right," remained high.

Reagan increased his popularity by his confrontation with student radicals in the state's colleges and with the man who conservatives thought was "coddling" the protestors. The governor took office holding an already-negative opinion of California universities, especially Berkeley. The "free speech"—or, as some called it, "filthy speech"—movement had begun there, and public anger at the university was widespread.

The president of the system, Clark Kerr, seemed unwilling or unable to restore order, and some on the board of regents wondered if he ought to be replaced. Reagan told Kerr that students should be taught to respect community moral standards, but Kerr thought instead that "youngsters should be taught a morality higher than that of the community."[26] Of course, many conservatives in "the community" resented paying to have children taught values different from those of their parents.

A more serious division between governor and president occurred when higher education officials were told that their proposed spending plans faced a 10 percent cut and that the era of free college tuition had to end.

Administrators, faculty, and students objected loudly to this, and Reagan blamed Kerr for the opposition. Kerr foolishly insisted on a vote of confidence by the regents and was dismissed. Reagan merely said that it was time for a change because Kerr had "outlived his usefulness," while the president's defenders complained that Reagan was politicizing a university system that had become great by transcending politics.

Ironically, in the final state budget, the proposed 10 percent cut had vanished and higher education actually received more money than the year before, not less. Kerr had lost his job but won his point. Conservatives, meanwhile, were happy that their new governor had faced down the man they regarded as chiefly responsible for student unrest.

Reagan's "tough on crime" image also helped to reassure his base. He was harshly critical of court decisions that, in his view, tilted the balance in favor of criminals and against law enforcement. In every state, governors had to sign death warrants for especially heinous murderers, and in the 1966 campaign, Reagan denounced Pat Brown for commuting more death sentences than any previous governor.

He himself, though, was quite uncomfortable with the ultimate toughness — sending murderers to the gas chamber. Reagan's first, the execution of a "cop-killer," was almost too much for him. He enforced the law but could not manage to face the murderer's mother with the grim news. Anti–death penalty protesters held a vigil at Reagan's house, and church bells chimed at the hour of execution. Because most Californians thought killers of policemen well deserved to die, the spectacle served only to increase the governor's popularity.

Despite his personal anguish, Reagan remained a firm believer in the death penalty, although he was unwittingly responsible for ending it. His most important judicial appointment was a new chief justice for the California Supreme Court, and in 1972 the man he chose, Donald Wright, ruled the death penalty unconstitutional, saving the lives of 100 convicted murderers. Reagan considered it a betrayal of trust because if the nominee had made clear his opposition to the death penalty, he would never have been appointed. Strangely, the governor had never bothered to ask.

Overall, Reagan's judicial choices turned out more to his liking. Reacting to Brown's last-minute court appointments, including dozens of personal friends and defeated legislators, Reagan came in determined to elevate the courts. Of course there was a deliberate effort to find qualified Republican judges to offset the previous eight years of liberal Democratic appointees, but he never appointed anyone graded as "unqualified" by the state bar. Judgeships, however, were useful bargaining chips, and several were traded to Speaker Unruh and Democratic legislators in return for favorable votes. Evaluating the hundreds of judicial appointments Reagan made in two terms, liberal journalist Lou Cannon concluded that, while the process was indeed partisan, it did produce good judges.

In the summer of his first year Reagan faced a crisis involving his chief of staff that might have hurt him with the voting public even more than the tax-increase and abortion decisions. Philip Battaglia had been the 1966 campaign chairman. As the governor's chief aide in 1967, he built a wall around Reagan, trying to control other staffers' access to the governor and to the media. This turned most of Reagan's other aides against Battaglia, but rumors of homosexual liaisons were what really alarmed them. In those years homosexuality meant political disaster and social disgrace, and a scandal involving the governor's chief of staff would be a serious wound to Reagan's national reputation.

Reagan himself was perfectly comfortable with homosexuals as individuals and apparently never thought about the larger social issue of discrimination. In his movie experience, being gay was no barrier to moving in the highest Hollywood circles or becoming a star actor. However, an ultimatum from virtually his entire top staff left the governor no real choice. He recognized, as they did, that a scandal would damage not only his administration but also his future.

On the other hand, Reagan liked Battaglia personally and was determined to protect his chief of staff's reputation. Even after the rumors were revealed by a muckraking columnist, Reagan continued to insist that Battaglia had left simply to return to his legal practice. The whole affair was distasteful to the administration's inner circle, but the one good result was a new and highly competent group of trusted advisors.

The new trio stayed with Reagan in Sacramento and later in Washington. William Clark had worked for both Goldwater's campaign and Reagan's. He became the new chief of staff, later a judge, and finally a justice of the California Supreme Court. Ed Meese succeeded Clark as chief of staff, and Michael Deaver served as assistant to both chiefs and as one of Nancy Reagan's closest allies in the administration.

All in all, the first year was eventful and often disappointing, and the next was little better. In early 1968, Reagan reversed himself on an issue even more emotional than his tax increase. Five years earlier, as the civil rights movement was growing nationwide, the California legislature passed a "fair housing" bill, the Rumford Act, prohibiting racial discrimination in the sale or rental of real estate. This produced an angry "white backlash," and a voter referendum repealed the law in 1964, only to have the state supreme court overrule the will of the voters and invalidate the law.

In his 1966 campaign, Reagan had promised to support repeal of the Rumford Act, and this helped him win large majorities among usually Democratic white working-class voters. In 1967, however, the new governor refused to lift a finger while anti-Rumford bills died in the legislature, and the next year he backtracked even more. He met with representatives of several minority organizations and was convinced by their complaints of discrimination in housing. He announced that he now favored the Rumford Act and would even veto a repeal bill if one ever did pass the legislature.

While Reagan wrestled with state issues, he and his advisors kept always in mind a larger goal: the White House. The front-runner for the Republican nomination was former Vice President Nixon, but even he assumed that Reagan's huge victory in 1966 made him a possible competitor. The Kitchen Cabinet agreed, one of them claiming, "we don't have gubernatorial material here, we have presidential material."[27]

Before Reagan was even sworn in as governor, his advisors had worked out a detailed plan for an eighteen-month drive to win the presidential nomination. The governor-elect was not sure he was up to the task and showed no sense of urgency. This attitude probably doomed his 1968 chances from the beginning, for while he dawdled, Nixon pushed ahead, rounding up convention delegates month by month.

Although new in office, Reagan was well positioned for a national race had he dedicated himself to it. He was governor of the largest state, one essential to a national Republican victory. His eight years touring the country for General Electric, his 1964 work for Goldwater, and his many speeches at Republican events had attracted a national network of eager acolytes. His relaxed self-confidence and actor's skill at connecting with diverse audiences was far more appealing than Nixon's stiffness.

Despite his own interest, Reagan sometimes seemed remarkably passive. All his life he had been guided by the belief, absorbed from his mother, that Providence ruled men's lives, and so it was now: "if God wanted him to be President He would see that it got done."[28] In truth, however, Reagan was not above helping God get it done.

As a national conservative icon, he spoke at Republican events across the country during 1967, dismissing with his "aw, shucks" smile any questions about higher office. A televised debate on Vietnam against Robert Kennedy, in which he was seen as outdoing the New York senator, increased his standing with the national media and the "political class." Still, respect was no substitute for delegates, and Nixon's determined campaign was scooping up more and more of those.

The dance of the noncandidate was best caught by a journalist's parody of the knightly "Sir Ronald" of the West who does battle in "the Thorny Thicket of the Legislature" but sees, far off, a "big White House" glittering in the East. His ever-faithful servant Nofziger says, "it is the Tantalizing Treasure" to be seized "lest some other knight captures it first." Sir Ronald, having promised to serve a full term in the Tangled Thicket, declares "a pox on fame and fortune; I shall not seek the Treasure" but tells his servant, "keep an eye on it, . . . in case it comes seeking me."[29]

An early 1968 survey of Republican county chairmen showed Reagan running second only to Nixon, but when he allowed his name to be put on a few primary ballots, the result was hugely disappointing. Reagan had no trouble holding California's delegates as a favorite son, but Nixon easily outran him elsewhere. Finally convinced that he must be more active, the formerly reluctant Reagan threw himself fully into the contest just weeks before the convention met in Miami.

Reagan quickly found that he had waited too long to court the delegates. He had broad emotional support from Southerners, many of whom longed to vote for him, but most had already been locked up by Nixon's managers. A frantic series of last-minute appeals to conservative delegates was fruitless, almost embarrassingly so, as he made a transparent appeal for Alabama Governor George Wallace's "white backlash" voters.

Although disgusted by Wallace's racist rhetoric, Reagan treated him lightly in public, not wishing to alienate Wallace's voters, who might be potential converts in the fall. It may have been a shrewd political judgment, but when Reagan followed this up at the National Governors Conference by refusing to support a resolution against housing discrimination, it hardly did honor to the memory of Jack Reagan's teachings about tolerance. Nor, for that matter, did it reflect Reagan's own record of appointing more minorities to office than any previous governor.

In the end, Nixon easily prevailed. His first-ballot total was nearly four times that of Reagan. The defeat in Miami confirmed Nancy Reagan's judgment that her husband should not have run. Mike Deaver, who was closest to her, noticed that "she would never again hold back her opinion on major political decisions, . . . it was always about protecting her husband, not about driving him on."[30]

Contrary to his wife's assessment, and despite the convention disappointment, the 1968 contest was good for Reagan. Nixon was impressed and needed the governor's help in California and with conservatives nationally. Responding to that need gave Reagan more visibility, more experience in navigating national politics, and a stack of IOUs from Nixon and others for whom he campaigned.

Reagan's work for his fellow Californian in the fall also increased the number of those who admired his skill. In San Diego, for example, Reagan spoke after a boring talk by Nixon and quickly had the crowd cheering and clapping. One observer marveled that "a man who can move an audience like that . . . is going to go a lot further than California." Another saw that "as soon as he entered a room, you could almost feel the aura about him. He could transform a rather stiff group into enthusiasts with that great smile and engaging manner of his."[31]

After the election, Reagan admitted that he had not been ready to operate at the presidential level. Still, his halfway campaign had taught him much about the hard realities of winning delegates, handling the national media, and appealing beyond his conservative base. As for the future and Reagan's place in it, he assumed that would unfold, as always, according to God's divine plan. In this belief, he remained all his life his mother's son.

One of the most surprising things about Reagan's governorship was his environmental record. He thought, as did many conservatives, that environmentalists seemed to care little for the human beings whose jobs were destroyed by their zeal for tough regulations. Yet he was more complicated than this. He owned several ranches in his lifetime, beginning with a small spread purchased in his mid-thirties and ending with the well-known Rancho del Cielo, where he spent leisure days during the presidency and afterward.

Thinking of himself as a rancher and cherishing the small-town values of his youth, Reagan was friendlier to the environmental movement than many other conservatives, including the business interests that helped elect him governor. He had often criticized the eager highway building that he felt marred the scenic landscape. Neither his friends nor his political enemies thought to notice this element of his experience and character; they fixed instead on his dismissive comment about the redwoods: "a tree is a tree. How many more do you need to look at?"[32] Ironically, it was his liberal predecessor who had favored roads over trees and housing developments over wetlands and rivers.

Reagan's director of resources, Norman Livermore, was a Sierra Club member and Republican lumber executive. Such people were not unusual; the conservation movement was bipartisan and crossed the ideological lines of conservative and liberal. Reagan was drawn to him as a fellow outdoorsman, and he was the only person to stay in the cabinet for the two full terms. Livermore subtly but persistently tugged Reagan toward a liberal environmental outlook, as shown by the hotly contested issue of logging in the redwood forests of California's North Shore.

For local residents, logging meant jobs and a decent living for their families; to them, environmentalists were saying that trees were more important than human beings. To conservationists, the issue was human greed versus natural beauty. After months of political wrangling and cabinet debates wore down Reagan's resistance, the governor agreed to create an eighty-square-mile redwood park. It gratified the Sierra Club but left enough land open to logging to preserve the local lumber industry.

Rivers were the next battleground. In his massive California Water Plan, Pat Brown had aggressively dammed one river after another to bring irrigation to farmers and drinking water to southern cities, and Reagan had no argument with this policy. Livermore did, however, and vowed to block a high dam on the Eel River that would flood a town, a valley full of farms, and an Indian reservation, and would wipe out the river's fishing business. To prevent this, Livermore worked all the levers that might move Reagan: the Indians would be devastated, local farmers would be driven out, and the cost would be huge. By early 1969 the governor was convinced. There was no dam and the river still flows free. It was his "finest environmental moment," in the words of one liberal.[33] A few years later, Reagan signed a bill saving the wild rivers forever. Environmentalists won more from a conservative than they had from the liberal he defeated.

Reagan finished his second year with a series of victories. He opposed a voter initiative to cap property-tax assessments and move financing for education and welfare from local real estate taxes to the state budget. It would have produced either a multi-billion-dollar increase in state taxes or deep cuts in government programs. Reagan saw it as merely burden shifting, not tax cutting, so he fought the plan and was pleased to see it lose by two to one. In the next four years, local property taxes soared—but, remarkably, once again no one blamed the governor. His anti-tax rhetoric seemed to trump reality.

In the November 1968, election, Republicans gained full control of the legislature, giving Reagan more friendly leaders to work with in the senate and assembly. Best of all, his 1967 tax increase had produced a budget surplus, and the governor was able to announce the first of four state tax rebates, gratifying his sometimes disgruntled conservative base.

He won even more applause for his hard-nosed handling of a new outburst of campus unrest. In January 1969, the radical "Third World Liberation Front" tried to shut Berkeley down with a strike, during which radicals attacked students going to class and tried to bomb college buildings. Reagan denounced the strikers as criminals and revolutionaries and finally called in the state police, to the approval of a huge majority of Californians, including liberals like Jesse Unruh himself.

Trouble broke out again in April with a much messier result, when radicals protesting the Vietnam War and other issues took over an empty patch of university ground and declared it a "People's Park." After police pushed them out and sealed off the "park," thousands of protesters counterattacked. Responding with the liberal use of teargas and buckshot, police injured a number of the radicals, killing one. Reagan reacted forcefully, putting Berkeley under a curfew and sending in the National Guard, which finally brought order out of chaos. The governor congratulated the Guard for restoring peace with "remarkable restraint," but both inside the university and out many expressed resentment at the military intervention. Nevertheless, most ordinary Californians continued to share Reagan's view that campus protesters were "rebels without a cause" and had only themselves to blame if law enforcement dealt with them ungently. Conservatives, in particular, saw him as a heroic bulwark against forces that would disintegrate American society. For them, his robust "law and order" reputation pushed out of mind the rapidly fading memory of his gigantic tax increase two years before.

Reagan's other big effort of 1969 turned out less successfully. For years, rapid growth in population and student enrollment had been driving municipal and school property taxes ever higher. The governor had helped defeat a tax relief proposal in 1968, but the state's rising revenue surplus changed his mind. Although Republicans controlled both houses of the legislature, tax-related bills needed a two-thirds vote to pass.

Hence, some Democrats had to be persuaded to support tax reform, causing one of Reagan's aides to complain that "we're doing business with the very people we came up here to get rid of."[34] Although the governor, his assembly speaker, and Democratic leader Unruh all wanted tax reform, there were too many competing plans and none of them could pass. Meanwhile, real estate taxes kept going up, squeezing family budgets.

All was not confrontation and frustration. Reagan went to Asia as Nixon's special emissary and then took a European tour as a break from politics and to introduce himself to important people overseas. He impressed an audience of Paris sophisticates and in London won praise from several thousand business executives. One of them told his wife, the Education Minister in the current government, of Reagan's masterful performance. A decade later, leading her own government in Westminster, Prime Minister Margaret Thatcher became President Reagan's partner in facing down the Soviet Union. The Asian and European trips raised his profile nationally, gave him a veneer of "foreign policy experience," and increased his own confidence in dealing with foreign leaders.

After this brief respite, he was back to the challenges of governing. A year after the failure of tax reform in 1969, Reagan tried again to use the state budget surplus to pay for a cut in local property taxes, but once again he failed. Along with this defeat came a reluctant reversal on one of Reagan's most cherished political principles. He had always opposed tax withholding, reasoning that if people had to pay their income tax in one lump sum, they would be less tolerant of tax increases. In 1968, he said that anyone who wanted to enact tax withholding would need to "walk over my dead body. With my feet set in concrete."

Legislators and state officials wanted withholding, arguing that it *would* make higher taxes less noticeable and because the state had to pay to borrow money before the one-time tax payments arrived. The media, too, became critical of Reagan's stubborn resistance, and by 1970 his own finance director finally convinced him that withholding was necessary. In announcing his surrender, the governor told reporters, "that sound you hear is the concrete cracking around my feet."[35]

Fortunately for Reagan, these were mere bumps on the road to a second term. A year before the 1970 election, polls gave him a twenty-point lead over his likely Democratic opponent, Jesse Unruh, whose campaign sagged beneath a load of difficulties. Unruh did not show well on television and had many enemies in his own party; even some of the usually Democratic unions defected to the Republican governor. Unruh also had less money than Reagan and had to spend much of it winning a bitter primary. Perhaps worst of all, he managed his own campaign, ignoring the rule that any candidate who does so has a fool for a client. He tried to portray himself as a "man of the people" and Reagan as "the rich man's friend." This theme did have some power in the recession year of 1970, but the Democrat overdid it and made himself look ridiculous.

Meanwhile, Reagan performed the exquisite feat of running the usual incumbent's ads, bragging of his achievements such as "the toughest air and water controls in history," while at the same time campaigning as an outsider against the government he himself had led for four years. As Lou Cannon put it, he ran "as if he were going to Sacramento to clean up a mess someone else had left behind."[36] The campaign also made history by introducing daily "tracking polls" of several hundred people, which have since become standard in the political world.

Three weeks from the election, Reagan led Unruh by 12 percent, but the race tightened as straying Democrats drifted back to their old party. The final November score was 53 to 45 percent, a 500,000-vote lead for Reagan over Unruh, including about a fifth of Democratic voters. Although Republicans lost the legislature and a U.S. Senate seat, this was a satisfying personal triumph for the governor and a classic example of what his friend and advisor Mike Deaver called the "Reagan mystique." He marveled that Reagan could win reelection "by running against the government. He campaigned as if he had not been part of it for four years."[37]

At Reagan's second inaugural in January 1971, radical protesters tried to disrupt the proceedings by jeering, shouting, and waving Viet Cong flags. Reagan shrugged off the protesters; they were "like mosquitoes and flies. They're part of the world and you have to put up with them."[38] The voters were not so casually tolerant. There is no doubt that the radicals, whether rioting at Berkeley or cheering the Viet Cong at Reagan's swearing-in, had made the governor an increasingly attractive figure in both California and the nation by the early 1970s. *LIFE* magazine put him on its cover as "the hottest candidate in either party."[39]

It was good for Reagan that he had such enemies, for the actual process of governing was becoming more difficult. Despite his triumphant reelection, Democrats regained control of the legislature, complicating the governor's ability to achieve his top priority for 1971: cutting welfare spending, which Reagan feared was bankrupting the state. In the 1960s welfare had turned from a short-term helping hand into a permanent "entitlement." Like his fellow conservatives, Reagan complained that bureaucrats actually sought out people to put on welfare because the bigger their empire of dependents, the more successful they appeared.

He agreed with his former idol, FDR, that dependence on welfare destroyed the human spirit; as he proclaimed in an essay in *The New York Times* in August 1971, "Welfare Is a Cancer." He tried to balance the interest of the taxpayer with that of the "truly needy" but had no sympathy for those who could work but chose to live on the dole. As with other issues, Reagan combined his critique of expensive, wasteful programs with a new determination actually to fix problems, not merely to bemoan them. For years he had been the frustrated citizen; now he had the power to act.

During Pat Brown's years, the welfare caseload had soared. There had been 400,000 people on public assistance in 1963; the number doubled by 1967 and doubled again by 1971, rising at 40,000 per month. This was an unsustainable trend, requiring either a huge tax increase or deep cuts in other state programs to offset welfare spending. Yet when Reagan proposed to reform California's welfare policy, even his own staff told him it was hopeless; the Democratic legislature would shoot any reform bill on sight. To invest his political credibility in such a lost cause might brand him a modern Don Quixote, foolishly tilting at the welfare windmill. Nevertheless, Reagan pushed on, driven by budget realities as much as conservative ideology.

First he had to deal with his own Republican president. For two years, Richard Nixon had been campaigning for a guaranteed minimum income for all Americans, which Reagan had opposed in congressional testimony, to the applause of conservatives nationwide. The president needed Reagan, who was governor of the largest state and the most popular conservative politician, so the two Californians came to an agreement. The governor would stop criticizing Nixon's plan, and the president would approve Reagan's "work for welfare" idea.

The next—and far more difficult—negotiation was with legislative Democrats, led by liberal House Speaker Bob Moretti. They foolishly refused to let Reagan speak to a joint session, so he outdid them by going directly to the voters on television. He told taxpayers that the welfare system was robbing them to support people who could perfectly well support themselves, while those who really needed help did not get enough.

His solution was to spend more on the "truly needy" but to require the able bodied to work for their money just as the taxpayers who supported them had to work. Newspapers across California liked his idea and so did the public, sending letters by the thousands to Democratic legislators. Reagan's attacks on "welfare cheats" and "soulless bureaucrats" were widely popular, and many lawmakers were shocked at the intensity of their constituents' resentment.

Much against his own convictions, Speaker Moretti was backed into a corner and finally sought a compromise. Both he and Reagan badly needed a major accomplishment, the speaker because he planned to run for governor in 1974 and Reagan because he intended to run for president in 1976. Moretti told Reagan, "I don't like you. And I know you don't like me, but we don't have to be in love to work together."[40]

The two of them worked for hours at a time for two intense weeks. As in his years as SAG president, when Reagan had to focus intently on something, he did it masterfully, holding firm on his "must have" items and trading away, when necessary, some of the "nice to haves." The result was a welfare reform plan that led California, and eventually the nation, toward a new approach, culminating a quarter-century later when President Clinton signed a Republican-sponsored national welfare reform.

After a summer of negotiating and maneuvering, welfare reform passed the legislature in August, and Moretti symbolically stood behind the governor as Reagan signed the bill into law. It pleased conservatives by weeding out fraud, improving efficiency, and forcing able-bodied recipients to work, while liberals could be happy that individual welfare payments rose by nearly 50 percent, along with cost-of-living increases and additional day-care centers.

By the end of Reagan's governorship, the law had moved 300,000 people off the welfare rolls and saved the state $2 billion. It even became a model for other states, and to many conservatives, welfare reform was Reagan's greatest accomplishment as governor. Democrats, who had helped pass the bill, later claimed that most of its supposed success was simply due to economic expansion and greater family planning.

The next year, Nixon finally dropped his idea of a guaranteed minimum income, leaving Reagan as the national Republican leader in welfare reform. His skill in proposing, negotiating, and passing his bill through a Democratic legislature showed the nation's political class that he could handle complicated, controversial issues. Furthermore, he became fixed even more firmly as the favorite of the Republican right wing.

Reagan gained yet more visibility when Nixon, having granted diplomatic recognition to the Communist regime in mainland China, sent him to smooth things over with Chiang Kai-shek's Nationalist Chinese government on Taiwan. He told Chiang—and later, conservatives nationwide—that "I don't like this any more than you do," but "we have to be . . . realistic about the changing face of the world." A less hostile China policy, Reagan thought, could mean a more peaceful planet in which "the great Armageddon is not inevitable, the great nuclear holocaust in which civilization disappears."[41] It was a remarkable foreshadowing of his monumental shift in policy toward the Soviet Union fifteen years later, and for the same reason—to wake the world from its long nuclear nightmare.

Reagan accepted another important trip as special envoy to Europe in July 1972, to reassure the NATO community about America's commitment to European security. He saw prime ministers, foreign ministers, the Pope, and NATO officials, gaining valuable experience dealing with foreign leaders that few other contemporary governors had.

Back home, Reagan made the environment his chief concern in 1972. He had followed up his protection of redwoods and rivers four years earlier with a tough water quality act in 1969 and the addition of more acres to state parks than any governor in modern times. The most highly publicized issue of 1972 was whether to build a major highway that would disrupt the 250-mile-long John Muir wildlife trail. On this, Reagan, the horse-loving outdoorsman, and the liberal environmentalists were fully agreed. As befit the practiced horseman, Reagan rode the trail personally, white hat and all; to conservationists "it was like the cavalry coming to the rescue."[42] On his recommendation, Congress killed the highway.

Nor was this all. Convinced that rapid development was degrading the clear waters of Lake Tahoe, one of California's most notable natural attractions, Reagan worked with his equally conservative friend, Nevada Governor Paul Laxalt, to save the lake. The two Republicans produced an interstate compact to slow down resort development and its attendant pollution, and Lake Tahoe is still a natural treasure.

The most striking of Reagan's environmental decisions came near the end of his governorship in 1974. He joined liberal Democrats to support a bill allowing state regulators to ban the sale of cars that did not meet California emission standards. Under threat of losing the nation's largest market, automakers had to comply, which of course increased the cost of each car to the purchaser. This was just the kind of "red-tape" rule that conservatives, including Reagan, had always denounced for imposing economic burdens on American families, but now he approved it.

One might expect that liberals would praise Reagan for achievements in conservation that reversed the "dam, pave, and cut" policy of Pat Brown, but the media and the Democratic party continued to portray him as a reactionary and a moron. Similarly, Reagan's environmental record ought to have disappointed many conservatives, but any dissent was so faint as to be unheard in their continuing adoration of "Mr. Conservative."

The governor finished up 1972 by working hard for Nixon's reelection, concentrating in the South and West, where his own popularity was greatest. In addition, his Kitchen Cabinet contributed or raised nearly $10 million for Nixon in order to accumulate IOUs, to be called in when Reagan made his own run four years later.

His other campaign in the fall of 1972 was a surprising one. California conservatives, responding to rising local real estate taxes, put a property-tax relief measure on the November ballot. It would have squeezed school district budgets, forced the state to take over the full cost of welfare, and raised state taxes to pay for the local tax relief. Arrayed against the proposition were the pillars of the political establishment: education leaders, major newspapers, liberal Democrats, and the man who usually denounced the liberal establishment: Ronald Reagan. Against such united opposition, the ballot measure had no chance. It lost by two to one.

Having defeated that plan, Reagan and Moretti produced their own, and this time it passed. It included $800 million of property tax relief (and an equally large state tax increase to balance it), plus $300 million in extra education spending. After working with Reagan on both welfare and property-tax reform, Moretti admitted that the governor was better than his predecessor, Pat Brown, and "miles, and planets, and universes better than Jerry Brown," Reagan's successor and Pat Brown's son.[43]

The highlight of Reagan's governorship in 1973 was his failed attempt to pass a "Taxpayer Bill of Rights," limiting the annual rise in state government spending to the inflation rate or the growth of per capita income. Almost every state's budget routinely grew much faster than this, pushing taxes up likewise, so Reagan believed that his idea would dramatically slow the expansion of government, leaving more money in the pockets of every family.

When legislative Democrats sneered at the idea, Reagan went directly to the people, rounding up hundreds of thousands of signatures to put his plan on the November ballot as a voter initiative, Proposition 1. Unfortunately for him, the proposition was 5,700 words long and hugely complicated. Reagan himself admitted that he did not understand it, and a suspicious electorate rejected it soundly.

This was the governor's only major policy defeat in eight years, and Reagan fell back on his lifelong belief that everything, even defeats, had a purpose in God's Great Plan. Events seemed to confirm his placid assumption that the setback was only temporary; five years later, voters gave a massive victory to Proposition 13, a property-tax limitation plan far stricter than Reagan's. The American anti-tax rebellion had begun, and it swept to victory in state after state for nearly twenty years. Reagan had been a prophet ahead of his time.

The fiasco of Proposition 1 was a sign of Reagan's weakening position in California during 1973 and 1974. Democrats controlled the legislature, and the continuing malaise of Watergate was demoralizing Republicans everywhere. He also suffered the wasting disease that afflicts all "lame duck" governors who cannot, or will not, run for another term.

As the weeks went by, politicians increasingly looked beyond him to the post-Reagan future. His last State of the State address in January 1974, had no new proposals, and a few weeks later his 797th veto was the first overridden by a rebellious legislature. Reagan himself was unsure what to do after the governorship: earn money on the speaking circuit, retire to the ranch he loved, or finally make that serious run for president?

He had expected, if he did run, to do so in an open race when Nixon retired. The president's Watergate troubles took Reagan quite by surprise, especially the sudden revelations at the end, which forced Nixon to resign. Although Reagan resolutely insisted that Nixon and his fellow Watergate perpetrators were not truly criminals, this blindness to the evidence did not hurt him with the public. In fact, biographer Lou Cannon believes that Watergate actually helped Reagan because it highlighted the "character issue," and he had always seemed a man of principle, even though he sometimes governed in opposition to his principles.

As he left office in 1975, Reagan regretted that his successful races in 1966 and 1970 did not revive Republican power in California. In the four decades since, the parties have divided the governorship, but Democrats have won 80 percent of the other statewide races and have controlled the state senate for the entire time and the state house for all but two years. In short, the "Reagan years" in California reflected his personal popularity and marked only a brief interruption in the state's steady drift to the Democrats since the shattering of Republican rule in 1958.

And what of his impact on state government? The California bureaucracy grew hardly at all, much less than in many other states. The three largest tax increases in California history to that time were somewhat mitigated by $4 billion in local property tax cuts and nearly $2 billion in state tax rebates. There were no major scandals, and his hardline rhetoric against criminals, rioters, and radicals was gratifying to most Californians.

Overall, however, Reagan's record was hardly what he or his supporters had expected the day he took office. The state budget more than doubled, and taxes took 15 percent more of a family's earnings in 1974 than in 1966. Public education spending per student grew three times as much as under his liberal predecessor, while the state's higher education budget rose almost 150 percent. Despite Reagan's "tough on crime" image, the rate of violent crimes doubled in his two terms.

Yet Reagan left office very popular with Californians and hugely so among conservatives. How did he do it? Beside the tax increases and higher spending, he signed a liberal abortion law, and his environmental policy favored trees, trails, and rivers over economic development. He reversed his opposition to fair-housing laws and tax withholding, and campaigned successfully to defeat two property-tax limitation initiatives. Yet despite all this, he remained the one great national conservative icon.

Part of the reason is the lack of competition. Most other party leaders were moderates, even liberals, and Nixon had been a sore disappointment even before Watergate. In a grim decade for Republicans, heavily outnumbered by triumphant Democrats, Reagan's conservative rhetoric never softened. Even with a mixed record in California, he remained the "first flower of their wilderness, star of their night."

Another reason for his appeal was apparent to his longtime opponent, Jesse Unruh, who said that "people believe Reagan . . . because Reagan believes himself. He sounds sincere because he is sincere, even when he should know better. Most politicians know when they're lying and so the people sense it. But in his own mind Reagan never lies and the people sense that, too."[44] Through two dozen years as candidate, governor, and president, Reagan saw himself as a "citizen-politician," undertaking government as a civic duty, not as a career ambition, and never compromising his principles—even when he did. This self-image of innocence set him apart from the common run of politician.

As he waited out the stale end of his second term, peering into the uncertainty of the mid-1970s, he might have asked himself Whitman's question from *Leaves of Grass*: "Where to? What next?" One possibility, certainly, was on his mind. A Democratic legislator challenged him with, "you're looking at that Oval Office, aren't you?" and Reagan's short reply was the same he had given to Bob Cummings thirty years before: "Yes."[45]

A diligent historian of the postwar conservative movement concluded in the mid-1970s that "conservatives were living in a revolutionary age" and noted their "disquieting perception of this fact." Many had come to doubt whether a successful defense of the traditional values that they treasured was possible. After two decades of wielding the *National Review* as a literary weapon against the liberal age, William F. Buckley came to the melancholy conclusion that victory "so far as I can see, is beyond our reach. Perhaps it was meant to be so."[46]

If the cause was to prosper and not to shuffle tiredly toward eventual irrelevance, as Buckley feared, one simple challenge must be met: "to defend enduring truths in a language appealing to America in the 1970s."[47] It was to this challenge that Ronald Reagan was called and to which he devoted the remainder of his life.

NOTES

1. Quoted in Colacello, *Ronnie and Nancy*, 334.
2. Spencer quoted *ibid.*, 338.
3. Quoted in Lee Edwards, *Reagan: A Political Biography* (San Diego, CA: Viewpoint Books, 1967), 101.
4. Lou Cannon, *Governor Reagan: His Rise to Power* (New York: Public Affairs, 2003), 140.
5. Quotations from Lyn Nofziger, *Nofziger* (Washington, DC: Regnery Gateway, 1992), 42.
6. Spencer quoted in Colacello, *Ronnie and Nancy*, 339.
7. Spencer quoted *ibid.*, 340.
8. Stanley Plog quoted in Morris, *Dutch*, 542.
9. Reagan quoted in Ross, *Hollywood Left and Right*, 176.
10. Reagan quoted *ibid.*, 177.
11. Quoted in Matthew Dallek, *The Right Moment: Ronald Reagan's First Victory and the Decisive Turning Point in American Politics* (New York: Oxford University Press, 2000), 204.
12. Reagan quoted in Ross, *Hollywood Left and Right*, 176.
13. Quoted in Neil Reagan, "Private Dimensions," UCLA Oral History Program, 28–29.
14. Quotations from Ross, *Hollywood Left and Right*, 179.
15. Fred Dutton quoted in Cannon, *Governor Reagan*, 161.
16. Quoted in Colacello, *Ronnie and Nancy*, 352.
17. Reagan quoted *ibid.*, 365.
18. Paul Haerle, "Ronald Reagan and Republican Party Politics in California, 1965–1968," Regional Oral History Office, Bancroft Library, University of California Berkeley, 13–14.
19. Gary G. Hamilton and Nicole W. Biggart in *Governor Reagan, Governor Brown: A Sociology of Executive Power* (New York: Columbia University Press, 1984), 186.
20. Lou Cannon, *Ronnie and Jesse; A Political Odyssey* (Garden City, NY: Doubleday, 1969), 161.
21. Nofziger quoted in Cannon, *Governor Reagan*, 184.
22. Colacello, *Ronnie and Nancy*, 360.
23. Quoted in Bill Boyarsky, *Ronald Reagan: His Life and Rise to the Presidency* (New York: Random House, 1981), 120.
24. Reagan quoted in Cannon, *Governor Reagan*, 206.
25. Reagan quoted in Colacello, *Ronnie and Nancy*, 361.
26. Boyarsky, *Ronald Reagan*, 142.
27. Reported by Colacello, *Ronnie and Nancy*, 377–378.
28. Nofziger, *Nofziger*, 69.
29. Art Hoppe quoted in Stephen Hess and David S. Broder, *The Republican Establishment: The Present and Future of the G.O.P.* (New York: Harper & Row, 1967), 288–289.
30. Michael K. Deaver, *Nancy: A Portrait of My Years with Nancy Reagan* (New York: Morrow, 2004), 44.
31. James Fuller and Caspar Weinberger, quoted in Peter Hannaford, *Recollections of Reagan: A Portrait of Ronald Reagan* (New York: William Morrow, 1997), 67–68, 184.
32. Reagan quoted in Boyarsky, *Ronald Reagan*, 167.
33. Cannon, *Governor Reagan*, 313.
34. *Ibid.*, 328.
35. Reagan quoted in Boyarsky, *Ronald Reagan*, 157, 159.
36. Cannon, *Governor Reagan*, 342.

37. Michael K. Deaver, *Behind the Scenes: In Which the Author Talks about Ronald and Nancy Reagan and Himself* (New York: Morrow, 1987), 44.
38. Reagan quoted in Peter Schweizer, *Reagan's War: The Epic Story of His Forty Year Struggle and Final Triumph over Communism* (New York: Doubleday, 2002), 65–66.
39. Richard Reeves, *President Nixon: Alone in the White House* (New York: Simon & Schuster, 2001), 246.
40. Moretti quoted in Morris, *Dutch*, 375.
41. Reagan quoted *ibid.*, 378.
42. Quoted in Cannon, *Governor Reagan*, 318.
43. Moretti quoted *ibid.*, 366.
44. Unruh quoted in Nofziger, *Nofziger*, 285.
45. Quoted in Morris, *Dutch*, 384.
46. William F. Buckley, Jr., *Let Us Talk of Many Things: The Collected Speeches* (NY: Basic Books, 2008), 95.
47. George H. Nash, *The Conservative Intellectual Movement in America since 1945* (New York: Basic Books, 1976), 344–345.

CHAPTER 5

RUNNING FOR PRESIDENT, 1976–1980

Ronald Reagan left the governorship with his popularity high and the grudging respect even of his political opponents. Jesse Unruh, who had no use for Reagan personally, summed him up quite favorably: "I think he has been better than most Democrats would concede and not nearly as good as most Republicans and conservatives might like to think. As a politician I think he has been nearly masterful."[1]

Both of the Reagans were relieved to put Sacramento behind them, eager to reclaim some sense of a private life. They had recently bought Rancho del Cielo, a full square mile of secluded mountain land, where the ex-governor spent most of his free time fixing things up. He also made very good money doing speeches at several thousand dollars each. That, plus a weekly column in nearly two hundred newspapers and a daily radio commentary on three hundred stations brought Reagan about $800,000 per year and kept his name before the public, reaching twenty million people weekly.

His message was the same as in the GE tours of the 1950s: America was threatened by big government and the world by Soviet Communism, and only conservatives could save the day. As he told the Conservative Political Action Conference (CPAC) in 1975, the country needed a revitalized Republican party, "raising a banner of no pale pastels but bold colors which make it unmistakably clear where we stand" and conveying a sense of America's mission and greatness. Of course, any picture of his own governorship would require quite a few "pale pastels" to depict Reagan's three tax increases and other lapses from pure conservatism.

Still, as he knew well, it was not his record in office but his vision for the future that inspired a growing band of followers. Even before he left Sacramento, Reagan and his advisors had discussed a second effort at the presidency, but when Nixon's resignation put Vice President Gerald Ford in the White House, Reagan hesitated. He really wanted Ford to succeed, and besides, Republicans were not supposed to challenge their own party's incumbent presidents.

The honeymoon proved brief, however. Conservatives quickly became disgusted with Ford's choice of liberal Nelson Rockefeller as vice president, his amnesty for Vietnam draft-dodgers and deserters, and his willingness to accept higher budget deficits to stimulate the economy. The entire Republican Party, tarnished by Watergate, seemed to be shrinking to permanent minority status. Less than one-fourth of voters called themselves Republicans, worse than in the Goldwater debacle.

In the spring of 1975, spurred by these desperate circumstances, Reagan decided to run against a sitting president. A *Newsweek* cover story proclaimed him "Ready on the Right," and his claim that "the free world . . . is crying out for strong American leadership" was the slap of a challenger's glove that set up the duel with Ford.[2] To continue making money from his radio and newspaper commentary, however, Reagan avoided an official announcement until November.

It would be a steep uphill climb; Ford was far ahead and journalists warned that Reagan would mean suicide for Republicans. One man who thought otherwise was John Sears, Reagan's manager. He worried that his candidate was too conservative but was sure that he was malleable and could be "moved to the center . . . if handled correctly."[3] The campaign strategy was simple: surprise Ford in New Hampshire, the first primary state, beat him again in Florida, and then Reagan would be unstoppable.

Reagan told his family in October that if he did not run, "I'd feel like the guy who always sat on the bench and never got into the game," a reminder of his disappointing first years in high school football.[4] The next month he formally announced, but he had already made the one mistake that probably cost him the nomination.

He had long believed that the federal government was uniquely inefficient and that the states could manage many programs better and for less, an idea he expressed in a Chicago speech. He suggested transferring welfare, public housing, food stamps, and Medicaid to the states, allowing a $90 billion cut in federal spending. Of course, this would mean a substantial increase in state spending, with tax increases to match.

The Ford campaign soon made the "Ninety Billion Speech" a prime exhibit in their effort to discredit Reagan as irresponsible and reckless. It was especially damaging in New Hampshire, whose residents felt lucky to have no state income or sales tax and who worried that Reagan's plan might require them. Reagan made a strong defense of what he called "financial federalism," but being on the defensive is the best way to lose an election.

Every day that Reagan remained stuck to the $90 billion tar baby was another day wasted in the race to catch Ford. In the end, he lost New Hampshire very narrowly and with it all hope of an early knockout.

Then he was on to Florida, where Ford showed why it is so difficult to unseat an incumbent. Conservatives often complained that, while it was against the law to buy one individual's vote, it was perfectly legal to appeal to large groups of voters by promising a new hospital here, a military contract there, and a mass-transit grant elsewhere. Presidents can do this; challengers cannot, and Ford made the most of it.

Reagan, meanwhile, began speaking less about big government and more about the decline of American power and the growth of Soviet influence in the world. Then, almost by accident, he hit upon the Panama Canal issue. Voters knew little about negotiations with Panama, but anger that the United States might give up control of the canal became a symbolic focus for the generalized feeling that America was in retreat.

Nevertheless, Ford still won Florida and then three more states, and by late March many in the Reagan campaign—including his wife—were ready to give up. Not the candidate. As his manager explained, "he made some pretty bad movies. . . . But he knows that if you make a bad movie, you don't stop making movies."[5] There was money to compete in just one more state, and North Carolina became the last stand. Reagan went on statewide television with an updated version of "The Speech" from 1964, casting himself rather than Goldwater as the cavalry riding to the rescue. The response was tremendous, and Reagan surprised even himself by winning North Carolina and changing the momentum of the race.

Moving on to Texas, he repeatedly hit Ford on the Panama Canal "giveaway," saying, "we bought it, we paid for it, it's ours, and we're going to keep it!" He also made an open pitch for George Wallace's voters in Texas, with a television ad showing a Wallace supporter saying, "much as I hate to admit it, George Wallace can't be nominated. Ronald Reagan can. He's right on the issues. . . . I'm gonna vote for Ronald Reagan."[6]

He swept Texas and several other states and briefly passed Ford in the delegate count, but the president gradually crept back ahead in the remaining primaries and conventions as the two candidates traded state for state. By the end of the process in July, Ford was forty votes short of a majority and Reagan was one hundred short, with 140 delegates still uncommitted. Then it was time for personal persuasion, and here Ford had clear advantage. He could bring a state's entire delegation to the White House for a fine meal, an ego massage, and a treasured memory, while Reagan had to make his plea on the telephone or by traveling.

Searching for some way to keep his candidate in the race, John Sears convinced Reagan to make a dramatic announcement of his choice for vice president—Senator Richard Schweiker of Pennsylvania. Although Schweiker was by no means a conservative, he was at least against abortion and gun control and was strong on national defense. He told Reagan, "I'm no knee-jerk liberal," and the reply was, "I'm no knee-jerk extremist." It was another proof of Reagan's willingness to put pragmatism above ideology, but not all conservatives were willing to do so; one said that Reagan had "betrayed the trust" of his supporters.[7]

Sears had hoped to pry loose some Pennsylvania delegates with the Schweiker ploy, but instead it cost Reagan Mississippi and sealed Ford's victory at the convention by the narrow margin of 117 votes. When defeat became clear, Schweiker's wife, overcome by the sad end of her husband's hopes, began to cry. Then she felt a comforting arm on her shoulder and heard Reagan's soft words: "Don't worry. It's all part of God's plan."[8]

This was one of the deepest-held aspects of Reagan's faith throughout his adult life: that all events great and small find their motive power in the purpose of the Creator. From the largest theme on his mental horizon—the planting of America as a beacon of hope for the world—to the mere outcome of a presidential nomination, all served a greater purpose, all marched toward a nobler end. The duty of man was simply to rest content in the ultimate goodness of God.

This faith sustained Reagan through disappointments and defeats, and it formed the most intimate part of the mystical connection he had with the American people in this vast nation of believers. It was also one of the things that most vexed his critics after 1980, that a president who held in his hands the literal existence of the planet and all who dwelt thereon, should be guided in the conduct of his great office by such an unworldly and, to them, simple-minded belief.

The next evening—the last of the convention—Ford, recognizing the need for a united party, asked Reagan to join him on stage. The delegates began to chant "We Want Ron," and down came Reagan to do what he had never done as an actor: steal a scene from the star. Cheers and applause swept the convention floor, and there was no doubt about the emotional favorite of the delegates. Reagan's duty now was to gather that emotion and turn it toward the man who had—just barely—beaten him.

This he did, in a brief speech praising Ford and the conservative party platform. He warned of the "erosion of freedom" under Democratic presidents and of the "horrible missiles of destruction" poised to wipe out life on Earth. He asked delegates to imagine what Americans a century later would say of them. Would they "thank God for those people in 1976 who headed off that loss of freedom, . . . who kept our world from nuclear destruction?"

The structure of his talk, like almost every other since "A Time for Choosing" in 1964, followed the timeworn pattern of political rhetoric.

One "viewed with alarm" the conduct of the other party and "pointed with pride" to one's own party, but with Reagan, there was also something more fundamental. In his mind the struggle from 1964 through 1976 and on into the future was about a stake far more vital than the victory of a candidate or a party or even an ideology. He believed that American freedom really was being eroded at home, that the West really was threatened by Soviet power, and that the world really was in danger of nuclear suicide.

In a goodbye talk to his supporters the next day, Reagan urged "don't get cynical. . . . [M]illions of Americans out there want what you want," and promised that "I shall rise and fight again."[9] On the way out of town, he passed a prophetic homemade sign, "Republicans: You Picked the Wrong Man." Back home, Reagan told his family that his greatest regret was not being able to negotiate arms control with Soviet dictator Leonid Brezhnev, who "would tell me all the things that our side would have to give up." Then Reagan would "whisper one little word in his ear: *Nyet.*"[10] It was a remarkable preview of his behavior as president, except that in the end, with Gorbachev, Reagan said "*da.*"

After losing to Ford, Reagan treated himself to plentiful downtime at the ranch, where he happily toiled away clearing brush and building fences. He also resumed his newspaper column, radio commentary, and speaking schedule. In his most important speech of 1977, to CPAC, he asked Republicans to escape their "country-club, big-business" past and become a populist party with "room for the man and woman in the factories, for the farmer, for the cop on the beat." Republicans should use "social issues" like abortion, "law and order," and forced busing of school children for racial balance, to win working-class Democrats, a prescription remarkably similar to that formerly used by George Wallace.

Conservatism itself had changed since the Goldwater days from a loose collection of individuals to an organized political movement. The lonely pioneers of the 1960s were now supported by "think tanks" like the Heritage Foundation, national groups like the American Conservative Union and its annual CPAC gathering, and a network of state taxpayer and conservative organizations. The Religious Right was also emerging as political force; evangelicals, many of whom had supported Carter in 1976 for his very public Baptist faith, were moving toward the Republicans.

Religion had been a powerful influence in American politics before— fighting slavery in the mid-nineteenth century, urban poverty in the late nineteenth century, and racial discrimination in the mid-twentieth century. These battles had enlisted what one might call the "Religious Left." When the Religious Right emerged in the 1980s, its issues were bringing prayer back into the schools and opposing abortion, pornography, and Communism.

The conservative movement had its internal tensions, over abortion and free trade, for instance. Yet beyond all such divisions, two overriding issues drew conservatives of every sort together: support for a strong national defense and the desire to preserve in a complex modern world the traditional private rights for which America had been founded. On these two themes hung most of Reagan's speeches and newspaper columns, and especially the radio talks he gave between 1975 and 1979.

In more than a thousand short broadcasts, Reagan's commentary on current issues laid out in detail his views on America, its government, and its place in the world. One-third of the talks dealt with economic issues; another third with defense and foreign policy; one-sixth with "big government"; and only a tiny fraction with social issues such as drugs, gun control, school prayer, immigration, and abortion. It was an accurate forecast of his presidency, where, despite the occasional rhetoric, there was virtually no actual effort to satisfy the "social issue conservatives."[11]

An even more emphatic, although little known, episode from 1978 might surprise many of today's social conservatives. On the California ballot that November was the "Briggs initiative," proposed by a Republican state senator. It would have removed homosexual teachers from California classrooms, and Reagan was chiefly responsible for defeating it, although doing so might have cost him some votes on the right.

Opponents of the ballot initiative knew that it would pass unless some powerful conservative voice spoke against it, and they persuaded Reagan that it was unfair to gays and could unjustly ruin teachers' reputations. The anti-Briggs campaign made sure his position was widely known, causing Briggs himself to accuse Reagan of pandering to the homosexual community. In one of his rare outbursts of anger, the former governor then charged headfirst into the campaign, and the ballot measure, which had been headed for easy victory, lost by a large margin.

Briggs knew very well who had beaten him: "that one single endorsement—Ronald Reagan's—turned the polls around." He was sure that he would get his revenge because Reagan had been "irrevocably damaged" by marching "to the drums of the homosexuals." Exactly two years later, Reagan won the presidency in a landslide.[12]

Reagan's 1980 victory was made easier by the fact that in the fifteen years since he spoke up for candidate Goldwater, the American population, and political power, had been migrating south and west. In 1964 the "Rust Belt" from Massachusetts through Illinois had cast eleven more electoral votes than the Southern and Western "Sun Belt." In the 1980 census, the Rust Belt would have thirty-two *fewer* votes than the more conservative Sun Belt, and the power shift became even more rapid in the next three decades. Even demography was smiling on Ronald Reagan.

The primary cause of his victory, however, was that by 1980 the American public could not wait to get rid of President Jimmy Carter. After Carter narrowly defeated Gerald Ford in November 1976, he entered the White House on a wave of good opinion, as a reform-minded outsider with a list of promises to keep—111 full pages of them. The sad result was that Carter rushed about from issue to issue and proposed policy after policy with no apparent theme or sense of priorities.

If Reagan managed his office too casually in Sacramento and Washington, Carter managed too minutely. He once proudly told a visitor, pointing to a two-foot stack of paper, "that's the Air Force budget. I've read every page of it."[13] The new president also made no effort to win friends among his fellow Democrats who controlled Congress and as a result kept almost none of his promised agenda: no tax reform or welfare reform, no national health insurance, no pro-union labor law, no energy policy, no arms limitation treaty.

The two greatest unsolved problems that dogged his presidency and finally cost him his office were in foreign and economic policy. The decline of American influence abroad was a universal topic by the late 1970s. Many on the political left, regarding their own country as a force for evil in the world, cheered the news. On the right, all bemoaned it, fearing with Kipling that "all our pomp of yesterday is one with Nineveh and Tyre." The U.S. share of the world economy had been shrinking since 1945, anti-Americanism was rife at the United Nations, Communist regimes had taken over Southeast Asia and Afghanistan, and Soviet influence was growing in Africa and Central America.

The Soviet dissident and author Aleksandr Solzhenitsyn, in a famous Harvard commencement speech, denounced the decay of Western culture and the triumph of materialism over moral duty. This survivor of the Communist slave labor camps warned that the world was at a dangerous turning point. Ronald Reagan agreed. The final blow to national prestige came in November 1979, with the capture of fifty-two American diplomats by Iranian radicals who stormed the embassy in Tehran and touched off the "hostage crisis" that consumed Carter's last year.

He also had the misfortune to preside during the latter stage of a long period in which the American economy was stuck in neutral. From 1966 to 1982 the stock market moved in a dispiriting cycle of decline, recovery, and decline, ending barely where it had been sixteen years before. The economy several times slipped into recession, and advocates of the free-market system grew pessimistic about the future. Marxists rejoiced, and articles began to appear with titles like "Crisis in U.S. Capitalism" and "The Demise of the World Capitalist System."

It was Reagan's good fortune and Carter's ill luck that by 1980 public distrust of government was at an all-time high. In the mid-1960s three-fourths of the population trusted government to do the right thing most of the time, but by 1980, after Vietnam and Watergate, only one-fourth did so. Carter was seen as an incompetent who could nag the nation but not lead it, while Reagan's long career of denouncing federal waste, corruption, regulation, and taxation fit this negative public mood to perfection. The man had found his moment.

Reagan officially became a candidate in November 1979, with a public rebuke of Carter's performance. America's affliction, Reagan said, was not a failure of national spirit but of leadership by those "who claim that our problems are too difficult to handle," that America "must learn to live with less, . . . resign itself to inevitable decline," and "no longer dream great dreams." The cure for the economy was simple: lower taxes and less government spending. He closed with a reminder that "mankind looks to us to keep our rendezvous with destiny," to be "that shining city on a hill."[14]

From the beginning, Reagan's 1980 effort suffered from a basic internal conflict. John Sears, returning as manager, knew that he could "sell" Reagan, but he had no very high opinion of his candidate's abilities. Worried about alienating moderates, he tried to put a lid on Reagan's opposition to abortion, only to touch off a rare explosion of temper: "I am running for president of the United States! You're not! Got it?"[15]

For Sears, Reagan was simply a product to be peddled, and he was a very good peddler, so he tried to accumulate all authority and began to marginalize or expel the old Reaganites. They, meanwhile—Nofziger, Meese, Deaver, and the others—knew Reagan's strengths as a candidate and believed that limiting his personal appearances and toning down his rhetoric, as Sears wanted, was wasting the campaign's greatest asset.

As 1980 began, Reagan was the clear Republican leader but was too conservative for some, haunted still by the nightmare of Goldwater's 1964 loss. To them, Reagan was simply Goldwater with a bigger smile and a smaller brain. Three men had a real chance to bar his way: Senate Minority Leader Howard Baker, ex-governor John Connally of Texas, and former Congressman and CIA director George Bush. Could one of them save the party from a Reagan nomination and another 1964?

Sears wanted his candidate to ignore the others, floating serenely above the "small ball" of local campaigning and protected from media ambushes. He expected to win easily in Iowa and New Hampshire and effectively end the primary battle in a few weeks. Instead, by ignoring Iowa, Reagan wound up losing to an energetic effort by Bush. It was a rude surprise, but the candidate and his manager learned their lesson. Reagan worked hard in New Hampshire, inspiring crowds and drawing enthusiasm from them. Fighting back, Bush branded Reagan's tax cut/military buildup/deficit reduction ideas as "voodoo economics."

The defining moment of 1980 came in Nashua, New Hampshire, where the local newspaper scheduled a debate between the two leaders the week-end before the primary. To satisfy federal law, the Reagan campaign paid for the event but wanted all the candidates on stage. As the room filled up on Saturday night, a tense discussion ensued: should there be two debaters, as Bush and the newspaper wanted, or all of them, as Reagan preferred? Finally the paper's editor, fed up with Reagan, told the sound man to turn off the governor's mike.

Reagan shot back, to the cheers of the audience, "I am paying for this microphone, Mr. Green!" It was typical Reagan: not entirely accurate—the editor's name was Breen—but perfectly suited to the occasion and com-pletely dominating the media story line. One short sentence at one small event, and the 1980 primary campaign was effectively over. The "Battle of the Microphone" was just what Reagan needed to get his blood up, and he crushed Bush on election day by two to one, although how many actual votes this one incident changed is open to question.

After that, only a monumental disaster could have kept Reagan from the nomination, and none occurred. On primary afternoon, he fired Sears, put his trusted Californians back in charge, and strode forth to battle. Baker and Connally quickly dropped out and then only Bush was left, the "eastern elitist" versus the "conservative cowboy," in the words of Lou Cannon. Another few weeks disposed of Bush as well, and the Republican conven-tion became a Reagan victory party.

Nearly everyone in the campaign, including the candidate, believed that choosing a moderate for vice president would make it easier to attract vot-ers uncertain about Reagan himself. Heading that list was George Bush, despite his sometimes pointed attacks in the primaries. After a frenzied and almost zany negotiation with Ford over a possible vice-presidential offer, which finally degenerated into a media circus, Reagan did the sensible thing and picked Bush, forgetting his vow of a few days earlier that "I'll never choose that man; he lied about my record!"[16]

Reagan's acceptance speech combined four powerful rhetorical elements. There was the usual partisan slap at the Carter administration's "direct political, personal, and moral responsibility" for economic hard times. They live "in the world of make-believe," he said, the very place many people thought Reagan himself spent his days. Next he warned the Soviet Union that the United States would never "let those who would destroy freedom dictate the future course of life on this planet." War, he said, "comes not when the forces of freedom are strong, it is when they are weak that tyrants are tempted."

The third element was Reagan's standard dose of patriotic nostalgia, rejecting those who say "that our nation has passed its zenith, . . . that the future will be one of sacrifice and few opportunities. . . . Can we doubt," he asked, "that only a Divine Providence placed this land, this island of freedom, here as a refuge for all those . . . who yearn to breathe free?" Finally came the direct religious note that often closed his speeches. "I've been a little afraid to suggest what I'm going to suggest. I'm more afraid not to. Can we begin our crusade joined together in a moment of silent prayer?" One witness said, "it is hard to think of another politician who could pull this off—or would try to."[17]

Reagan left his convention as the clear favorite for election in November, while President Carter, fighting off a challenge from Ted Kennedy, seemed helpless to deal with inflation, unemployment, and the hostage crisis. Many Democrats were almost desperate about Carter, who for a brief time was barely ahead of independent candidate John Anderson in the polls. Fortunately for Carter, Reagan lost his early advantage by stumbling through the summer committing one gaffe after another.

He spoke up for "states' rights" in a Mississippi town where civil rights workers had been lynched, called the Vietnam War a noble cause (which, true or not, cost him votes), and made statements about Taiwan that threatened to damage relations with China. Had this continued, it could have been fatal, so the campaign brought back Stuart Spencer, the strategist of 1966 and 1970. Accepting his guidance, Reagan finally settled down.

Meanwhile, Carter had to fight all the way to the Democratic convention. In state after state he beat Ted Kennedy, but occasionally the senator won a primary, renewed his hopes, and fought doggedly on. A contested nomination is never helpful to a sitting president, and Kennedy's challenge was especially dangerous because the issues he raised against Carter were the same ones Reagan would use in the fall: the economy and foreign policy.

Carter finally stumbled to victory even as 80 percent of American voters thought his economic policy was a flat failure. In his own acceptance speech, he called the election "a stark choice between . . . two futures," something on which he and Reagan fully agreed. As one politico summed up the contrast of platforms, Democrats called for expanding government power to secure "justice," while Republicans wanted to limit government power in order to preserve "freedom." There could hardly be a more concise statement of the way in which liberals and conservatives defined themselves.

The Democratic convention, despite Carter's unpopularity, did at least succeed in rallying his party. Reagan's large lead after his own convention had vanished, and the two candidates began the home stretch almost even. The official start of the two campaigns was instructive. Reagan used his kick-off in Detroit to appeal to blue-collar ethnics by hugging the father of Polish patriot Lech Walesa; Carter, needing to hold his Southern base, opened his campaign by hugging the former segregationist leader, George Wallace.

The "wild card" in 1980 was Illinois Congressman John Anderson, who, having flopped in the Republican primaries, ran as an independent in November. Although he denounced both major-party candidates, he especially complained about Reagan, who "thinks in terms of a holy war against Communism" and sees himself as "destined to lead the charge against it."[18] This was precisely what Reagan did think, and he was only puzzled that Anderson seemed to criticize such a crusade against tyranny. How far the self-confessed "hemophiliac liberal" of 1945 had come!

Carter's people knew that the terrible economy and the frustrating Iran hostage deadlock made defeat likely unless they could demonize Reagan and make him an unacceptable alternative. Voters would still reelect Carter, much as they disliked him, if they feared the challenger more. Or, as one admitted, the campaign message had gone from "Why Not the Best?" in 1976, to "It Could Be Worse."[19]

Reagan's job was simpler and easier. He did not have to persuade people that Carter should be sent home; they had already convinced themselves of that. He had only to soothe the uncertainties about himself and soften fears into mild doubts. His message would be, "I'm not nearly as bad as you thought." To this end, the dominant subject of Reagan's television ads was his time as governor, portraying him as a competent and successful manager, not a nuclear-armed cowboy. In his own speeches, he probably uttered the word "peace" more often than any other.

Like every sensible campaign, Ronald Reagan's wanted to convey the candidate's message clearly to the public. The best way to achieve this is to follow an "issue of the day" strategy, where speeches by the candidate and surrogates, briefings to the media, and paid advertising all focus on one dominant issue. The hope is that this single-minded pattern will allow the candidate to set both the topic and the tone of reporting.

Of course election campaigns, like football plays and military battles, have a life of their own, and slippery reality often escapes the bounds of any premade plan. A controlled strategy is much easier when the candidate himself has media experience. No other presidential nominee has ever had the benefit of Reagan's background in Hollywood, speaking for General Electric, and hosting a popular television show. If Ronald Reagan had begun in the 1930s with a lifetime plan to prepare for a presidential campaign in the media age, he could not have done better.

As the fall race began, Reagan was secure in the Plains states, the Southwest, and the West. The decisive battle would be in the industrial states of the East and Midwest—New York, Pennsylvania, Ohio, Michigan, and Illinois—where Reagan's appeal to blue-collar Catholic Democrats made him dangerous. With his evangelical support he might even threaten Carter's Southern base. The president needed a heavy turnout of black voters to hold the South, and what journalists call "playing the race card" was one way to encourage this, so Carter denounced Reagan for opposing the 1964 Civil Rights Act and accused him of encouraging racial hatred.

His black supporters went even further. One said, "when I hear Reagan's name, I see the spectre of white sheets," and another claimed that Reagan had given the word "that it's going to be all right to kill niggers again when he's president."[20] Reagan was hurt and angry that African-American politicians would brand him—the boy who had brought black teammates to sleep in his house, the governor who had put more blacks in office than any other in California history—a racist.

However, all this fed a growing media theme that Carter was running a "mean" and "vindictive" campaign. He had been warned by fellow Democrats that personal attacks on Reagan would fail as they had in California and would undermine voters' impression of Carter himself as a fair and decent man. As one said, to "attack a nice guy is certain to result in a backlash which could really hurt us."[21]

When the "race card" failed to trump Reagan's "nice guy" image, Carter next played the "warmonger card," and here he had more luck. In years of public speaking, Reagan had often suggested using American military force in international disputes. Simply highlighting some of Reagan's own past statements raised fears that he would be dangerously reckless in a world overstocked with atomic weapons. Secretary of State Edmund Muskie warned, for instance, that Reagan's election would produce a "perpetual state of war." Carter worked this lever to raise Reagan's "negatives," as political consultants say, but again he went too far too often and drew media criticism for being vicious and dishonorable. Still, he made his point; by more than two to one, people said Carter would be more likely than Reagan to prevent future wars.

Meanwhile, Reagan himself tried to focus on the economy as the major issue, and he found the perfect wording: "A recession is when your neighbor loses his job. A depression is when you lose yours. And recovery is when Jimmy Carter loses his." It was a short, simple, and endlessly repeated mantra, although two years later President Reagan must have winced at the memory when America fell into a recession far deeper than Carter's. Nevertheless, in the fall of 1980 it struck home among union audiences in the steel-and-auto country of the industrial North.

One of the most effective Reagan ads, and no doubt the one most galling to Democrats, was simply a clip from one of Ted Kennedy's primary speeches in which the Senator declaims, "It's time to say, 'No more American hostages! No more high interest rates! No more high inflation! And no more Jimmy Carter!'" Here was Reagan's case in a nutshell, from the mouth of perhaps the most popular Democrat in America. It played powerfully upon Carter's miserable approval ratings: less than one-fifth of Americans liked his management of the economy and foreign policy.

As the autumn wore on, one thing became quite clear. Many people, fed up with the double pain of inflation *and* recession, wanted to vote Jimmy Carter out of the Oval Office but were still reluctant to put Reagan in it. Typical of this conflicted mood were the endorsements of two leading newspapers. The Philadelphia *Inquirer* supported Carter but only with "grave misgivings," while the Chicago *Tribune* backed Reagan, while admitting "there is good reason to worry" about him.[22]

Public opinion polls were mixed, implying a close contest where many voters might change their minds. As Carter and Reagan prepared for their only debate of the long campaign, a new Gallup Poll showed the president moving into a three-point lead after trailing two weeks earlier. The nation's senior newscaster, Walter Cronkite, was among those who thought that the debate might be the decisive moment of the year.

On the big night, Reagan immediately established physical dominance of the stage, striding across to shake the hand of the startled president, a perfect picture of confident strength versus nervous uncertainty. As the contest got underway, both candidates held closely to their scripts. Carter did his best to portray Reagan as a risky choice—too uninformed, too ideological, too belligerent to be trusted in the Oval Office. He clearly outclassed Reagan in detailed knowledge of the issues and caught him on several factual errors.

Reagan, meanwhile, had two goals—to calm fears that he was a warmonger, and to pound home his year-long critique of the growing economic damage and shrinking international prestige that afflicted "Carter's America." Asked why he should be president rather than Carter, Reagan replied with a capsule summary of conservative beliefs: he promised "less government . . . less taxes . . . more freedom."

Voters want to feel comfortable with the person who will steer their country through the dangerous currents of the future, and in this Reagan had a natural advantage; he simply had to be himself. He showed this with four simple words in response to one of Carter's many attacks on his past record of careless and extreme statements. Rather than defend himself, Reagan said with a regretful shake of his head, "there you go again." He had as much as branded the president a liar, with a tone like that of an uncle reluctantly calling a wayward nephew to account.

Voters also want a president who sees the world as they do, whose values and instincts agree with theirs. Reagan understood and reflected the values of the "common man" because he actually was one, while Carter was a nuclear engineer. Although he came from the same rural stock as Reagan and was equally religious, those qualities seemed lost beneath his awkward, humorless stiffness. It was, in Sunday cartoon terms, a contest between Mark Trail and Dilbert.

Nearly every election with a sitting president is a referendum on the incumbent's performance. With inflation and unemployment high, the Soviet Union on the march in Afghanistan and Africa, and Americans still hostage in Iran, it was impossible for Carter to win the contest over issues. Reagan sealed his advantage with a masterful set of closing questions. "Are you better off than you were four years ago . . . ? Is there more or less unemployment . . . ? Is America as respected throughout the world as it was?"[23] Considering the state of things, his questions answered themselves.

Asked afterward if he had been nervous on the same stage as the most powerful man in the world, Reagan said, "No, I've been on the same stage with John Wayne."[24] Most media critics thought Carter had won on points; he knew the issues and often put Reagan on the defensive. The American public—over 100 million of them—must have watched a different debate. For the great majority, it was their first extended look at Reagan, and they liked what they saw. In barely more than a week, he went from a slight underdog to a landslide lead.

Reagan left the debate energized and eager for the final push, while the Carter people seemed to realize that the end was near. Crowds were subdued, staffers grim, and the president's own remarks more strained and desperate at each succeeding stop. Throughout the fall, Reagan had repeatedly "stolen" the Democrats' great heroes, quoting FDR and John Kennedy, and now he even stole their theme song as a band played "Happy Days Are Here Again" at preelection rallies.

The only thing that Reagan had really feared all year long, an "October surprise" release of the hostages, never occurred. Instead, in perhaps the best television of his life, Reagan talked to the nation on election eve, asking, "does history still have a place for America, . . . for her great ideals?" He brushed aside the claim that "our energy is spent, our days of greatness at an end. . . . That we must tell our children . . . not to dream as we once dreamed."

Reagan spoke of religion, of the faith that from the nation's youth and his own been a guiding light, "this hope of divine providence." He closed with the assurance "that America is still united, still strong, . . . clinging fast to the dream of peace and freedom" so that the future would say of "our generation that we did keep faith with our God, . . . act worthy of ourselves," and "pass on lovingly that shining city on a hill."[25]

Remarkably, coming from a candidate on the eve of an election, it was not so much a political speech as a sermon on America's "civic religion" in the manner of Abraham Lincoln. It summed up the values formed over a lifetime and forecast the beliefs that would power a presidency. That evening it rained in Dixon, Illinois, and a rainbow settled just over the old Reagan homestead where once had dwelt a boy who learned to believe in God's overruling Providence.

On election day itself, two vignettes foretold the outcome. At Reagan headquarters in St. Louis, five hundred people showed up to work the twenty-five telephones, while on Air Force One, Carter's pollster called to tell him that in the weekend surveys "the bottom had fallen out." As soon as the early state polls closed at 7:00 p.m., the networks called two states for Reagan, then three more at 7:30, and at 8:00 six more and quickly another six. By 8:15, it was over and Jimmy Carter became the first Democratic president in ninety-two years to lose reelection.

Reagan carried all but six states, won 489 electoral votes to Carter's 49, and carried the popular vote by 51 percent to 41 percent (with 7 percent for Anderson), a margin of nearly 9 million. A bigger surprise even than the magnitude of Reagan's victory was the Republican capture of a 53–47 majority in the U.S. Senate, the first since Dwight Eisenhower's days. No one had expected this astounding result; a full dozen Senate seats changed hands, and not a single Republican lost.

The stunning defeat of so many Democratic senators produced talk of a conservative sweep in 1980, perhaps even a fundamental shift of the nation's voters to the right. A closer analysis of the results, however, shows that, while Reagan won a convincing personal victory over Carter, Democrats remained the nation's long-term majority party. Despite winning only twelve of the thirty-four Senate races in 1980, Democratic candidates actually outpolled their Republican opponents by 4 million votes.

In the House of Representatives, Democrats had a 2-million-vote margin over Republicans, although they lost thirty-four seats to Reagan's coattails. The overall Democratic majority was 243–192 in the House, leaving the new president dependent upon "boll weevils"—conservative Southern Democratic congressmen—if his policies were ever to become law. At the state level, despite Republican gains, Democrats still had more governors and elected 4,400 legislators to only 2,900 Republicans.

So, while the 1980 election produced a shift to the right in the federal government, it was not *caused* by a shift to the right among American voters. Reagan, a Republican Senate, and a conservative coalition in the House certainly governed differently than Carter and a liberal Democratic Congress. But neither Ronald Reagan nor his conservative issues won the 1980 election. Jimmy Carter lost it.

After nearly a year of intense campaigning, even the least attentive person should have known that, on the issues of federal spending and taxation, Reagan was for less and Carter was for more. The reality was quite otherwise. According to the National Election Survey, only half the voters correctly knew that Carter opposed cutting nondefense spending. The other half either wrongly thought that Carter did want to spend less, or had no idea what his position was. Likewise, only a third of the voters knew that Reagan wanted to reduce federal domestic spending; the remaining two-thirds either incorrectly believed that he opposed spending cuts or simply did not know. This was after Reagan had been denouncing "big government" spending for the last twenty-five years.

Furthermore, the voters themselves, by a three-to-two margin, opposed what Reagan was demanding and supported Carter's position. A narrow majority agreed with Carter that the United States should be satisfied with military parity with the USSR rather than Reagan's idea of military superiority. A majority also opposed Reagan's tax cut plan. In short, Ronald Reagan won not because the voters agreed with him, but in spite of the fact that they disagreed with him.

In summary, more than 60 percent thought inflation was the biggest issue and were going to punish Jimmy Carter for that regardless of what Reagan said. One-fifth of the voters changed their minds in the last four days, producing Reagan's landslide victory, and for them the economy and the hostages were the driving issues, not taxes, government spending, or the Soviet threat.

To be sure, even after the election, there were those who still feared Reagan more than Carter, and one of the places where he was least popular was his old stomping ground: Hollywood. Actors who knew him there had such angry comments as, "he's destroying everything . . . I've lived my life for" and "every profession has its John Wilkes Booth. Reagan is ours." Others were simply fearful: "I think we're headed for disaster," or "I just hope we can get through the next four years."[26]

Perhaps the Californians' lament was best expressed by the man Reagan had tossed out of the governorship by a million votes in 1966, Pat Brown: "I am chilled to the bone at the possibility of Ronald Reagan . . . becoming President of the United States."[27] As it turned out, the people who should have been "chilled to the bone" were the rulers of the Soviet Union. A month after the election, France's intelligence agency director told Reagan that "you are the American president who will lead the free world to final victory over Communism."[28]

Notes

1. Unruh quoted in Whalen article, *New York Times Magazine,* February 22, 1976, in Colacello, *Ronnie and Nancy,* 428.
2. Reagan quoted in Colacello, *Ronnie and Nancy,* 440.

3. Jules Witcover, *Marathon: The Pursuit of the Presidency, 1972–1976* (New York: Viking Press, 1977), 69.

4. Reagan quoted in Nancy Reagan, *My Turn*, 181.

5. John Sears quoted in Witcover, *Marathon*, 409.

6. Quoted *ibid.*, 419.

7. *Ibid.*, 461, 463.

8. Author's interview with John Miller, Reagan Museum, Eureka College.

9. Reagan quoted in Cannon, *Governor Reagan*, 432.

10. Reagan quoted in Nancy Reagan, *My Turn*, 193.

11. Tabulation of radio talks from Kiron Skinner *et al.*, ed., *Reagan in His Own Hand* (New York: Free Press, 2001).

12. Briggs quoted in Boyarsky, *Ronald Reagan*, 181.

13. Carter quoted in Theodore H. White, *America in Search of Itself: The Making of the President, 1956–1980* (New York: Harper & Row, 1982), 200.

14. For Reagan's announcement, see www.reagan.utexas.edu/archives/reference/11.13.79.html

15. Reagan quoted in Craig Shirley, *Rendezvous with Destiny: Ronald Reagan and the Campaign That Changed America* (Wilmington, DE: ISI Books, 2009), 108.

16. Reagan quoted *ibid.*, 336.

17. Elizabeth Drew, *Portrait of an Election: The 1980 Presidential Campaign* (New York: Simon and Schuster, 1981), 220.

18. Anderson quoted in Shirley, *Rendezvous with Destiny*, 225, n38.

19. Drew, *Portrait of an Election*, 184.

20. Patricia Harris and Andrew Young, quoted in Shirley, *Rendezvous with Destiny*, 457, 502.

21. Les Francis quoted in Cannon, *Governor Reagan*, 490.

22. Shirley, *Rendezvous with Destiny*, 529.

23. For the transcript of the debate, see www.reagan.utexas.edu/archives/reference/10.28.80debate.html

24. Quoted in Shirley, *Rendezvous with Destiny*, 545.

25. Quotes from reagan.utexas.edu/archives/reference/11.3.80.html

26. Actors' comments in McClelland, *Hollywood on Reagan*.

27. Edmund G. Brown, *Reagan and Reality: The Two Californias* (New York: Praeger Publishers, 1970), 32.

28. Morris, *Dutch*, 472.

CHAPTER 6

PRESIDENT REAGAN, 1981:
LEARNING A NEW ROLE

Carly Simon's song says, "let all the dreamers wake the nation," and Ronald Reagan was nothing if not a dreamer. Others might placidly accept, or eagerly welcome, the restraints of current reality, but not he. He dreamt of new worlds, new possibilities. Was it not possible to halt the relentless reach of government into the lives of Americans? To end the Soviet empire's rule over one-third of a billion subjects? To free humanity from the fear of nuclear holocaust? To Reagan and his followers these were noble dreams, dreams that could change the world.

Reagan's detractors, and there were many even in his own party, might grant that dreams were fine things, but those who governed must do so in the stark daylight of reality, not the fuzzy shadows of dreamland. These dreams, expounded countless times across the years made Reagan, as he took office, seem to Washington sophisticates to be breathtakingly naïve or abysmally stupid about the actual world in which people must live, governments govern, and nations negotiate.

For Reagan himself, the most immediately prosaic aspect of the actual postelection world was the need to staff his new administration. Unlike all too many presidential transitions, Reagan's was thoroughly organized both as to policy and personnel. He and his people were not going to enter Washington as they had Sacramento in January 1967, wondering, "what do we do now?" His trusted Californian, Ed Meese, set up dozens of task forces to study national issues, and the search for competent and conservative people to fill the top positions actually began almost a year earlier. There was also a "palace guard" recruited from the "Old Brigade," a supporting team of personal advisors—Richard Wirthlin, the pollster; Stuart Spencer, the strategist; Michael Deaver, the "keeper of the image"; and Lyn Nofziger in public relations, as well as Meese.

To bring some order to the usual scramble for office in a new administration, Reagan asked an informal personnel committee of old "Kitchen Cabinet" friends to give him three candidates for each available spot. The California conservatives, and Meese himself, assumed that he would be the new president's chief of staff. Instead, that key position went to Texan James Baker, George Bush's manager in the primary campaign and a Ford supporter in the 1976 contest. Reagan thought that Baker would get along better with the Washington sophisticates, members of Congress, and the media.

The choice of Baker—a pragmatist and, even worse, a supposed moderate—was a rude shock to conservative activists who had anticipated a "Reagan Revolution." It seemed an early sign that the Reagan presidency might be, as his Sacramento years had been, a constant skirmish between true-believer ideologues and more pragmatic compromisers. Would the constant day-to-day advice from Baker seduce the new president from his principles? The conservatives hoped not, but they had their doubts.

His assistant for presidential appointments said of one meeting with Meese, Deaver, and Baker that "we were discussing the usual things, Reaganites versus pragmatists," but what bothered the "Reaganites" more than anything else was that the chief pragmatist was Ronald Reagan himself.[1] Decades before, he had learned as SAG president to talk tough but compromise when necessary, and he lived by the same code as governor and president, even when "compromise" looked to some of his most fervent followers like "surrender."

Reagan got some early advice, for the higher offices and for general strategy, from Richard Nixon, eager to work his way back into a position of influence in Republican politics. Among his recommendations were the men who wound up in the top three cabinet positions connected with foreign affairs: Caspar Weinberger, William Casey, and Alexander Haig.

"Cap" Weinberger had been a "green eyeshade" cost-cutter in Sacramento, picking out hundreds of budget items for Reagan's vetoes, and he had the same record in Nixon's Cabinet. This was a major reason he became Secretary of Defense, to be a ruthless weeder of wasteful spending in the military. Instead, he almost "out-Reaganed" Reagan in arguing for increased defense spending, no matter what the budgetary impact. He was a good fit for his new position and served for almost the entire span of Reagan's presidency until he, like several others, was brought low by the Iran-Contra scandal.

Casey had taken over from John Sears as manager of the 1980 campaign, and before that had been Nixon's chairman of the Securities and Exchange Commission and then a Wall Street lawyer. Like Weinberger and Reagan himself, Casey believed that the Soviet Union's expanding influence in the

1970s posed a serious threat, and as Director of the Central Intelligence Agency he funneled substantial aid to the Afghan resistance and to the Solidarity labor movement in Poland. He, too, was caught up in Iran-Contra and only his death prevented a date in court.

While Casey and Weinberger served more than half a dozen years with Reagan, his first Secretary of State, former general Alexander Haig, had a short and anguished tenure. Nixon's White House Chief of Staff and commander of NATO forces in Europe, Haig was experienced in the ways of Washington and in foreign policy. He seemed a good choice for Secretary of State, but from the beginning he was on the wrong foot with the men closest to Reagan. Furthermore, combining his military experience with his new position, he expected to be in full charge of national security policy, an assumption naturally not acceptable to the Secretary of Defense and the National Security Advisor.

Haig also neither understood nor approved of Reagan's management style, which required cabinet officers to deal with him through his personal staff, the Baker-Deaver-Meese triumvirate. As if this were not enough, Haig was sensitive to any remark or action that did not accord him the respect he thought his position merited and was perennially suspicious that others were trying to undermine him. Hence, his tenure as Secretary was uncomfortable from the beginning.

Haig's real problem, though, was one of priorities and ideologies. For Reagan, as well as Baker and Deaver, nothing was more important in the beginning than to tackle the dual economic problems of inflation and unemployment, while Haig thought it vital to make an early foreign-policy challenge to the Soviet Union. This put him out of step with the president's timetable as well as with Baker's and Deaver's desire to moderate the Cold War confrontation. Haig's hardline attitude exploded in a discussion about Castro's Communist regime in Cuba: "Give me the word and I'll make that island a f___g parking lot."[2]

In domestic policy, the two chief appointments went to Treasury Secretary Donald Regan and Budget Director William Stockman. Regan had been chairman of the Merrill Lynch brokerage firm and a Wall Street reformer before he came to Washington. Like Haig, he was a stranger to Reagan but became a powerful force advocating the president's economic policies of tax cuts, spending cuts, and a balanced budget, although ultimately achieving only the first of these.

Finally, there was David Stockman, the one true revolutionary in Reagan's entourage—far more so than the president himself, much to Stockman's eventual distress. A two-term Congressman from Michigan, he had prepared his new boss for the 1980 debates with John Anderson and Carter, and he came to the Office of Management and Budget determined to wage war on the welfare state. Like Haig, Stockman had problems from the beginning understanding Ronald Reagan and dealing with the White House staff.

His journey to disillusionment began in the earliest days of the administration. It quickly became apparent that while he was intensely committed to achieving one of Reagan's primary goals by cutting spending to balance the budget, he would have to fight others who were equally determined to achieve the president's other goals—cutting taxes, increasing military spending, and protecting Social Security—all of which were incompatible with Stockman's. Even more disturbing for Stockman, the president himself put economic recovery ahead of balancing the budget. Who would have thought Ronald Reagan was a Keynesian?

One top position that was never fully effective until Reagan's later years was that of National Security Advisor. Believing in "cabinet government," Reagan did not see where this person would fit and hence neglected the office, to his misfortune. As governor, domestic issues had been his entire concern, but for a modern president foreign policy was at least as important, especially during the Cold War.

In many presidencies the secretaries of Defense and State have different views on national security issues, and the president needs an advisor who can manage the personal rivalries and policy differences between these competing cabinet members. Reagan ran through half a dozen national security advisors; although most were quite competent, he did not grant any of them sufficient authority until late in the second term. The result was often confusion and poor decisions at the intersection of foreign and military policy.

Reagan's choices for the top spots in his administration show that, like Abraham Lincoln, he had no problem whatever surrounding himself with men who had been his opponents. He picked George Bush, who had denounced Reagan's "voodoo economics," as his vice president and Jim Baker, who helped Gerald Ford defeat Reagan in 1976, as his chief of staff. Drew Lewis, who kept Pennsylvania delegates from switching to Reagan in 1976, was appointed to the Cabinet, and James Brady, who worked for John Connally's 1980 campaign, became Reagan's own press secretary.

His Cabinet and the inner circle of old Californians helped the president polish and express his ideas, but the ideas were his own. From the influence of his parents, his reading in political theory, his eye-opening experience speaking with General Electric workers, and his eight years as governor, Reagan's view of the world, of government, and of America was set solid by 1980. Lower taxes, less government spending, and a stronger military were his bedrock principles on the campaign trail and in the Oval Office. Still, ideas are not actions, and when his principles did not fit the practical realities of a situation, he was to prove quite flexibly pragmatic, often disappointing his conservative devotees.

As he prepared to take office, his Hollywood experience, honed by the years in Sacramento and his last two presidential races, had taught Reagan how to identify and then cultivate the people who mattered. Even before inauguration day, he and his wife began circulating among the Washington insiders, the powerful names not only in politics but also in business, the media, and the cultural world. He was especially careful to begin on a cordial note with the congressional leaders of both parties, whom Jimmy Carter had coldly ignored. He even tried to build friendly relations with Carter himself; Reagan understood how it felt to be rejected.

The inaugural ceremony on January 20, 1981, took place for the first time on the west front of the Capitol, facing the Washington Monument, the Jefferson Memorial, and the Lincoln Memorial. Not satisfied with the draft that his speechwriter had produced, Reagan sat down and wrote his own. As usual with his speeches, it combined stretches of boilerplate political rhetoric with higher moments of eloquence. Most of it merely summarized the issues of the recent campaign—a stalled economy, high taxes, excessive federal spending. In short, "government is not the solution to our problem; government *is* the problem."

This had been his standard message ever since the "Time for Choosing" speech that launched his public career in 1964, and in fact even before, in the later General Electric years. He promised to unleash prosperity, tame government, and restore the proper balance between Washington and the states. In foreign policy, the new president made no threats and extolled peace, but he warned unnamed adversaries that while "we will negotiate for it, sacrifice for it; we will not surrender for it."

As he often did, Reagan dwelt upon American exceptionalism. "The orderly transfer of authority," he said, "routinely takes place, as it has for almost two centuries, and few of us stop to think how unique we really are. In the eyes of many in the world, this every-four-year ceremony we accept as normal is nothing less than a miracle." This was to some degree hyperbole, as democratic elections were also "normal" in Western Europe, Canada, Japan, Australia, New Zealand, Israel, India, most of the Caribbean, and a few Central and South American countries.

Yet Reagan's larger meaning was clear: fully half of humanity lived under authoritarian rule, and several on the list of democratic nations—Japan, India, Germany, Italy, and others—had only recently become free. In all the world only Iceland could match the American example of two hundred years of rule by the people. Using stories of wartime heroes to make his point, Reagan proclaimed that "no weapon . . . is so formidable as the will and moral courage of free men and women." He closed by urging his listeners to believe in "our capacity to perform great deeds. . . . And after all, why shouldn't we believe that? We are Americans."

On a personal level, Reagan, unlike almost every other occupant of the White House, seemed unchanged by the presidency. It is a lonely office, but he had always been able to exist contentedly within himself, needing no one, except, of course, his wife. If anything, he seemed to open up a bit more in his eight Washington years, especially with his children, from whom he had so often been disappointingly remote. His eldest daughter, Maureen, sometimes stayed at the White House, and he saw the others occasionally in Washington or California.

Even so, he still shied away from too much emotional closeness with them, possibly because he had never known much from his own father. Nevertheless, the children loved him, although they were always hoping he would let down his guard and share something more of himself with them. Michael, for instance, lamented that "he can give his heart to the country, but he just finds it difficult to hug his own children."[3] Even his wife of half a century sometimes found that a part of him was unreachable.

The presidency certainly feeds egos, as witness the haughty bearing of a Johnson or a Nixon, but Reagan already possessed what anyone might need to feel confidently important. A Hollywood career that rose to the edge of stardom, eight years speaking to appreciative audiences on the General Electric circuit, another eight as governor of the largest state, a secure spot as the idol of American conservatives—Reagan did not need the presidency to make himself a "big man." He was always in awe of his office, but never of himself. Early in the first term, when the band played "Hail to the Chief," the president said, "I don't think I'm ever going to get used to the fact that they're playing that song for me."[4] And he never did.

The words most often used to describe him as president, by those who worked for him, worked with him, and simply met him, are "serene," "secure," "genuine," and "happy." As more than one said, Reagan knew who he was and had no need to impress anybody. He even asked his secretaries whether they would rather have him write out his letters or dictate them. What other president of the United States would offer to do what his secretary preferred?

One reason he took to the presidency with such serenity is that he spent as much time as possible away from its stressful center in the Oval Office. He always seemed to be watching movies, either in the residence quarters or at Camp David, the presidential retreat in the Maryland hills, where he spent nearly two hundred of his weekends. He also rode as much as possible at Camp David and especially at Rancho del Cielo. Time at the ranch—or, indeed, the outdoor life generally—left Reagan relaxed and recharged for facing anew the frustrations of governing. He agreed with

Lord Palmerston that "there is nothing so good for the inside of a man as the outside of a horse."

When he was not riding, he was clearing brush or doing something else unusually vigorous for a person his age. It is likely that few of his sedentary critics, or allies either, could have kept pace with him. House Speaker Tip O'Neill had "never met a man in better physical condition" for his age and decided that he would copy Reagan's workout of chopping wood. He confessed that he "survived about fifteen minutes before I had to come inside, tired and sore." O'Neill was two years younger than Reagan, who thought nothing of wielding the axe for hours at a time.[5] The widely broadcast image of Reagan in checkered shirt, Levis, and cowboy hat, acting every bit like a rancher on the old frontier, was not only important relaxation. It was also one more way Reagan connected the future-oriented idea of building America by hard work with the historical past of a nation defined by its long frontier experience.

As an actor, Reagan had learned to stick to a script and follow direction, both vital requirements of a good political candidate, who must regard himself as simply another resource for his manager to employ. This is what Reagan did when he ran for office, and it is how he conducted his governorship and presidency, faithfully keeping to the daily schedule his aides drew up for him. Asked on one occasion where he might be next, the president said, "I can't tell until somebody tells me. . . . I never know where I'm going."[6] This makes him sound a mere puppet, but every good candidate knows to let the campaign manager plan each day's events and every sensible high executive, whether in business, education, or the military, has a scheduler to map out the daily calendar.

Although willing to follow a routine prepared by someone else, Reagan was now the "star of the show" and insisted that the schedule be a relatively easy one. His campaign manager had warned him in 1980 that he would have to put in long days at the White House, beginning with a National Security Council briefer who would show up at 7:30 in the morning. Reagan merely said, "well, he's going to have a helluva long wait." The NSC gentleman quickly learned to arrive at 9:30 a.m., when the President began his workday.[7]

He tried to keep a couple of daytime hours free to unwind with aides or answer personal mail, and at around 5:30 he clocked out, although he might take a stack of material up to the residence for evening reading. Reagan especially liked to read letters from ordinary people and, if they had some financial problem, he often sent them a personal check. Sam Donaldson recalled that once when Reagan read of "a boy who needed a kidney transplant, he sent the family $1,000 of his own money, without a word to anyone."[8] He felt a special responsibility to console those who lost family members in the service of their country, and if he could not meet them in person he would make a sympathetic phone call.

Generally speaking, Reagan had a good time in the presidency, as he had done in most of his life's experiences. While it must have aged him—how could it not?—he was not ground down by the weight of its responsibilities, as Carter, Nixon, and Johnson had been. He had tremendous respect for the office and its trappings—for example, he always wore a jacket and tie in the Oval Office—but he escaped as often as he could. In all, Reagan spent nearly one-eighth of his entire presidential term out at the California ranch, as well as nearly every possible weekend at Camp David, where he enjoyed his horseback riding.

While his relaxed approach to being president may have done him much good personally, it hindered the proper functioning of his office. Reagan's management style in the White House can best be described as "Extreme Hands-Off." Management involves three steps: gathering information, making decisions, and seeing that those decisions are carried out. Some executives have difficulty deciding policy because they are always searching for that last piece of information; others are micro-managers, constantly peering over the shoulders of their subordinates to direct every detail in the execution of policy.

Reagan did neither. He almost never took the initiative to gather information, relying on subordinates to bring him policy alternatives with the accompanying reasoning and factual information. After making a decision, he again depended entirely on his aides and cabinet members for follow-up. This approach to management left Reagan, as governor and especially as president, in a difficult position.

The title of every vast government department suggested a unity of purpose—Defense, Commerce, Agriculture, and a dozen more. But this was a facade behind which lay a whole forest of separate fiefdoms, each with its own corporate culture, its own shibboleths to trip up the unwary, and its own paths—both official and hidden—by which one might push through the tangled thicket of bureaucracy to influence policy. Changing this culture was going to be much harder than the new president imagined.

All that was necessary to move the government rightward, he thought, was to appoint good conservatives to run the various departments. In short, he believed that the establishment of policy could be separated from its execution. Reagan did not realize that while cabinet secretaries might come and go, a department's permanent bureaucrats would remain from administration to administration. When a new chief was appointed, they would first resist and then ensnare him. Before long the new head would represent not the policy views of the president who chose him, but the desires of the bureaucrats who actually ran the department and the outside constituency the department served.

Reagan depended on his staff to recommend the best people for cabinet positions, and then he left them largely alone to run their departments, almost never seeing some of them individually. This arms' length relationship demoralized many who felt almost deserted by the president. It also led to one of the most embarrassing of all Reagan gaffes. Samuel Pierce, Secretary of Housing and Urban Development, brought a group of African-American mayors to the Oval Office and when the meeting was over the president shook all their hands—Pierce's included—and told him, "nice to meet you, Mr. Mayor."

The President did make regular "pep talks" to the political appointees, encouraging them to guard against being "absorbed" by the bureaucratic culture of the career civil service personnel in their respective departments. However, that was the extent of his involvement in making sure that his people carried out his policies. It was hardly enough.

A prime example was what happened to the Department of Education, which had been created, according to *The New York Times* and *Washington Post*, to reward the National Education Association for supporting President Carter in 1976. Before his election, Reagan had promised to abolish the department, believing that the federal government had no constitutional power over education, which had been—and he thought always should be—a state and local responsibility. His first Secretary of Education, Terrel Bell, never understood the firmness of Reagan's constitutional view and thought that evil "movement conservatives" had misled the president.

Therefore, Bell, who believed that Washington should be a powerful force in education, did his best to undermine his boss's desires. Needless to say, Bell's tenure as Secretary was troublesome and he left office with no friendly view of Reagan. Bell did, however, with powerful allies in Congress, the teachers' unions, and the educational bureaucracy, succeed in his goal. Despite Reagan's campaign promise and the conservatives' desires, the federal Department of Education remained, spending even more money and exerting more power over local schools than in 1980.

Bell's quiet sabotage was hardly the worst of Reagan's early personnel problems. He picked as his first Secretary of the Interior James Watt, not only an opponent of restrictions on economic development in the West, but an extreme one. He was the exact opposite of the conservationist advisors who had helped Reagan compile an environmental record in California that even many liberals grudgingly approved. Watt had no political skills whatsoever. Environmental groups were terrified of his rhetoric, but Congress and the courts blocked most of what he wanted to do in easing restrictions on public lands, mining, and other issues. Even many congressional

Republicans opposed Watt's agenda and after two ineffective and frustrating years, he resigned.

The initial experience of the Environmental Protection Agency was even more embarrassing, leading to the prosecution and conviction of one high official and the forced resignation of the EPA's director in 1983. After these early stumbles, Reagan brought in more moderate, experienced, and politically capable people to run the EPA and the Interior Department. Even so, relatively little was done about the growing problem of several hundred thousand toxic waste dumps or the "acid rain" produced by emissions from cars and industrial smokestacks. These issues, like many others, were simply low priorities for Reagan, compared to the economy and foreign policy.

His aloofness from a president's management function not only led to public embarrassments such as these, it often frustrated the conservatives mightily. The Office of Presidential Personnel was expected to make sure "that the Reagan Revolution was being waged by true Reaganites," and one of its members "could spot a liberal at twenty paces." Yet the conservatives found themselves "outmaneuvered . . . by the moderates" because Reagan "rarely had the heart to fight about it."[9] The president did invite a group of conservative intellectuals to consult regularly with White House senior staff, but it was a feeble effort, abandoned after just two meetings, "symptomatic of a Republican party problem," according to one disappointed intellectual.[10]

Even the history-making appointment of Sandra Day O'Connor as the first woman to serve on the Supreme Court caused anguish on the right. She had been a Republican state senator and a Superior Court judge in Arizona, and her record there made pro-life groups suspicious of her views on abortion. Several conservative senators complained to Reagan about the appointment, although in the end none voted against her confirmation. In her years on the Court, she usually voted with the conservative bloc, especially in the close 5–4 decisions, and although she would not overturn the *Roe v. Wade* decision legalizing abortion, she did vote to expand the ability of state legislatures to restrict the procedure.

While conservatives might grumble about hands-off personnel decisions, Reagan's staff wrestled with another problem. Reagan's inclination to believe anything he read was a pre-computer version of the gullible newbie who accepts whatever shows up on the Internet. Michael Deaver "used to caution colleagues . . . that they needed to be extremely careful about the information they passed on. . . . Anything they gave him would be entered into his mental computer and could be spit back at any time in the future."[11]

This handicap was doubled by the fact that when he did get reliable briefings from his staff, he sometimes paid scant attention, until people learned that if they used anecdotes themselves or presented information in video form, Reagan would drink it in. The Secretary of Defense frequently used colorful charts to make his point, while the National Security Advisor went "full Hollywood" and made short films to brief Reagan visually on world leaders he was to meet. The president enjoyed them.

Sometimes he liked movies too much. Although a constant reader, Reagan—like most people—found briefing papers boring and preferred watching a good film. This was a perfectly sensible response to the bureaucratic jargon that often clogged the pages of policy briefs, except that it was Reagan's job to read them nevertheless, a duty he often ignored. Before a 1983 economic summit in Virginia, Jim Baker brought in a detailed "briefing book" for the president to study. The next day, Reagan confessed he had not even opened it because *The Sound of Music* had been on television. As one biographer summed up, "it was never safe to assume that Reagan was informed, unless the material was before him on cue cards."[12]

Reagan was often uninformed but almost never indecisive, providing his advisors brought him a consensus proposal. He rarely agonized before making a major decision and never second-guessed himself afterward. When he was well advised, this trait was beneficial; when he was not, decisiveness based on faulty or no information could be quite harmful, as in the Lebanon and Iran-Contra disasters.

A list of the factual mistakes and dubious ideas uttered during eight years would be quite long, and this fed the widely held impression that the president was not terribly smart. Democrats, of course, were glad to spread this idea, and many in the media agreed with them. Even some who worked with Reagan came to think that his intelligence was, at best, average. Certainly he was often uninformed, even about important matters, but ignorance is not lack of intelligence. Reagan concentrated his attention on a few vitally important concerns—taming inflation, reviving the economy, rebuilding the military, ending the Cold War, eliminating nuclear weapons. All else, for him, was peripheral detail, residing in the outer suburbs of his consciousness.

In fact, Reagan's closest associates concluded from long acquaintance that he was quite smart enough in things that mattered. He had, above all, a clearer understanding of the American people—what moved them, what worried them, and how they saw themselves—than any other politician of his generation. He also had the capacity not to fear thoughts that roamed beyond the bounds of current consensus, to imagine an end to the growth of government, to the Cold War, and to nuclear weapons. Usually the consensus is correct and far-ranging fancy is not. But what if the runaway thought, the wild hope, should become the new reality? Then, the world would change. It takes intelligence, as Lou Cannon said, and of a kind seldom seen, to spy out such an unmarked path and follow where it led.

On the whole, Reagan did extremely well as head of state, with the ceremonial functions of the presidency. He was far less effective as head of government because of his assumption that policies, once decided, would be executed faithfully and well by his subordinates. Oversight of the government he led was, to him, by far the least interesting part of his duties and the part to which he paid least attention, sometimes with serious consequences. Yet no executive, president or not, is good at everything, and if one has to choose, perhaps it was better for Reagan to work on changing world realities than riding herd on the bureaucracy.

In short, he seemed an excellent king but a poor prime minister. This is the conclusion of most of the people who worked with him and of those journalists who studied him during the whole of the White House years, but this is only half true. Reagan was actually quite diligent in one of the most important aspects of governing: getting his policy ideas passed into law by Congress. He had learned from the hard experience of his first frustrating year as governor that working effectively with the legislative branch is essential to an executive's success.

As President, he devoted many an hour to rounding up votes for his economic and foreign-policy proposals, making phone calls to members, inviting others to the White House for personal persuasion, and of course his true forte: using his skills as the Great Communicator to mobilize Americans at the grassroots to put upward pressure on their members of Congress. Reagan was helped mightily by the fact that his diligence was a welcome contrast to the past four years of Jimmy Carter's studied neglect—almost to the level of contempt—toward Congress as an institution and the members of Congress as individuals.

When he settled into the big chair in the Oval Office, the greatest challenge Reagan took up—as for every president since Truman—was what Thomas Patterson called *The Mortal Duel*, the Cold War with the Soviet Union. This was not the grand heroic war, where one could hear the music and see the flags and perhaps forget the body bags and mourning families. The Cold War was a different thing, less bloody but more anxious, less frantic but more protracted. It required not the noble act in the moment of crisis, but the constant small sacrifice—higher taxes, fear of The Bomb, the inconvenience of tighter security. And this was not for a week, a month, or even a year, but for decades—for half a human life span as it turned out, ever since the late 1940s. There seemed no end in sight until Ronald Reagan and Mikhail Gorbachev said: "Enough."

Before Reagan, the attitude of the United States, and indeed of the West, was that the Soviet Union was here to stay as one of the two great powers of the planet. It was foolish to imagine anything different, and hence Western diplomacy should be carefully polite so as not to anger the Russian Bear and unsettle a fragile detente. For many, this was a true saying, worthy of all men to be received.

To this longstanding consensus Ronald Reagan dissented. He believed that noble ideals such as human liberty, religious freedom, and national self-determination should rule the modern world. In Reagan's world there was no place for a totalitarian empire based on Marxist ideology and brute force. The day of kings and kaisers was long gone, and the day of the commissar was fast fading into twilight. The Soviet Union, the world's last great empire, had overstayed its time on earth.

The "Wise Men" of the West—they who inhabited the halls of academe, the corridors of the State Department, and the chancelleries of Europe—scoffed at this juvenile fantasy. Long study and experience had taught them that the Soviet Union was a fixed star in the political firmament and that in the 1970s it was waxing, not waning in power.

Sporadic attempts to reject Russian rule—by East Germans in 1953, Hungarians in 1956, Czechs in 1968—had all been crushed by the tanks and machine guns of the Red Army. Abroad, an invading army of Soviet troops fought to put down resistance in Afghanistan, and local Marxist regimes in Ethiopia and Angola survived on Russian military and financial aid. In the Western Hemisphere, Cuba was a loyal Soviet satellite, and there were friendly Marxist governments in Nicaragua and Grenada.

When Reagan took office, many believed that the Cold War military balance had tipped dangerously against the West, as described in a flurry of anxious books with titles like *The Crisis in Western Security* and *Europe Without Defense?* Even with the creation of the North Atlantic Treaty Organization and the long-term stationing of American troops in Germany, it had never been likely that conventional military forces alone could prevent a Soviet conquest of Western Europe. Until the 1960s, it was at least possible for Europeans, sheltered beneath the American nuclear umbrella, to feel a certain degree of security.

Then, however, a Soviet crash program to develop intercontinental missiles gradually eroded U.S. nuclear superiority. At the same time, the Communist bloc began what Democratic Senator Sam Nunn described as a "military buildup in Europe unprecedented in peacetime since Hitler's rearming of Germany in the 1930s." The combination of these two changes had raised the scary possibility, as Nunn said, that the "Soviet Union and its Warsaw Pact allies could conquer Germany east of the Rhine within forty-eight hours."[13]

These were not foolish fears. East German documents found after the fall of the Berlin Wall revealed a massive Soviet contingency plan to overrun

Western Europe by 1980, "blasting their way forward with plentiful use of tactical nuclear weapons"—a total of more than five hundred atomic strikes in Germany alone. Communist East Germany "had even struck a victory medal and decided how to rename West German cities."[14]

In the 1980 campaign, Reagan had said, "What I think the Russians would fear more than anything else is a United States that all of a sudden would hitch up our belt and say, 'O.K., Buster, . . . We are now going to build what is necessary to surpass you.' And this is the last thing they want from us, an arms race, because they are already running as fast as they can and we haven't started running.'"[15]

Reagan set the new tone in his very first press conference, charging that the Soviets "reserve unto themselves the right to commit any crime: to lie, to cheat" in pursuit of world domination. The assembled journalists could hardly believe it; no president since Harry Truman had so insulted the USSR. Walking back from the event, Reagan asked his national security advisor, Richard Allen, "Dick, the Soviets do lie and steal and cheat, don't they?" When Allen answered, "yes, sir, they do," the president smiled: "I thought so."[16]

The Soviet rulers were not used to being talked about in those terms. They were accustomed to Western leaders and diplomats who kindly overlooked the slave labor camps of the Gulag and the Red Army in Eastern Europe and treated the Soviet Union as a respected superpower. Anatoly Dobrynin, ambassador to the United States, asked of Reagan, "how is he going to do business with us?" He rated the new president "far worse and far more threatening" than Jimmy Carter.[17]

Before Reagan could devote himself to foreign policy, he had to restore the economic health of his own country. This was Richard Nixon's earnest advice as well as Reagan's own inclination. The former president sent the incoming one a detailed memo urging a focus on the economy first and foremost, with foreign affairs distinctly secondary. The same message was coming to Reagan from public opinion surveys, which put the economy at the very top of voters' concerns.

He had read some of the major conservative economists and talked with others, and he came into office totally convinced that he could rescue America from Carter's twin legacy of inflation and unemployment. His plan was simple: cut inflation, cut spending (except on defense), cut regulations, cut taxes, and balance the budget. This is what liberals came derisively to label "Reaganomics."

Immediately after the election, Congressman David Stockman, soon to be Reagan's budget director, sent in a dire memo. He warned that only swift, bold action to undo the "big government" behemoth created by the New Deal could prevent economic chaos for the country and political disaster for Republicans. Pollster Richard Wirthlin advised the opposite course in an "Initial Actions Project," suggesting that Reagan capitalize on his high public approval rating to convey a message of confidence, stability, and hope, as FDR had done in his famous first Hundred Days.

Thus there emerged, even before the beginning of the new administration, a tension between ideological "Reaganites" and the pragmatic conservatives, at whose head stood Reagan himself. The same arguments had flowed like an undercurrent through the gubernatorial years, between those whose goal was to roll back liberalism and those who thought their duty was to "govern"—which meant, in practice, to work within the existing system rather than upsetting it.

Unwilling, as he often was, to choose among arguing subordinates, Reagan tried to accommodate both tendencies. With his preexisting bias against high taxes and "red tape," he readily lapped up Stockman's "supply side" economics theory, that lower taxes, less spending, and less regulation would unleash initiative and boost productivity, increasing both individual prosperity and government revenues. On his first day as president, Reagan froze all federal hiring and equipment purchases, and soon after ordered spending cuts on travel and consultants.

The cautious pragmatists, on the other hand, liked Reagan's pledge to protect Social Security, Medicare, and the "social safety net" of welfare programs. This highlighted the most difficult problem conservatives face with the federal budget: while most people often believe that government spending is too lavish and should be cut, nearly all of them oppose cutting programs that benefit themselves. As political scientists would put it, people are "theoretical conservatives" but "operational liberals."

Reagan presented his budget, primarily the work of Stockman, less than a month after being sworn in. It was a bold plan, asking Congress to increase defense spending (one-fourth of the budget); trim the growth rate of domestic discretionary spending (one-sixth of the budget); allow "entitlements" like Social Security, Medicare, and welfare, to rise modestly; cut income taxes by 30 percent; and balance the budget by 1984. A somewhat contradictory set of proposals, to be sure, but Congress applauded and the public approved.

Then the real battle began, fought out in a multitude of White House number-crunching sessions and congressional committee hearings. Reagan himself applied public rhetoric and private persuasion to win over reluctant Democrats and hold wavering Republicans. It was the first test of his ability to govern; the Senate's Republican majority would be no problem, but the verdict of the Democratic House was uncertain.

While the president was in the midst of his quest for votes, he was shot down outside the Washington Hilton on March 30 by John Hinckley, who hoped thereby to impress the actress Jodie Foster. A lunchtime speech to the labor leaders of the AFL-CIO was on Reagan's schedule that day. The Secret Service let him go without his usual bulletproof vest because he would be exposed to the public only for a minute or two on the way to his limousine. That was enough for Hinckley, who from about ten feet fired six pistol shots. All of them missed hitting the president directly.

One got Press Secretary James Brady in the head, two others struck down a police officer and a Secret Service agent, and another, although it missed Reagan at first, glanced off the limousine and hit him under the arm, stopping in his lung just one inch from the heart. If Agent Jerry Parr had not grabbed Reagan an instant before and thrown him into the back seat of the car, the president would have been hit directly in the head and probably killed. He would likely have died anyway if Parr had not deduced that the bullet had hit a lung and ordered the limousine directly to a hospital instead of to the White House. Reagan's "Brass Bancroft" movies had enthralled Parr in his boyhood and made him vow to join the Secret Service. Now he had saved his favorite actor's life.

When the car swooped to a stop at the hospital's emergency entrance, Reagan got out, straightened his pants, buttoned his jacket, and walked through the door by himself, as though being shot by an assassin was a mere distraction in the day's events. Then he collapsed and was whisked into the emergency room. An admitting room intern asked Deaver the name of the person who was just brought in, penciling the information on his form. "It's Reagan. R-E-A-G-A-N." "First name?" "Ron." "Address?" "1600 Pennsylvania." The pencil stopped. "You mean . . . ?" "Yes. You have the president of the United States in there."[18]

When his wife arrived at the hospital, Reagan said only, "honey, I forgot to duck," and when his aides showed up, he asked, "who's minding the store?" To the doctors waiting to operate, he joked, "I hope you're all Republicans." No would-be killer was going to quell Reagan's sense of humor. In the recovery room with a tube in his throat, he had to write his one-liners: "I'd like to do that scene again—starting at the hotel" and "send me to L.A. where I can see the air I'm breathing."

Learning of the injuries to his press secretary and the policeman, the wounded president became serious. Praying for them, he "realized that if I was going to do what was right, I'd have to pray for that boy who shot us, too."[19] When his daughter Patti saw him, Reagan told her, "'I prayed for that young man when I was lying there,' . . . 'For Hinckley?' I asked incredulously. 'Yes. He's disturbed. I prayed that God would forgive him. And that he would ask for God's forgiveness.'" She marveled, "No one has ever amazed me as much as my father did at that moment."[20]

Within little more than a week, he was feeling well enough to write a Fourth of July column for *Parade*, the magazine carried by Sunday newspapers across the country. The American Revolution, he wrote, was "the only true philosophical revolution in all history. . . . Ours was a revolution that changed the very concept of government"; he declared "that man is born with certain God-given rights; that government is only a convenience." It was pure Reagan.

Being so close to death caused the president to reflect upon how to spend his remaining years. He told a visiting cleric that "whatever time I have left belongs to Him," and he especially began to seek ways to pull back from confrontation with the Soviet Union. Reagan never lost his conviction that Communism was an insult to the human spirit and Soviet power a threat to human freedom. Like FDR, however, he believed that making a personal connection with his adversary might discover common ground on which to build a less dangerous relationship.

While still recovering from his wound, Reagan labored over a six-page handwritten letter to Soviet ruler Leonid Brezhnev, suggesting a meeting to discuss their common responsibility for a safe and peaceful world. State Department bureaucrats turned his personal appeal into a dull collection of "boilerplate" diplomatic clichés, but Reagan rebelled and ordered, "send it the way I wrote it."[21] Brezhnev ignored it.

A life of vigorous exercise and his unflappable optimism made Reagan's recovery quite swift for such a serious wound. His HUD Secretary said that when Reagan "walked into that Cabinet Room that first time back, he was exactly like he was before the assassination attempt. I said to myself, 'is this really the man who was shot?'"[22]

There was one more casualty from the Hinckley attack besides those who were physically stricken. On the day Reagan was shot, Secretary of State Alexander Haig was closeted with other high-level aides. He thought that the acting press secretary was doing a poor job with the media, so he rushed into the press briefing, panting and excitable, and announced: "I am in control here, in the White House." He looked as though he was not even in control of himself, and his blurted statement became a running joke in Washington. After this, only two months into his tenure, Al Haig was on a slow but terminal glide to dismissal a year and a half later.

The president, although compelled by his doctors and his staff to return only gradually to a full schedule, still argued for his "Economic Recovery Plan" in a televised address to Congress less than a month after he had been shot down outside the Hilton. Needless to say, it was the warmest reception he ever received from that body. He made light of his ordeal by reading a note from a second grader who hoped "you get well quick or you might have to make a speech in your pajamas" and who added a "P.S. If you have to make a speech in your pajamas, I warned you."

Then he quickly turned to "getting spending and inflation under control and cutting your tax rates," pointing out that in the past six months unemployment had remained high and inflation had actually reduced people's real incomes. He asked the Democratic majority in the House to reject its own party's alternative budget and approve the bipartisan plan worked out by Stockman and Texas Congressman Phil Gramm, including a personal income-tax cut of 25 percent over three years.

Reagan warned that it was no longer acceptable "to shave a little here and there" from spending (although in the end, a shave—and not even a close one—was all that he wound up with). "All we need to begin with," he said "is a dream that we can do better than before. All we need to have is faith, and that dream will come true." Encouraging words, but expecting a room full of politicians to make a dream reality through mere faith was one of the most unusual things an American Congress has ever been asked.

What the House proceeded to do instead was to shatter Reagan's dream by paying attention to the demands of their constituents. Stockman himself, strangely for someone who had served in Congress, seemed unaware that the "pork-barrel" spending he wanted to wipe out existed because voters wanted it and congressmen were not about to disappoint them. The same was even more true for the entitlement programs like Social Security, Medicare, Medicaid, and welfare.

In the aftermath of disillusionment, Stockman mourned that "the true Reagan Revolution never had a chance."[23] He was wrong; it was the Stockman Revolution that never had a chance, not the Reagan Revolution. Stockman wanted to repeal the New Deal, which had been settled policy in America for nearly fifty years. Reagan accepted the New Deal; he merely wanted to stop the *growth* of government spending and regulatory power and to reduce tax rates.

His revolution, if it deserves to be called one, took a very big step toward success in the congressional votes of summer 1981, and the president's own efforts at persuasion were a large part of the reason. House Democratic Majority Leader Jim Wright said that Reagan was "terribly shallow," did not know the details of his program, and "his philosophical approach is super-ficial. . . . What he preaches is pure economic pap. . . . Yet so far the guy is making it work. . . . I stand in awe nevertheless of his political skill. I am not sure that I have ever seen its equal."[24]

House Speaker Tip O'Neill had to agree. Soon after election day, he had condescendingly warned Reagan that Washington would be tough, that his governorship had been only the "minor leagues." By midsummer, when a Bostonian asked the Speaker how things were going in the capital, his rueful response was, "I'm getting the shit kicked out of me." Once again confounding those who underestimated him, the "minor league" player had become Rookie of the Year in the Bigs.[25]

The 25 percent tax cut was real; it saved American families billions of dollars in the near term and hundreds of billions in future years. Democrats complained that Reagan would starve the government of needed revenue and drive up the national debt (something they had never worried about with Democratic presidents). Supply-side advocates responded that, as the economy boomed after 1982, federal tax collections rose along with people's incomes and business profits. By Reagan's last year, federal revenue was 65 percent greater than when he took office.

The Democrats were right about the national debt, but not from insufficient tax revenue. The supply-side formula for a balanced budget required not only tax cuts but real spending cuts as well, and these never occurred. Reagan's second congressional victory in July—the budget plan—was purely symbolic. By the time the House and Senate cast their final votes in July, Stockman's fierce assault on both pork-barrel and entitlement spending had failed and he was in full retreat. There were "pretend spending cuts" aplenty, but very few were actually carried out.

However, Reagan's victory lay in drastically slowing the growth of government (aside from its responsibility for national defense). Military spending, in "real" dollars after inflation, grew 40 percent faster than under Jimmy Carter (4.1 percent yearly versus 2.9 percent), much to the new president's satisfaction. However, domestic discretionary spending—everything but defense, entitlement programs, and interest on the debt—actually declined in real dollars during Reagan's two terms.

Stockman, in his fight for a "lean" budget, had done much better than he realized. He did not smash the pork-barrel and welfare state as he had hoped, but it was quite enough for Reagan's own purposes, which were to put the brakes on the government, not to yank it into reverse.

One other episode reinforced the perception of Reagan as a strong leader in the aftermath of the congressional budget and tax votes. In the 1980 campaign, the Professional Air Traffic Controllers Association, almost alone among labor unions, had supported Reagan and expected good treatment after the election. However, when PATCO controllers, dissatisfied at the progress of contract negotiations with the Federal Aviation Administration, went on strike in August, they were unpleasantly surprised by the president's reaction.

This was an illegal strike; federal law prohibits strikes by government unions. Reagan denounced the walkout, ordered the controllers back to work, and threatened to fire any who stayed out. Two days later, he did dismiss 11,000 striking controllers (nearly 90 percent of the total) and banned all of them from any future federal job. The union itself went out of existence by the end of 1981. This immediate harsh response by the president to an illegal action was a rude shock to organized labor, but the public overwhelmingly approved, even though airline service was curtailed until more controllers could be trained.

Probably no single action of Reagan's presidency did more to establish his reputation for decisive leadership and toughness when challenged. One historian called it "the strike that changed America," partly because it encouraged private businesses to take a more robust attitude in their own labor negotiations. It even affected foreign policy, as Soviet leaders saw that Reagan would be a more resolute opponent than previous presidents who had mildly accepted the Soviet Union's superpower status and expanding influence in the Third World.

Congressional victories over Democratic opposition and his rapid response to the PATCO strike burnished Reagan's reputation as summer ended, but his one great disappointment was failing to achieve a balanced budget. What ruined that hope, besides his increased defense spending, was the sharp recession that began in the fall. If the administration's economic assumptions had held true for 1982, and if Congress had actually made all of Stockman's proposed spending "cuts," the excess of spending above tax revenues would have been lower than the deficit in Carter's last budget and within three years there would have been a small surplus.

By far the largest single domestic expense in the federal budget was Social Security, and here Reagan suffered his one major defeat of 1981. Regardless of what happened to the multitude of lesser programs and "pork projects," any hope of serious fiscal restraint depended on reforming Social Security. Created in the Depression as a modest supplementary retirement income for the few people who then lived past age sixty-five, it had by 1980 become an increasingly shaky financial proposition.

Many people believed that the taxes they paid into Social Security were set aside for them, earning interest, and upon retirement this fund would generate their monthly check. This was completely erroneous. The taxes a worker paid in were immediately paid out again to some retired person; nothing was saved up for the worker's own retirement. When a worker did reach sixty-five, his or her monthly Social Security checks would come from the taxes then being paid in by younger workers.

So long as there were eight or ten current workers paying into Social Security for every retired person receiving a check, all would be well. When the system began, it worked because most people died before age sixty-five and never received a dime from Social Security for all the taxes they had paid during their working lives. Then, as better medicine and healthier habits extended the average life span, more and more people lived long enough to get a Social Security check.

Furthermore, Congress, to win senior citizens' votes, frequently made benefits more generous, until the typical retired person by 1980 was expected to receive five times as much from Social Security as he or she had paid in during his or her working lifetime, plus interest. This could not continue indefinitely. Eventually the system would go bankrupt, or taxes on working people must rise to punitive levels, or benefits must be scaled back.

Before he became president, Reagan had been willing to consider ideas for reforming and saving Social Security for the long term, but his White House advisors warned him to keep away from this "third rail of American politics" that might electrocute his popularity. Liberal Democrats had become experts at accusing Republicans of undermining Social Security, and the only way to avoid this partisan barrage was to keep hands off the system even though every responsible person could see that it was headed for financial disaster.

Only someone willing to think boldly, as Reagan was on other important issues, could have made the changes that would put Social Security on a path to long-term health. His best chance was early in his presidency, when he could use his considerable popularity as a lever to move timid members of Congress. A bipartisan group of senators had actually discussed a plan to restrain the yearly cost-of-living rise in Social Security payments and, with the president's support, might have achieved something. But Reagan had already let his advisors put him in a box on the issue by promising in 1980 that he would not cut Social Security. What the senators proposed was, of course, not a cut at all but simply a lower yearly increase, but the president would not budge and an opportunity was lost.

Instead of approving this moderate plan, which had some congressional support, Reagan inexplicably wound up a few months later with a much stronger proposal by Stockman that had no chance whatsoever in Congress. Furthermore, this let Democrats attack the administration and the Republican Party as anti-Social Security, which they eagerly did. According to Tip O'Neill's biographer, the Speaker "made a far-reaching decision to politicize Social Security" and "for the next twenty years, . . . Democrats would follow O'Neill's lead and cry, 'Save Social Security!' or 'Republicans want to cut Medicare!'"[26]

Stockman had outmaneuvered Jim Baker's more cautious White House team by appealing to the president's sense of himself as a man of destiny, as "the first President in history to honestly and permanently fix Social Security" because "no one else had had the courage to do it."[27] Congressional Republicans hid from the predictable political backlash as best they could, while Democrats used the Social Security issue to frighten senior citizens and win votes in the 1982 midterm elections.

Temporarily disappointed in his desire to reform Social Security, Reagan had much better luck curing the number-one problem on voters' minds in 1981: high prices. Inflation had eaten away the value of the dollar by nearly 10 percent each year in Carter's presidency. Reagan called this "the cruelest tax of all" because, although it struck rich and poor alike, the wealthy could afford such annual losses in real family income far better than working families and people on fixed incomes.

He came into office resolved to kill inflation, and although he did not actually slay the beast—no one ever has—he left it weaker, wounded and far less dangerous. In the first twenty-five years since Reagan left office, yearly price increases averaged less than 3 percent, with enormous benefits to Americans up and down the income scale. Winning the war against 10 percent inflation was Reagan's greatest domestic triumph.

It came, however, at a terrible price, as wartime victories often do. The Federal Reserve System, acting with the president's full support, "tightened" the money supply, reducing the flow of dollars in circulation and hence slowing down the rise in prices. This was all to the good, but the bad consequence of tighter money was a serious recession, the worst economic downturn—or at any rate the worst unemployment—since the Great Depression of the 1930s.

Consumers bought less, businesses laid off workers, and the suffering spread quickly during the last half of 1981 and all through 1982. Millions of families had less to live on, like a besieged garrison on half rations, and could only wait hopefully for rescue in the form of renewed economic growth, which finally arrived by mid-1983. As the economic decline worsened, Reagan's approval ratings sank, from 60 percent in the summer of 1981 to 50 percent by year's end and even lower in 1982. The decline was sharpest among blue-collar families, the "Reagan Democrats."

With Reagan's attention consumed almost entirely by economic concerns—the budget, taxes, inflation, and now recession—foreign policy was almost a passing afterthought during his first year. Three issues, however, began to emerge during 1981 that were to vex the administration in succeeding years. The most important was the life-and-death question of military strategy in the atomic age. U.S. nuclear policy had for two decades been framed around a "triad" of land-based missiles, submarine-launched missiles, and manned bombers, allowing the nation to absorb a Soviet first strike and still be able to inflict unacceptable damage in retaliation.

President Carter, afraid that missiles in fixed silos were too vulnerable, had proposed a new experimental missile—the MX—that would be shuttled around the landscape and hence would be more difficult to destroy. The

Reagan administration inherited this idea but could make no firm decision about the MX during 1981, so debate dragged on into the new year with ultimately unsatisfactory results.

Another Cold War problem arose in Central America when the forty-year dictatorship of the Somoza family in Nicaragua was overthrown in 1979 by Marxist Sandinista rebels. Although the Somozas had long enjoyed American support, the U.S. granted the new government more than $100 million in economic aid, provided the Sandinistas did not help Marxist rebels in other Central American countries.

When it became clear that the new Nicaraguan President, Daniel Ortega, was in fact allowing his country to be a conduit for Russian and Cuban aid to rebels in El Salvador, President Carter suspended American aid. In the meantime, Ortega began suppressing democratic groups that believed he was merely replacing the Somoza dictatorship with his own. This became Reagan's problem in 1981 just as anti-Marxists were organizing an opposition force, the contras.

CIA Director Casey proposed giving secret aid to the contras in hopes of forcing Ortega to liberalize his regime, but this touched off a heated debate within the administration. Would helping the contras be the first step into a new Vietnam-like quicksand? It was an instructive debate. Secretary of Defense Weinberger (a civilian) opposed strong action, while the Secretary of State, Al Haig (a former four-star general), demanded it. In the end both compromised on the Casey plan, and in December 1981, Reagan approved the first covert assistance to the contras, a decision that would lead to the most damaging crisis of his presidency.

The third foreign policy arena that caught Reagan's attention amid the first-year battles over taxes, budget, and economy was the Middle East. Since the 1940s, this region had seen its own mini–Cold War between Israel and the Arab nations pledged to its destruction. As a lifelong supporter of Israel, the new president wanted both to ease tensions in the Middle East and to keep Soviet influence out.

This was a difficult assignment, especially after the Israelis bombed a nuclear reactor in Iraq in June and the Palestine Liberation Organization's headquarters in Lebanon the next month, killing many civilians. Relations with Israel were further strained by Reagan's decision to sell an air defense system to Saudi Arabia, a move that barely won congressional approval over heavy Israeli opposition. Still, as 1981 ended, the president remained committed to an "honest broker" role in the Middle East, despite the danger that the United States might be drawn into an impossible situation—as in fact happened over the next two years.

With his victorious tax cut and budget votes and the show of presidential toughness with the air traffic controllers, and with foreign problems still in the future, one might think that Reagan was in a relatively strong position at the close of his first year. Some of his conservative supporters were not so sure, worrying that their earlier fears about "creeping moderation" in the administration were becoming reality. One very telling sign was the isolation and eventual resignation of Lyn Nofziger, who had been among the earliest and most loyal of Reagan's Californians. Baker, Deaver, and even Nancy Reagan seemed to be slowly excluding him from the inner circle as part of a presumed campaign to reduce conservative influence around the president.

When Nofziger left in December 1981, it marked, to some, a discouraging turning point in the politics of the administration. With the economy and Reagan's popularity now both declining, the year that began with the exciting prospect of a "Reagan Revolution," was ending with conservatives confused, frustrated, and concerned about the future. Nofziger himself expressed the fears of many Reaganites that the president was being guided in the wrong direction because there were too few "true believers" in the administration. Conservatives were asking, "'What's this Bush guy doing in here? What are these Ford people doing in here? Where the hell are the Reagan people?' . . . If the Reagan people could have controlled the White House, Reagan would have been a better President."[28]

NOTES

1. Helene Von Damm, *At Reagan's Side* (New York: Doubleday, 1989), 254.
2. Haig quoted in Lou Cannon, *President Reagan: The Role of a Lifetime* (New York: Public Affairs, 2000), 163.
3. Michael Reagan, *On the Outside Looking In* (New York: Zebra Books, 1988), 33.
4. Reagan quoted in Jim Kuhn, *Ronald Reagan in Private: A Memoir of My Years in the White House* (New York: Sentinel, 1984), 81.
5. Tip O'Neill, *Man of the House: The Life and Political Memoirs of Speaker Tip O'Neill* (New York: Random House, 1987), 335.
6. Reagan quoted in Cannon, *President Reagan*, 130.
7. Cannon, *Reagan*, 304.
8. Sam Donaldson quoted in Hannaford, *Recollections of Reagan*, 45.
9. Von Damm, *At Reagan's Side*, 212.
10. Emmett Tyrell quoted in Hannaford, *Recollections*, 176.
11. Michael K. Deaver, *A Different Drummer: My Thirty Years with Ronald Reagan* (New York: Harper Collins, 2001), 35.
12. Cannon, *President Reagan*, 37, 250.
13. Nunn quoted in Robert Close, *Europe Without Defense?: 48 Hours That Could Change the Face of the World* (New York: Pergamon Press, 1979), viii–ix.
14. Richard Brooks, *Atlas of World Military History* (New York: Barnes & Noble, 2000), 245.
15. Reagan quoted in Drew, *Portrait of an Election*, 119.
16. Richard V. Allen interview, Presidential Oral History Program, Ronald Reagan Oral History Project, Miller Center of Public Affairs, University of Virginia, 57.
17. Anatoly Dobrynin, *In Confidence: Moscow's Ambassador to America's Six Cold War Presidents, 1962–1986* (New York: Times Books, 1995), 484.

18. Quoted in Deaver, *Behind the Scenes*, 19.
19. Reagan quoted in Deaver, *A Different Drummer*, 142.
20. Patti Davis, *The Way I See It: An Autobiography* (New York: Putnam, 1992), 273.
21. Reagan quoted in Deaver, *A Different Drummer*, 152.
22. Richard Schweiker quoted in Hannaford, *Recollections*, 161.
23. David A. Stockman, *The Triumph of Politics: How the Reagan Revolution Failed* (New York: Harper & Row, 1986), 9.
24. Wright quoted in John A. Farrell, *Tip O'Neill and the Democratic Century* (Boston: Little Brown, 2001), 561.
25. O'Neill quoted *ibid.*, 558.
26. *Ibid.*, 580.
27. Anderson quoted in Stockman, *Triumph of Politics*, 188.
28. Lyn Nofziger interview, Ronald Reagan Oral History Project, Miller Center of Public Affairs, University of Virginia, 40.

CHAPTER 7

PRESIDENT REAGAN, 1982–1984:
RECESSION TO REELECTION

A visitor to the White House once remarked on the "merry twinkle" in the president's eyes and the "'tone of familiarity' that instantly set people at ease."[1] He was speaking of Abraham Lincoln in the 1860s, but the description fit Ronald Reagan just as snugly. Like Lincoln, Reagan told endless jokes, stories, and parables.

In Hollywood, he began a lifetime's work collecting funny stories until, as biographer Lou Cannon observed, in the White House years "anecdotes were Reagan's fundamental form of communication."[2] Like any good performer, he used jokes to break the ice in political gatherings, in cabinet meetings, and even high-level international conferences.

With individuals, his banter served to diminish the interpersonal distance between *The President* and his companion, whether a fellow politician, a White House visitor, or an ordinary citizen. It was his method of "descending from the throne" and was among the ways in which he was the most egalitarian president since Lincoln himself. Unlike such predecessors as Nixon or Johnson, he was secure enough with the "inner Reagan" to make his age, his habits, and even his lack of knowledge the butt of many of his own jokes.

Entering his second year, Reagan would need all his optimism and self-confidence. If the midsummer political victories of 1981 had faded into disappointment by December, 1982 promised to be even worse. The economy shrank, unemployment rose, and deficits grew. Overseas, allies and adversaries worried that Reagan was a combative cowboy. Ending the Cold War seemed less attainable than ever, as the Soviets reacted angrily to Reagan's military buildup and harsh rhetoric.

Reagan's approach to foreign policy was, like that of many in his generation, shaped by memories of the late 1930s when the failure of Britain and

France to face down Hitler's aggression led to the catastrophe of world war. The conclusion seemed clear: weakness in democratic nations encouraged aggression by tyrants; military strength could prevent war. For Reagan, on these two lessons hung "all the law and the prophets."

His Cold War policy was a five-front offensive against the USSR. First was a rhetorical effort to delegitimize the adversary, casting it as a leftover from the age of empires, out of place in a world where democracy and human rights should be the ruling values. This began with the "lie, cheat, and steal" comment in his first press conference of 1981 and continued through his speeches to the United Nations and to the British Parliament in 1982, to his "Evil Empire" address the next year.

The second tactic was to rebuild American military strength, as he had often promised in the 1980 campaign. Reagan believed that the USSR could not afford to keep up with American rearmament and would have to negotiate mutual cuts in nuclear weapons. Until then, he saw little use in talking because the Soviets would never consider serious arms reductions until they truly feared being left behind by growing American power.

Third, Reagan challenged the Soviets within their own sphere of control. There was a massive program of economic, technical, and rhetorical aid to Poland's Solidarity movement as it worked to undermine Communist rule in that country. Building on President Carter's response to the Soviet invasion of Afghanistan, Reagan steadily increased American military aid to the Afghan rebels, driving Soviet military casualties to uncomfortable levels. This became known as the "Reagan Doctrine."

Fourth, he tried to apply pressure to the already-ailing Soviet economy by reducing the USSR's ability to earn foreign exchange from its energy exports. Reagan attempted to use economic sanctions to block a Soviet gas pipeline to Western European markets, and he lobbied Saudi Arabia to increase oil production so as to drive down world oil prices and the value of Russia's petroleum exports.

And finally, in 1983, Reagan's Strategic Defense Initiative ("Star Wars") faced the Soviets with a "technology race" they knew they could not win. Many liberals, as well as some in his own administration, thought Star Wars was simply an expensive folly, but there is no question that the leadership of the USSR was terrified of it, as some later admitted.

This multipronged plan to put pressure on the Soviet Union did not mean that Reagan wanted to prolong the Cold War; rather, he hoped that increasing the cost of confrontation would make the Communist regime see that cooperation and liberalization were in its own interest. He continued to make occasional conciliatory gestures in the meantime; for instance, in April 1981, he ended the embargo Jimmy Carter had imposed on selling grain to the USSR, which had also hurt American farmers.

Even more significant was the handwritten letter the president sent to Leonid Brezhnev that same month, over the objections of his "hardline" Secretary of State, Alexander Haig. He asked whether ideological rigidity might have kept the two superpowers from working together, and told Brezhnev that he had repealed the grain embargo to stimulate "constructive dialogue" and to fulfill "our joint obligation to find lasting peace." Reagan had wanted to suggest even more, raising the suggestion of actual nuclear disarmament, but Haig talked him out of going that far.

Nothing came of this "olive branch" letter, largely because repeated deaths caused a shuffling of Soviet leadership that lasted through Reagan's entire first term. Brezhnev died in 1982, his equally ancient successor, Yuri Andropov, in 1984, and Andropov's successor, Konstanstin Chernenko, in 1985. Mikhail Gorbachev then became the fourth ruler of the USSR in five years, and finally Reagan found someone he could talk to.

Inside the administration, George Shultz replaced Haig as Secretary of State in mid-1982. He was Reagan's chief guide, as Cold War policy became a White House skirmish between pragmatists and hardline Reaganites for the entire first term. Both sides agreed on the president's rapid expansion of American military strength, but not on its purpose.

The pragmatists included Deaver and Baker in the White House, Nancy Reagan in the residence, Shultz, and Ronald Reagan himself. To them, military strength would let the United States negotiate to reduce tensions and armament from a position of security. Those who considered themselves true Reaganites—Meese in the White House, Weinberger at Defense, Jeane Kirkpatrick at the United Nations, Casey of the CIA, and the new National Security Advisor, William Clark—saw the buildup as an end in itself because they could envisage no future but an ongoing Cold War with all its dangers.

Unfortunately for the Reaganites, Reagan himself was not one of their number. Reading his speeches, one finds a man of sharp ideological conviction, but for him dreams outranked ideology. The two dreams he clung to most tenaciously were the end of the Soviet empire and the end of nuclear weapons. Neither could become reality without also ending the Cold War, and here Reagan parted company with the Reaganites and found himself working with the pragmatists they distrusted. The cry of his fervent supporters was always, "Let Reagan Be Reagan!" but some were quite startled to see the real Reagan who emerged in the second term.

In 1982, however, he was still the man of tough talk and sometimes unrealistic proposals. Speaking at his old alma mater, Eureka College, in May, he suggested a 30 percent cut in land-based ICBMs and told the Soviets that they "have nothing to fear from the United States." However, cutting land-based missiles would leave the U.S. submarine-launched ICBMs untouched and produce a large American lead in total warheads. The Soviet high command replied that Reagan was a "warmonger" out to destroy Communism—which, of course, he was, although not by warfare.

The next month, on a trip to keep the Western allies from financing a Soviet pipeline, Reagan delivered one of his most significant speeches, to the British Parliament in Westminster Hall. He posed the dire alternative: "Must civilization perish in a hail of fiery atoms? Must freedom wither in a quiet, deadening accommodation with totalitarian evil?"

He predicted a third, more hopeful future, flowing from his belief that there was a crisis "in the home of Marxism-Leninism" because the Soviet Union "runs against the tide of history by denying human freedom and human dignity to its citizens." Freedom, Reagan said, belonged not to a "lucky few" but was the "universal right of all human beings," guaranteed by the UN Declaration of Human Rights.

He urged the free nations to "foster the infrastructure of democracy" in the unfree world, as the United States was doing by aiding the Solidarity movement in Soviet-occupied Poland. This would be a "march of freedom and democracy which will leave Marxism-Leninism on the ash heap of history. . . ." After Westminster, Reagan made a quick visit to Berlin, observing that the Wall was "as ugly as the idea behind it."[3] Five years later, he would use that very spot for the most memorable words of his long life.

The Soviet leadership did not appreciate Reagan's assumption that they were doomed, and even American analysts thought the president was engaging in wishful thinking about a "crisis" behind the Iron Curtain. "Everyone" knew that the Soviet Union was a superpower, not a mere shell of armor encasing a hollowed-out and decaying body—everyone but this foolish actor flopping about in the too-large shoes of a president.

In fact, a realistic few in the USSR did understand that Reagan was all too accurate about their economic decline. The West was beginning the technological boom known as the "Computer Age" and the United States, wringing inflation from its economy, was only a year away from the longest peacetime boom in its history. Meantime, despite vast farmlands, the Soviet Union had to import food for its people. A mocking billboard in the American Midwest announced, "Kansas: Breadbasket of the Soviet Union."

Nevertheless, anger at Reagan's tough talk kept Brezhnev from making any overtures, and in the fall the Soviets even walked out of a Geneva arms conference. Brezhnev died in December, but his replacement seemed even worse. While Brezhnev had been unyielding and difficult, Yuri Andropov was actively hostile. As the year ended, even Congress dealt Reagan a blow, refusing money for the MX missile that he had counted on as a major part of the military buildup that would let him negotiate from strength.

If Reagan was discouraged by lack of progress in his Cold War strategy, a minor "hot war" in the South Atlantic drew him and his chief diplomatic partner, Prime Minister Margaret Thatcher, closer together. Argentina had long claimed ownership of the Falkland Islands (the Malvinas to them), which Britain had governed for 150 years. The military rulers of Argentina, hoping to improve their popularity at home, seized the islands in April, assuming Britain would be unable to respond.

Instead, Thatcher sent a naval force to the Falklands and other nations took sides. The United States at first hesitated; most of its European allies supported Britain, while Latin America sided with Argentina. However, like many of his generation, Reagan remembered that in the dark days of 1940 and 1941, when Hitler stalked across Europe devouring one nation after another, it was the British people who held the gate and kept the beast at bay until a tardy America awoke at last to her duty. He was in no doubt as to where the United States should stand, though UN Ambassador Jeane Kirkpatrick and a few others in his administration sympathized with Argentina.

During April, when the British force sailed the 8,000 miles southward, and throughout air and naval battles in May, the United States provided military intelligence and logistical support and even offered to lend an amphibious warship. Reagan ordered, "give Maggie everything she needs to get on with it."[4] British troops landed, the Argentines surrendered after some sharp resistance, and Thatcher was a hero at home.

Supporting Britain damaged U.S. relations with Latin America, but not nearly so much as Reagan's ongoing support for the contras' "war by proxy" against Nicaragua's Sandinista government. The president worried that the Caribbean might become a "Marxist lake." Soviet bloc advisors, equipment, and money were flowing through Cuba to support Marxist rulers in Nicaragua, the island of Grenada, and Suriname on the northern coast of South America, as well as rebels in El Salvador.

Reagan hoped that the contra war would force President Daniel Ortega to end his aid to the Marxist rebellion in neighboring El Salvador and liberalize the regime in Nicaragua itself. Some of his advisors wanted to go further and build up the contras to the point that they could actually over-throw Ortega by military force. This would have been nothing new for the United States, which had intervened in Nicaragua almost a dozen times since the 1850s, including a twenty-year military occupation that ended only in 1933.

Reagan was pushed toward a more belligerent role by Clark, Kirkpatrick, and Casey. Trying to hold him back from what they saw as a potential Vietnam-like quagmire were the moderate "usual suspects," Baker and Deaver, joined by Shultz and Weinberger, Secretaries of State and Defense.

It was the usual tug-of-war, or as Reagan once jokingly said, "what's called the battle for my mind."

American financial help during 1982 allowed the contra military force to grow far beyond its original core of ex-Somoza guardsmen. As with almost every revolution that simply replaces one authoritarian government with another, some former Sandinistas became disillusioned with Ortega's failure to fulfill his democratic promise and joined the resistance when he began vigorously suppressing dissent.

Ironically, the growing contra military activity gave the Sandinista government a perfect excuse to become more oppressive and to portray itself as a victim of the North American bully. Having brought a viable contra force into being, Reagan failed for many months to speak up for the anti-Sandinista guerillas, while the Ortega regime and its allies on the American left launched a vigorous campaign to tarnish the contras' reputation in the United States. They were joined by many Democrats who saw Reagan's Central America policy as a public-relations disaster, reversing nearly fifty years of the "Good Neighbor Policy."

If confrontation seemed Reagan's method in Central America, peace-keeping was his goal in the Middle East, which had seen wars between Israel and the Arab states in 1956, 1967, and 1976. President Carter had negotiated the Camp David peace agreement between Israel and Egypt, and the chief remaining controversy was over the question of an independent Palestinian state.

Reagan, like most Americans, strongly supported Israel's right to a secure and peaceful existence. However, he also believed that solving the "Palestinian issue" was a necessity for peace in the Middle East and that any realistic solution must include a Palestinian state of some sort, an idea strongly opposed by the Israelis because Palestinian leaders had always proclaimed that the destruction of Israel was their ultimate aim.

Five years of civil war in Lebanon between Muslims and pro-Israeli Christian groups, and the intervention of the Syrian Army, complicated the situation hugely. The Palestine Liberation Organization, taking advantage of Lebanon's helplessness, used that country as a base to launch attacks on Israeli civilians. Finally, in June 1982, Israel sent troops into southern Lebanon to stop the PLO, and many Lebanese civilians died in the fighting. Reagan tried to get Israeli Prime Minister Menachem Begin to agree to a cease fire, but fighting continued through the summer, including a week-long Israeli air attack on Beirut that killed still more civilians. Reagan grew quite frustrated with Begin's hardline attitude, exclaiming, "Boy, that guy makes it hard for you to be his friend."[5] The American public was also losing patience with Israel as civilian casualties grew.

Hoping to guarantee security for Israel, peace in war-torn Lebanon, and a solution for the Palestinian issue, the president decided in August to send in U.S. Marines as part of a peacekeeping force. Some of his advisors were wary, and congressional Democrats gave only cautious bipartisan support, but the Marine presence seemed to produce calm. Reagan then proposed a far-reaching peace plan in which Israel would return land captured in the 1967 war and Palestinians would have their own state associated with Jordan. The Israelis were not happy, but Egypt and Jordan were enthusiastic, and the Marines left Lebanon on a wave of goodwill.

Then in mid-September, Lebanon exploded. The Christian president was assassinated, and Christian militiamen slaughtered hundreds of Palestinians in a refugee camp, as Israeli troops allegedly stood by. With the support of Senate Republicans as well as Tip O'Neill, the president sent Marines back in, uncomfortably wedged between Israeli troops, Syrian troops, and the mutually hostile Christian and Muslim Lebanese. There they sat for months until, by the next year, discomfort became disaster.

Almost overshadowing all the foreign-policy issues was the steady, relentless decline of the American economy. Although the effort to curb inflation was working, the cost was high. By November unemployment was over 10 percent, the worst since before World War II, and the number of families sinking into poverty was the greatest in a dozen years.

As the recession deepened, television stories about its human impact multiplied, each of them embarrassing to a president who lived by the media and regarded himself as a master of it. Himself a "sucker" for hard-luck stories, Reagan could only protest that cutting inflation in half helped far more families than were hurt by the economic tightening, which was the price of victory over inflation. Ever the optimist, he called the downturn temporary and complained that negative media stories were only depressing public confidence and prolonging the recession.

Others were not so serene; the decline in business activity and jobs meant fewer tax dollars coming in, while unemployment compensation and welfare spending rose, so the budget deficit exploded. Republican senators and congressmen, facing a difficult election climate, begged the president to raise taxes to reduce the embarrassingly large deficit.

Protesting to the end, he finally gave in and signed the largest corporate tax increase ever, wiping out almost a third of his historic tax cut enacted just a year earlier. Congressional Democrats agreed to reduce spending by $3 for every $1 of higher taxes but never did so. Reagan could only denounce their broken promise and swear never to be fooled again, but the tax increase remained.

Still he remained cheerful, believing that things would turn out well, although his own approval rating from the voters sank to 35 percent, the lowest of any postwar president at the two-year mark. Republicans cringed and Democrats salivated as the November election approached. Reagan had agreed not to campaign against any congressional Democrats in 1982 who had voted for his budget and tax cuts, but with his popularity fading they had little to fear anyway from presidential opposition.

The voters' verdict was a stinging defeat for Reagan; Democrats gained twenty-six seats in the House, more than half of them from Republicans who had been swept in on his coattails just two years before. It could have been much worse. Twelve additional Republicans barely avoided defeat, and Democrats led the nationwide popular vote by landslide proportions, 55 percent to 43 percent.

Republicans did better in the Senate, losing two seats and gaining another two, keeping their 54–46 majority. The popular vote, however, told a different story; the total vote for senator in all thirty-three contests showed a 5,000,000 majority for the Democratic candidates. At the state level, Democrats won across the board, defeating seven Republican governors and winning many new legislative seats. Republicans were left with only sixteen out of fifty governors and control of only eleven state legislatures. Altogether, it was a sad result for a president who had hoped to reshape American politics, and Democrats who had feared just such a "Reagan Realignment" were vastly encouraged about the future. Astute analysts wondered whether Reagan would even run for a second term.

Although 1983 opened with Reagan's approval stuck at 35 percent, he kept blithely insisting that recovery was at hand. He was soon proved right—and not merely right, but spectacularly so. The economic boom that began in 1983 became the longest ever in American history, generating nearly 20 million jobs, while across the Atlantic other industrialized nations fell far behind. With their new purchasing power, Americans bought record quantities of imported goods, so that ironically prosperity pushed the United States into a trade deficit with the rest of the world.

In May, it was Reagan's turn to act as host for the annual G-7 economic meeting, and with inflation collapsing and the economy rising while Europe's recession still lingered, the other heads of government gathered round in jealous admiration. Chancellor Helmut Kohl of Germany urged Reagan to "tell us about the American miracle." When the conversation turned to putting American missiles in Europe, things were not so genial, but Reagan and his ally Margaret Thatcher won their point. She marveled that the president "managed to get all he wanted, . . . while allowing everyone to feel that they had got at least some of what *they* wanted, and he did all this with an immense geniality."[6]

If the economic news was good, the government's fiscal outlook was much less so. The recession's legacy of lower revenue and increased spending lasted long after the recession itself ended. Congress, worried about the stubbornly high budget deficit, compelled Reagan once more to accept higher taxes for the second year in a row. He approved a bipartisan plan that increased Social Security taxes, raised the retirement age to sixty-seven, cut the monthly benefit for early retirees, and imposed a new tax on Social Security benefit checks for all but the lowest-income retirees.

Revenue from the new tax increases and lower spending from the higher retirement age saved Social Security from financial crisis for the next two decades. Both Tip O'Neill and Reagan praised the agreement, but for the president it meant putting his signature on a multibillion-dollar tax increase for American workers and retirees. This, combined with the large cuts in the top income-tax rates from 1981, made the federal tax system more regressive than it had been for many years.

In addition to accepting a tax increase, Reagan had to face unwelcome staff changes. His Interior Secretary, James Watt, became so controversial that he had to be replaced, much to the relief of environmentalists. His guiding principle was, "we will mine more, drill more, cut more timber." He took the Endangered Species Act quite casually and even discouraged people from donating their own land for conservation purposes because he believed that the Second Coming and the end of human history was near. The immediate cause of his resignation, though, was a speech in which he mocked diversity in government, saying, "I have a black, a woman, two Jews, and a cripple" on one board. In a week, he was gone.

Three other cabinet members also left in 1983. The shuffling was in part a result of the president's management style. He relied heavily on his aides but was withdrawn and distant in his relations with them, and one of the most frequent complaints of those who left his service was that they felt unappreciated. This was compounded by the fact that, even as governor, he had always had trouble remembering even the names of people outside his inner circle.

Meanwhile, if domestic politics looked more hopeful as the economy rebounded, foreign problems seemed as intractable as ever. The two most complicated situations, as before, were in Central America and Lebanon. Reagan continued to believe, as did many conservatives, that the shaky efforts toward a more democratic politics in Central America were threatened by troublemaking from Cuba and Nicaragua.

Guerillas were still fighting to oust the government of El Salvador, and their savage tactics were met by equal viciousness from right-wing "death squads" supporting the government. Meanwhile, Sandinista leader Daniel Ortega in Nicaragua was steadily increasing his suppression of dissenters there, following the model of his Soviet and Cuban allies.

Reagan was as much disturbed by all this as he had been in his first two years but was determined not to be drawn into a direct military venture in

Central America. Besides, the lines were blurry. The government of El Salvador, while pro-American, was no less brutal in fighting the guerillas than the Marxists were in fighting the government. In Nicaragua, the United States had actually helped the Sandinistas (though very tardily) in overthrowing right-wing dictator Anastasio Somoza, and the growing contra army had attracted an embarrassing group of former Somoza soldiers.

All through 1983, critics of Reagan's policy in the media and the Democratic Party steadily turned American opinion against intervention in Central America. In December 1982, Congress had passed the Boland Amendment, forbidding any U.S. effort to overthrow the Nicaraguan government, and opposition to funding the contras for any purpose at all was growing both in and out of Washington. Reagan grumbled about Congress intruding into the president's constitutional control of foreign policy, but he passively refrained from launching any concerted or continuing rhetorical defense of his policy. For a man who had often shown great mastery of public relations, it was a surprising lapse, and it led indirectly to the Iran-Contra scandal three years later.

In the other major trouble spot, Lebanon, hopes for peace had become worn and tattered since the Marines returned the previous September. Syria was the roadblock, helping Islamic terrorists and targeting Lebanese Christian leaders. The U.S. Marine detachment, originally welcomed in 1982 as peacekeepers, was now regarded as an alien force helping to keep a minority Christian government ruling a Muslim-majority country.

Throughout the year, while diplomacy was failing, Reagan paid little attention to Lebanon, presuming, as he often did, that his team was "getting the job done." In his mind, the Marines were keeping Lebanon from disintegrating into hostile parts, when in reality the fragmenting was already a fact, and the Marines were simply easy targets for militants.

By August they were being fired on sporadically, and there had been warnings of major terrorist threats. Still, the president believed that standing firm in Lebanon was vital to curb Soviet influence in the Middle East, and he kept the Marines in Beirut, exposed though they were. Finally, the inevitable happened; on October 23 a suicide bomber blew up the Marine barracks, killing 241. The noble hope of reducing Middle East conflict had ended in months of frustrating diplomacy and the greatest American casualties of Reagan's presidency.

The president demanded retaliation, but there were no clear targets to strike. As he stewed in frustration, his popularity took a sharp, though temporary, dive. It was easy for suspicious people, at home and abroad, to assume that the American invasion of Grenada, just two days after the Beirut blast, was designed to distract public attention from the body bags that were coming home from Lebanon.

In fact, the Grenada operation had been planned for some time. The elected government of that small Caribbean island had been overthrown by a Marxist military coup in 1979, which in turn was ousted in October 1983, by a more hardline Communist group that aligned itself with Castro's Cuba and the Soviet Union. The leaders of six Caribbean nations who feared for their own security, as well as the British governor-general of Grenada, all pleaded with Reagan to oust the Communists and restore a democratic government.

Always worried about the pro-Soviet axis of Cuba, Nicaragua, and the Salvadorian rebels, Reagan was receptive to the islanders' request. Perhaps even more to the point, there were eight hundred American medical students in Grenada, whose seizure, he feared, might produce a hostage crisis far worse than the Iranian one of 1980 that had haunted Carter's presidency.

A military plan (Operation Urgent Fury) was quickly drawn up, and on October 25 over 7,000 U.S. troops and several hundred from the Caribbean nations landed. Two days of occasionally hard fighting against Cubans and local forces secured the island. The Americans found, besides eight hundred armed Cubans, a gigantic arsenal of machine guns, artillery, rocket launchers, and armored cars sufficient for a 10,000-man army—this in a country with only 30,000 adult males.

As with almost anything Ronald Reagan did, there was the usual mixed reaction at home. The medical students were thankful, some of them believing that the invasion probably saved their lives. The Congressional Black Caucus and some other liberal Democrats denounced the operation, although Tip O'Neill, who had earlier been opposed to it, now said Reagan had done the right thing.

Reaction overseas was almost uniformly negative. Of course the Communist bloc, led by the USSR and China, denounced Reagan, but even friendly countries disapproved, as shown in the overwhelming 108–9 vote for a UN resolution branding the invasion an offense against international law. Even Margaret Thatcher was angry at American military action against a member of the British Commonwealth. However, public opinion polls showed that ordinary Americans thoroughly approved Reagan's action, which allowed him to shrug off the critics.

The focus of foreign policy, as always, was the apparently perpetual Cold War, and the events of 1983 were almost relentlessly discouraging. The president increased his criticism of the Soviets, proposed building a defense against enemy missiles, ousted the Marxists from Grenada, and put nuclear missiles in Europe. To all this, the men in Moscow reacted angrily and the superpower confrontation reached alarming levels.

Addressing evangelical leaders in March 1983, Reagan made what instantly became known as the "evil empire" speech, although this was a small fraction of his remarks. The greatest part praised Americans' strong religious faith because "freedom prospers only where the blessings of God are avidly sought and humbly accepted." Criticizing liberals who, he said, wanted to constrict the role of faith in public life, Reagan claimed that the Founding Fathers "never intended to construct a wall of hostility between government and . . . religious belief." He pledged support for returning prayer to public schools and restricting "abortion on demand."

This part of his talk would have been controversial enough to many liberals, but then Reagan proceeded to launch an extended attack on the "nuclear freeze" movement that was demanding a halt in the production of atomic weapons. The idea of a freeze was "a very dangerous fraud," he said, because it would "reward the Soviet Union" for its arms buildup and prevent the West from catching up.

Then came the words that produced shock and outrage among liberals in America, Marxists everywhere, and especially the rulers of the Kremlin. Reagan said that so long as the Soviets "preach the supremacy of the state, declare its omnipotence over individual man, and predict its eventual domination of all peoples on the earth, they are the focus of evil in the modern world." He urged his listeners not to "ignore the facts of history and the aggressive impulses of an evil empire," but assured them that Communism was only "another sad, bizarre chapter in human history whose last pages even now are being written."

The reaction from Soviet leaders was predictable: Reagan was a dangerous warmonger. Liberals in the United States and left-wing critics in Europe endorsed the Soviet complaint; one American professor called this the worst speech ever by any American president. Conservatives of course grumbled that these people had no difficulty branding South African *apartheid* as an evil system, but thought it imprudent for Reagan to say the same of a nuclear-armed Soviet Russia.

Outside the Kremlin, in the streets of Moscow, the response was quite different, admissions of "self-disgust and self-acknowledgement . . . spreading through society."[7] In the prisons and slave labor camps of the Gulag, where Reagan's words spread through the tap-tap-tap grapevine from cell to cell, there was joy: "finally, someone has said it."

For decades, dissidents had been tortured and shot by the thousands in the cells of the KGB's prisons, or frozen, starved, and worked to death by the millions in Siberian slave labor camps, the "Gulag." The scale of persecution was greatly reduced after Stalin, but stern repression of dissent continued into the 1980s. To Reagan and Americans like him, if this was not evil, then the word had no meaning. It baffled them that some could not bring themselves to utter the word for fear of offending the evildoers. To Reagan's critics, however, it was a simple case of preferring realism to meaningless rhetorical gestures that sounded noble but only complicated relations with the world's other superpower.

Within weeks of the "evil empire" controversy, Reagan made an even more significant speech on missile defense, whose consequences were felt to the end of his presidency. The episode had its beginning in an aspect of the president's thought that was seldom understood. The man was a "nuclear abolitionist." Others might seek national safety in the doctrine of Mutual Assured Destruction, or in a "nuclear freeze" that stopped the arms race, or even in a reduction of atomic weapons. Ronald Reagan dreamt of a world far beyond all this, where nuclear weapons were only a bad memory in a brighter human future.

He had warned his fellow Republicans at the 1976 convention that "the great powers have poised and aimed at each other horrible missiles of destruction that can, in a matter of minutes, arrive in each other's country and destroy virtually the civilized world." That sentence would have brought applause at any meeting of the left-wing "peace movement." If Reagan's critics in the nuclear-freeze campaign had heard it, they might have realized that their goal was also his, or rather, that his goal of nuclear abolition went far beyond their more modest demand.

As a deeply religious man, Reagan believed in Armageddon, the final battle between good and evil on earth. He even said in the 1980 campaign that Armageddon might be near at hand, by which he meant the prospect of nuclear war. To him, the strategy of Mutual Assured Destruction was MADness indeed. Surely there had to be a defense against missiles. Every offensive weapon in the history of war had been matched by a defensive response: shields against swords, armor against arrows, tanks against machine guns. He believed it his destiny to produce that defense against nuclear missiles, not just for his own nation, but to be shared with the world. It was a throwback to his early post–World War II call for international control of atomic weapons.

The idea of missile defense was not new with Reagan. It had been considered in the 1960s as the Soviet arsenal grew to threatening proportions but was rejected as impossible for the technology of that day. Even if it were feasible, a missile-defense system might look to the Soviets like a threatening offensive tactic. Mutual Assured Destruction depended on each side having enough missiles remaining after an enemy's first strike to rain down an unacceptable degree of retaliation. If the United States could stop a large percentage of Soviet missiles, then mutual destruction would no longer be assured, and the United States, so the Russians feared, might be tempted to risk a preemptive first-strike attack.

When he was governor, Reagan learned on a tour of an air-defense base that there was no way to knock down incoming missiles: "Are you telling me then that we can't defend this country?"[8] When he later heard from Dr. Edward Teller, father of the hydrogen bomb, of the theoretical possibility of destroying missiles in flight, he tucked this idea away. It emerged to the forefront of his consciousness after a 1979 briefing at the North American Air Defense Command, where once again he was told that if missiles were fired at the United States, there was no defense, only massive retaliation and worldwide atomic war. He was amazed that "we have spent all that money and have all that equipment, and there is nothing we can do to prevent a nuclear missile from hitting us."[9]

The 1980 Republican platform advocated missile defense and, once he became president, Reagan began actively thinking about an alternative to Mutual Assured Destruction. He was confident that American scientific genius could hurdle any technical barriers (although a space-based system is still not possible today), and U.S. strategists were sure that the Soviet Union could not compete in the "research arms race" necessary for a complex missile defense system.

Although there was widespread skepticism in the scientific community "outside the Beltway," the chiefs of the military services endorsed the idea. However, no one was prepared for Reagan's surprise announcement of a Strategic Defense Initiative in what was supposed to be a routine televised speech on defense issues in March 1983.

After many minutes of detailing how the USSR had been out-producing the United States in conventional arms, the president suddenly marched to higher rhetorical ground: humanity must rise above "dealing with other nations . . . by threatening their existence. . . . Wouldn't it be better to save lives than to avenge them?" It would be a huge task, he said, to "intercept and destroy ballistic missiles before they reached our own soil," but well worth it "if free people could live secure in the knowledge that their security did not rest upon the threat of instant U.S. retaliation."

The reaction was hardly encouraging. In Moscow, Yuri Andropov called the idea "insane" and American liberals agreed. Even Reagan's own Secretary of State, George Shultz, thought it was a lurch into the realm of fantasy, and it would probably have violated the U.S.-Soviet anti-ballistic missile treaty. However, once Reagan had absorbed an idea, it was almost impossible to purge it from his system. He clung to SDI as a more humane alternative to Mutual Assured Destruction and even offered frequently to share the secret with the Soviets if it worked.

The strong Soviet reaction against Reagan's "evil empire" speech and the SDI announcement was only the beginning of the slump in superpower relations during 1983. The low point was reached in September, when a Soviet fighter plane shot down a Korean civilian airliner, killing 269 people, including an American congressman.

Doubly angry at the event and at an initial Soviet denial, Reagan went on national television to denounce the act. "This was the Soviet Union against the world," he said, "an act of barbarism, born of a society which wantonly disregards . . . human life and seeks constantly to expand and dominate other nations." He reported with satisfaction that "from every corner of the globe the word is defiance in the face of this unspeakable act. . . . There is a righteous and terrible anger."

Then, however, he cautioned that "vengeance . . . is not a proper answer." It was more important that the United States "not give up our effort to bring them into the world community of nations" and "to bring peace closer." In short, he did not want to overreact. His advisors urged tough retaliation, but Reagan told them, "I don't think we need to do a damn thing. . . . The entire world will . . . condemn the Soviets," but "we need to remember our long-term objectives."[10] He announced a few largely symbolic "slap on the wrist" responses and frustrated his conservative supporters by continuing arms reduction talks in Geneva.

Unused to being talked to in such contemptuous terms, Soviet leaders saw the speech as more confirmation of their hardening belief that Reagan was an utterly belligerent enemy from whom only insulting words and dangerous actions could be expected. Two months later, despite persistent lobbying by the USSR and Western "peace" activists, Germany agreed to Reagan's plan for basing intermediate-range Pershing missile in Europe. For Moscow, one push too many from the American "warmonger" prompted Soviet delegates to walk out of the Geneva arms talks.

This series of public actions in 1983, from the "evil empire" speech to the Geneva boycott, seemed to put U.S.-Soviet relations in a dangerous tailspin, but below the surface tide of events, an undercurrent was pulling Reagan steadily and with increasing earnestness toward a historic turning point. His view of the nuclear issue began to change fundamentally, and three events during the year seem to have been responsible for this shift.

One was the made-for-television movie *The Day After*, viewed by 100 million people, depicting the aftermath of a Soviet missile strike on Lawrence, Kansas. The movie showed in graphic detail the horrible human cost of the bomb blast, the lingering radiation, and the collapse of civil society, with the implication that multiple nuclear attacks had produced similar catastrophes throughout the country. The conclusion has one survivor desperately broadcasting on a homemade radio, "Hello? This is Lawrence, Kansas. Is anybody there? Anybody? Anybody at all?"

Many conservatives believed that *The Day After* was designed to weaken support for Reagan's defense policy, especially since the presidential voice in the film was an imitation of Reagan's. They were amused to find that opinion surveys taken after the movie's release actually showed a rise in the president's job-approval rating. But if *The Day After* had little impact on the public, it had a powerful influence on Reagan himself, who saw a private screening. His diary records that it "left me greatly depressed" and determined "to see there is never a nuclear war."[11]

The second event that shook Reagan was a Pentagon briefing on nuclear war fighting. He had always declined to attend such sessions, but after seeing *The Day After*, he changed his mind and went to one. He discovered that the United States had targeted 50,000 Soviet sites, both military and civilian, and it was almost certain that the USSR had attack plans on the same scale. He was amazed that people were talking seriously about winning a nuclear war: "I thought they were crazy."[12]

The final push toward a new appreciation of the nuclear danger was the Soviet reaction to a NATO war game called "Able Archer 83." Both the West and the USSR conducted such exercises to detect and correct flaws in military preparedness, but this one had a startlingly dangerous result. For ten days in November, NATO's political and military leadership rehearsed command procedures for fighting a nuclear war.

Each side always monitored the other's exercises, and this time Soviet leaders began to wonder whether the United States, led by the "madman" Reagan, might actually be planning a nuclear first strike disguised as a war game. This was believable because the USSR itself actually did have plans for launching such a surprise attack. KGB agents worldwide were urgently told to report any evidence of an impending attack, nuclear-capable aircraft were alerted, and plans were made for a retaliatory atomic strike.

Fortunately, Able Archer ended before a "red line" was passed, but American officials were astounded at the level of Soviet panic. Reagan, especially, was alarmed that anyone could believe that the United States would start a nuclear war. He had not understood before the level of fear that infected many in the Soviet political and military high command. With his long-held belief in the reality of Armageddon, Reagan took the Able Archer scare extremely seriously, realizing that "many Soviet officials feared us not only as adversaries but as potential aggressors . . . in a first strike."[13]

His new attitude, although sincere, was politically providential going into the 1984 election. The economic expansion would be nearly two years old by November, and Reagan's popularity rose with the stock market and the job numbers, but foreign affairs told a more discouraging story. In a February Gallup Poll, Americans disapproved of the president's foreign policy by 49 to 38 percent. The numbers were even worse for his actions in Central America (49–29 negative) and in Lebanon (59–28 negative).

The Democrats who had criticized Reagan over Nicaragua, Lebanon, and Soviet relations seemed on the right side of public opinion; the president was on the wrong side. This was not a comfortable place for him at the start of an election year, no matter how well the economy was doing or how much he was liked personally. Only a tone-deaf president would allow this to continue, and Reagan was expert in judging America's mood.

For the next ten months to election day, he hardly opened his mouth in public without pronouncing soothing words such as "peace," "negotiation," or "arms reduction." He was encouraged in this by the pragmatists who now completely dominated his White House team—Baker, Deaver, Shultz, and the new National Security Advisor, Bud McFarlane, with Nancy Reagan pushing behind the scenes, all wanting a softer line toward Soviets.

This was more than a vote-getting ploy, however. Reagan's "nuclear abolitionism" was becoming a paramount objective. The only way to end the Great Fear was to end the Cold War. For three years Reagan had rebuilt the military so that America could negotiate from a position of strength. This he was now ready to do, just as the Soviet system was about to bring forth, in Mikhail Gorbachev, the first ruler to see that internal reform and ending the Cold War were necessary to save that system.

Reagan's "peace offensive" began with a speech on Soviet relations broadcast to both Americans and Europeans in January, calling 1984 "a year of opportunities for peace." He recalled the dangerous 1970s, when "the United States seemed filled with self-doubt and neglected its defenses," while the USSR built "six times as many ICBM's, four times as many tanks, twice as many combat aircraft."

Now that America was stronger, one could talk about arms reduction, he said, because Soviet leaders will no longer "underestimate our strength or question our resolve." Americans "do not threaten the Soviet Union," Reagan said. "Freedom poses no threat." Some later called this address the turning point in the Cold War, although it was strongly criticized as too "soft" by conservatives like Pat Buchanan. Reagan also pulled the Marines out of Lebanon, easing fears that the United States might be drawn into a long and frustrating Middle Eastern war against terrorism.

His Democratic opponent, Walter Mondale (Carter's vice president), emerged only after a difficult primary contest against Colorado Senator Gary Hart and the Reverend Jesse Jackson. Hart surprised everyone with a strong early showing, winning three of the first four states as the forward-looking candidate of new ideas compared to Mondale's old interest-group politics. However, Mondale's organizational support, especially from labor unions, let him retake the lead and survive a late surge from Hart, who won eight of the final ten primaries.

Jackson ran to impress on the Democratic Party how much it depended on African Americans, and he amply proved it by winning over 3 million primary votes to about 6 million each for Hart and Mondale. Although the former vice president struggled through to victory, he won only 40 percent of the total primary vote and only twenty-three states to twenty-seven for his two opponents.

While Democrats fought one another through the spring and summer, Reagan coasted to an unopposed renomination by a united and optimistic party. He took advantage of the lull to improve his foreign-policy ratings by two major foreign trips. In April he met with China's Communist leaders, cautioning them that despite increasingly friendly relations, the United States would stand by Taiwan's *de facto* independence.

The Chinese had promised to broadcast his major speech in Beijing live throughout the country, but instead they taped it and cut out Reagan's remarks about religious faith, freedom, and democracy. When he repeated those sentiments in a television interview, once more they were edited out, but on a third try the regime relented and finally let Reagan speak directly and in full to the Chinese people.

Two months later, he was in Europe for the fortieth anniversary of the D-Day landings at Pointe du Hoc. Speaking before the surviving Rangers, he said "these are the men who took the cliffs. . . . These are the heroes who helped end a war." It was perhaps the most superb rhetorical moment of his career; among the solders, the spectators, and even the reporters there was hardly a dry eye. Not forgetting the Allies, he praised their part in the war, and especially the Russians who bore most of the burden of defeating Hitler and suffered 20 million dead. Later, at Omaha Beach, Reagan spoke again, promising that "we will always remember. We will always be proud. We will always be prepared, so we may always be free."

As the president enjoyed himself abroad, Mondale was trying to use the Democratic national convention to pull his quarreling party together. To satisfy the Gary Hart voters, who thought Mondale too stodgy and too much rooted in the past, the nominee had to show that he could reach toward the future. What bolder stroke could there be than picking New York Congresswoman Geraldine Ferraro for vice president, the first woman on the national ticket of a major political party? This could send him into the fall campaign with at least some possibility of winning.

Then Mondale ruined it all by promising a tax increase. He said in his acceptance speech, "Mr. Reagan will raise taxes, and so will I. He won't tell you. I just did." Reagan's managers could hardly believe their good luck. Stuart Spencer was "in ecstasy. . . . The political graveyard is full of tax increasers."[14] Of course, one who avoided the graveyard was Reagan himself, who, after his trademark 1981 tax cut, had signed a major tax hike in 1982 and another, for Social Security, in 1983, as well as the huge state tax increase in his first year as governor.

Despite the tax-hike *faux pas*, Mondale did get a temporary boost from the convention, as Democrats emerged more united and enthusiastic than one might have expected. This was a reminder, however brief, that the New Deal party system might be weakened but was still alive. Despite Reagan's personal popularity, the Democrats were still the dominant party in the electorate. It remained true, as it had been since the Great Depression, that there were more votes to be had by promising benefits to people than by preaching fiscal restraint and lower taxes.

To meet this challenge, the basic Reagan strategy was outlined in a midsummer memo. First, tie Mondale to the failed Carter years when he was vice president; then brand him as weak, a "special-interest liberal," soft on national defense. For Reagan, emphasize peace, strength, traditional values, prosperity, and "America's future." In short, "paint RR as the person-ification of all that is right with, or heroized by, America. Leave Mondale in a position where an attack on Reagan is tantamount to an attack on America's idealized image of itself."[15]

Ed Rollins, Reagan's campaign manager, allocated millions of dollars to build up a grassroots network during the campaign, including finding and registering 6 million new Republican voters. With that massive "ground game" in place, he believed that a popular president hardly needed to flood the country with expensive television ads. He was set straight by the campaign's media consultant, Stuart Spencer, who insisted that the Reagans wanted a strong visual media effort.

The result was a masterful television campaign featuring some of the most effective ads ever used in a presidential election. It included two short television spots that many students of the art would rank in the top dozen ever produced. Between them, they aimed at putting the president firmly in control of the two dominant political issues in Cold War America: the economy and national security.

The more famous of the two proclaimed that "it's morning again in America," and against a visual background of workers, families, and flags, detailed in just sixty seconds the points Reagan wanted voters to take to the ballot box. More people were working than ever before, interest rates and inflation were half what they were in 1980, and "our country is prouder and stronger and better." It closed by asking, "why would we ever want to return to where we were less than four short years ago?"

Less well known, but perhaps even more effective, were thirty seconds entitled, "The Bear in the Woods." The words were simple but powerful, encapsulating the decades-long tension of the Cold War without ever mentioning the Soviet Union or the nuclear threat. The script ran, *in toto*:

"There's a bear in the woods. For some people, the bear is easy to see. Others don't see it at all. Some people say the bear is tame. Others say it's vicious and dangerous. Since no one can really be sure who's right, isn't it smart to be as strong as the bear—if there is a bear?"

A third spot, aimed at women, played emotionally on the theme of peace. "In my lifetime," Reagan says against a slide show montage of children at play, "we've faced two world wars. . . . I want our children never to face another. A president's most important job is to secure peace—not just now, but for the lifetimes of our children. But it takes a strong America to build a peace that lasts."

Democrats tried the same image-mongering, but it was much harder to "demonize" a smiling, optimistic Reagan, and almost impossible to turn Mondale's dour expression and years of interest-group insider politics into the picture of a "happy warrior." They foolishly tried to attack Reagan as heartless, caring little for the poor and showering benefits on the rich. Not only was this partly false—the president did care, remembering his own childhood—but, more to the point, it conflicted with the impression voters had formed of Reagan. Instead of changing their minds about him, people blamed the Democrats for being "mean."

Tip O'Neill himself saw this during the campaign when a Boston construction worker, paralyzed by a fall, was upset at the administration's plan to tax workers' compensation benefits but also complained that O'Neill was "too tough on the president." The Speaker was stunned. "Who do you think is cutting your benefits?" The worker assured him, "Not the president. . . . He's got nothing to do with it. It's the people around him." O'Neill concluded, "that's the amazing thing about Ronald Reagan. People just wouldn't believe he would do anything to hurt them. Even while he was cutting the heart out of the American dream. . . ."[16]

The Reagan mystique was never so apparent as in a reporter's interview with a young unemployed Michigan couple. They said Reagan "likes the rich" and "sides with the special interests"; Mondale "sides with the average citizen" and was "more likely to keep the United States out of war." Who were they voting for? Reagan, because "he's brought the country back together."[17]

Democrats made another mistake in denouncing SDI by repeating the Soviet claim that "Star Wars" was a dangerous escalation of the arms race. To most Americans, a plan to defend them against attack was a good thing, far preferable to the policy of Mutual Assured Destruction that Reagan's critics supported. Much to Mondale's frustration, when he ran ads against SDI, they made people *more* likely to vote for Reagan.

Reagan himself did not work very hard during the campaign; there were few extended swings and usually the president flew out and back on day trips. Spencer, Baker, and the others planning the schedule wanted to "sit" on his lead over Mondale and take few risks of an unscripted "Reagan moment" that might cost votes. Overall, this was a sound approach, as Richard Wirthlin's daily tracking polls showed.

Only three times did the president's lead fall below ten points—once in the aftermath of the Democratic convention, once after Reagan joked about bombing the Soviet Union, and the last time after the first presidential debate raised the "age issue." Each of these dips in popularity laid bare one of Reagan's potential weaknesses, but fortunately for him all were fleeting.

To avoid any game-changing gaffes, the campaign kept their candidate carefully scripted, avoiding news conferences for months, but they could not refuse face-to-face debates with Mondale. Reagan had previously shown himself a master of one-on-one debating. He had outshone Robert Kennedy, John Anderson, George Bush, and Jimmy Carter, if not always by mastery of the facts, then by a memorable punch line.

All were shocked, then, when his performance against Mondale in a Louisville debate on October 7 was Reagan's worst ever. He had approached it passively, letting his aides "over-brief" him with far too much information. Meanwhile, his opponent had prepared masterfully. Pat Caddell, a brilliant young strategist who had worked for Hart against Mondale in the primaries, urged him to keep Reagan off-balance by alternating aggressive and deferential tactics. The result was that Mondale looked cool, in control, and presidential, while the president himself seemed tentative, out of focus, and old, stumbling over details.

In the following two weeks, the age issue, always Reagan's potential nemesis, was increasingly raised in television and the press—sometimes subtly, sometimes bluntly. Years later, after he was diagnosed with Alzheimer's disease, some people wondered whether the debate performance had been an early sign of that affliction. However, the editor of Reagan's handwritten diaries has said that he detected no change in the president's mental sharpness as reflected in eight years of diary entries, and Reagan's doctors have unanimously given their professional medical opinion that no signs of Alzheimer's appeared during the presidency. The medical correspondent of *The New York Times*, who covered Reagan's health during both terms, gave the same opinion.

Reagan knew that he had floundered in the first debate, as did his wife, who lashed out at the campaign staff. She and everyone else spent the intervening days building up the president's confidence, and he prepared himself carefully for the return bout. Just before he faced Mondale again in Kansas City on October 21, one of his handlers warned Reagan that he should be prepared for a question about the age issue. After a moment's thought, the president said, "I can handle that."[18] And handle it he did.

Reagan's pollster, Richard Wirthlin, merging the standard "focus group" with new technology, put several dozen people in a room to judge the second debate. Each one was told to punch positive or negative reactions into a handheld device hooked up to Wirthlin's computer. (This has become routine in political debates, but it was relatively new in 1984.)

As the debate rolled on, Wirthlin could tell that Mondale was scoring no points in his effort to drive home the idea that Reagan was simply mentally and physically worn out, too old to be president. Reagan, for his part, was adequate but not compelling at the podium until he got the question that was on everyone's mind: was he, in fact, too old for the job?

With his trademark smile and tilt of the head, Reagan brushed away such concerns and then struck home with his counterthrust. "I will not make age an issue of this campaign," he said. "I am not going to exploit for political purposes my opponent's youth and inexperience." The audience exploded; even Mondale had to chuckle, and in Wirthlin's focus group the approval lines shot right off the graph. The age issue had breathed its last.

Campaigning, especially when he was headed for victory, energized Reagan even as the long hours (which he did not share) wore out his staff and the traveling journalists. Flying back to Washington on Air Force One on election eve, Charlton Heston saw that people were exhausted and was amazed that "the only one in high spirits was the President. He was older than anyone else aboard, but his eyes were shining."[19]

And well might they shine, for the next day Reagan won every state but Mondale's own Minnesota (losing that by fewer than 4,000 votes) and took 525 electoral votes (the highest total ever) to 13 for Mondale. Of the nationwide popular vote, he polled nearly 59 percent, a majority of 17,000,000, carrying every region of the country, every age group, every occupation but the unemployed, and every income group but the very poorest. Reagan even won nearly half the union households, a quarter of the Democrats, and 30 percent of liberal voters.

His one great disappointment was his weakness among black voters. Reagan had grown up absorbing from his parents a vigorously emotional dislike of racial prejudice, and in Hollywood he had been one of the few whites who made any effort to improve opportunities and conditions for African Americans in the movie industry. As governor and as president he spoke up for racial understanding, but he was forever distressed that black voters, and their advocates in the political world, were more hostile to him and his administration than any other group in the population.

Repelled by Goldwater's 1964 campaign and pleased by LBJ's civil rights program, blacks had since the mid-1960s been by far the most monolithically Democratic voting group. Besides, in the 1980s African Americans saw Reagan, whatever his personal convictions, as completely unhelpful in aiding them to overcome the barriers hindering their dreams for a good life in modern America. He had opposed the Civil Rights Acts of the 1960s, for example, as an unconstitutional overreach of federal power. The reason for his opposition might be "pure" as opposed to the racism of some Southern Democrats, but the result was the same: blacks would get no help from Reagan in securing their right to vote in the South.

As president, while he personally and often preached racial equality, his budgets eroded the funding for social programs like Aid to Families With Dependent Children, housing subsidies, and school lunches, on which a larger proportion of blacks than whites depended. On a very important symbolic issue, Reagan, despite praising Martin Luther King, opposed a national holiday in King's name because of the expense to the government of another paid day off for federal workers. He even threatened to veto the bill, but gave in when it passed Congress by huge majorities.

To all these offenses in the eyes of African-American voters, Reagan added a very tepid policy toward South Africa's racist *apartheid* regime. In addition, he appointed very few blacks to administrative or judicial positions because there simply were not many African-American conservatives to begin with. With such a public record, it was natural for the Congressional Black Caucus to form the bitter core of opposition to Reagan's policies and for huge majorities of blacks to vote against him.

Except for this group, Reagan won a broad and deep majority in 1984, partly because he embodied the mythic America of the past—the sturdy frontiersman who valued hard work (despite his easy schedule), thrift (despite the growing national debt), and family (despite troubles with his own children). More than this, he also encouraged Americans to imagine a wonderful future—a world free of trade barriers, nuclear bombs, and Soviet Communism. As one voter summed it up, Reagan "really isn't like a Republican. He's more like an American."[20]

For those less entranced by visions of the past or the future, the booming economy of the prosperous present was sufficient reason to reelect the president. Half of those who voted said they were better off than in 1980 and of those, five of every six went for Reagan. A college student told the president that "with you in office when we graduate, we can get a job." In addition, Mondale's promise to raise federal taxes hurt him badly with people who voted on economic issues. Not surprisingly, those who felt left on the beach as the tide of prosperity rose—blacks, the poor, and the unemployed—were among the few groups giving Mondale a majority.

Among other voters, specific issues seemed to matter less than general impressions. Exit polls showed that while Reagan was considered as a strong leader, people saw Mondale as too "weak." Furthermore, the president's emphasis on the "peace and prosperity" theme seemed to address broad national problems. By contrast, too many people thought, as one pollster put it, that Mondale "kowtowed to special interests," becoming, as a Democratic governor mourned, "the perfect reflection of the left wing" of his party.

It is sometimes said that the 1984 landslide was a purely personal one, that even though people disagreed with Reagan on most issues, they liked him personally and felt more comfortable with him than with Mondale in the Oval Office. In other words, Reagan won despite his conservative policies, not because of them. This is untrue. The *Los Angeles Times* made the most thorough study of voter attitudes during 1984, conducting polls in February, April, and October. Of the twenty-one issues polled by the *Times*, Reagan had the advantage throughout the year on fourteen or fifteen of them, and the few where Mondale led ranked low on people's priorities.

As the campaign ended, Reagan led Mondale by four to one on the issue of national defense; three to one on controlling inflation and fighting crime; two to one on taxes; and three to two on controlling the federal deficit, making America competitive in trade, keeping the peace, dealing with the Middle East and Central America, and prayer in the schools.

Voters did prefer Mondale by three to one on civil rights, two to one on helping the poor, and three to two on protecting the environment. Unfortunately for Mondale, few people considered these questions very important in deciding their presidential vote. Americans were much more concerned about the economy (58 percent) than foreign policy (19 percent), social issues (10 percent), or the candidates' personal qualities (6 percent).

These results on major issues do not mean, however, that people approved of all the president's specific actions. A survey by *The New York Times*, for example, was not unusual in finding that voters were critical of Reagan's help for the contras in Nicaragua and blamed him for American military deaths in Lebanon. But most people doubted that Mondale would do any better because Reagan continued to have a substantial lead on the generic question of "who do you want handling foreign policy?"

Some journalists and political analysts described Reagan's victory as an issueless campaign, leaving him without a mandate for his next four years. If one compares the promises Reagan ran on in 1980 with what he accomplished—or, at least, what occurred while he was in office—there appear to have been quite a few "issues" in 1984. He promised to revive the economy, and he did. He promised to rebuild American military power, and he did. He promised to cut taxes, to cut inflation, and to cut discretionary federal spending, and he did all three.

The fact that these problems were no longer "issues" in 1984 was a sign, not of a meaningless election, but of a successful presidency, at least as Reagan—and the voters themselves—defined success. The one great failure was the promise to balance the federal budget, and that apparently could be overlooked as long as there was no war and no recession. And if one seeks a mandate for the future in the 1984 landslide, it was Reagan's hope for easing Cold War tensions and reducing nuclear armament—and that hope was to be spectacularly fulfilled, sooner and more fully than anyone could have imagined.

NOTES

1. Doris Kearns Goodwin, *Team of Rivals: The Political Genius of Abraham Lincoln* (New York: Simon & Schuster, 2005), 615.
2. Cannon, *President Reagan*, 96.
3. Reagan quoted in Morris, *Dutch*, 461.
4. Reagan quoted in U.S. Naval Institute *News*, June 27, 2012.
5. Reagan quoted in Laurence I. Barrett, *Gambling with History: Ronald Reagan in the White House* (Garden City, NY: Doubleday, 1983), 271.
6. Kohl quoted in Reagan, *An American Life*, 351; Margaret Thatcher, *The Downing Street Years* (New York: Harper Collins, 1993), 300–301.
7. Morris, *Dutch*, 474.
8. Reagan quoted in Frederick H. Hartman, *Naval Renaissance: The U.S. Navy in the 1980s* (Annapolis, MD: Naval Institute Press, 1990), 257.
9. Reagan quoted in Martin Anderson, *Revolution* (New York: Harcourt Brace Jovanovich, 1988), 83.
10. Deaver, *A Different Drummer*, 95.
11. Douglas Brinkley, ed., *The Reagan Diaries* (New York: Harper Collins, 2007), 186.
12. Reagan, *An American Life*, 586.
13. *Ibid.*, 588.
14. Mondale and Spencer quoted in Jack W. Germond and Jules Witcover, *Wake Us When It's Over: Presidential Politics of 1984* (New York: Macmillan, 1985), 413.
15. Peter L. Goldman, *et al.*, *Quest For the Presidency 1984* (New York: Bantam Books, 1985), 413.
16. O'Neill, *Man of the House*, 357.
17. Washington Post, September 23, 1984, quoted in Cannon, *President Reagan*, 450–451.
18. Reagan quoted in Goldman, *Quest for the Presidency*, 339.
19. Charlton Heston quoted in Hannaford, *Recollections of Reagan*, 70–71.
20. Quotations in this and the next two paragraphs from "Election '84", *Time* magazine, November 19, 1984, 45–47.

PRESIDENT REAGAN, 1985–1989:
"WE WIN, THEY LOSE"

"The Wall." From 1961 to 1989, only one structure could be meant by those words—the wall in Berlin. It was a symbol of the boundary between freedom and tyranny for all the world to see. When Reagan took his oath of office for the second time, the Wall had barely five years to stand and the empire that erected it less than seven. If one could have sensed it, the earthquake was already building that would bring down the Wall and the regime that hid behind it, afraid to let its subjects see the contrast between their drab world and the brighter one beyond.

As it was, when 1985 began, it seemed that the next few years would be occupied by the same familiar issues: the economy, fiscal policy, and the Cold War. In his State of the Union message in February, Reagan told how he saw things at the halfway point of his presidency. Mostly he repeated what he had been saying even before 1980: cut government subsidies, eliminate wasteful spending, stand firm against Soviet power, and help those who fight Marxist dictatorships.

Then he proposed something that became the highlight of domestic policy in the second term: tax reform. The system, he said, "remains unfair and limits our potential for growth," and taxes on low-income families "make hard lives even harder." He suggested cutting both personal and corporate tax rates, curbing business tax breaks, and making the poorest families "totally exempt from Federal income tax." After nearly two years and much tinkering, this became the famous Tax Reform Act of 1986.

The president had to operate in his second term without the protective group, mostly of "old Californians," who had guarded his image and guided his actions in the first four years. In January, Jim Baker left for the Treasury Department and during the year, Deaver and Stockman both departed. Clark had already left for the Interior Department, and Meese had become Attorney General the previous year.

Almost worse than the departures were some of the newcomers, especially the new Chief of Staff, Don Regan. A Wall Street executive, he was used to wielding unquestioned authority rather than the collegial consensus of the Baker-Meese-Deaver troika. As a result, there was only one referee, instead of several, to raise a "yellow card" to warn Reagan off some impolitic action. If Regan did not catch the potential danger—and he often did not—there was no one else.

One result was Bitburg. As if by some divine law of compensation, Reagan's masterful D-Day rhetoric in June 1984, led to one of his most troubling performances, the 1985 visit to Bitburg Cemetery. West German Chancellor Helmut Kohl was the most important American ally on the Continent. To balance his exclusion from the Normandy event, he wanted a joint appearance with Reagan at some German site, to mark 1945 not as victory over Germany, but rather as the rebirth of a free Germany. Reagan appreciated Kohl's loyalty and agreed that the two heads of government would visit a German military cemetery and a concentration camp.

When Deaver flew over to check the Bitburg cemetery, he was told that it included no war criminals. That was technically true, but by the time firm plans were made for a presidential trip, news broke that several dozen soldiers of the Waffen SS were interred there. These were not the infamous concentration camp guards, but the Waffen SS had committed its own atrocities during the war against Jews, other civilians, and Allied troops. During the postwar Nuremburg trials, it had been declared a criminal organization.

The impact of the SS story was magnified because it broke during Passover week. The American Jewish community was appalled and angry; even those who had been loyal Reagan supporters were distressed. As if that were not enough, Republican Jewish leaders were invited to the White House to convey their concern on the very day of the official Bitburg announcement, much to their embarrassment.

There was worse to come at a public ceremony in which Reagan gave the Congressional Medal of Freedom to concentration-camp survivor Elie Wiesel, the country's most famous Jewish leader. Wiesel had asked the president privately, but in vain, to reverse the Bitburg decision. Now, on national television, he spoke out again: "May I, Mr. President, . . . implore you to do something else, . . . to find another way, another site. That place, Mr. President, is not your place. Your place is with the victims of the SS. The issue is . . . good and evil. . . . I have seen the SS at work, and I have seen their victims—they were my friends, they were my parents."[1]

The outrage and opposition to Bitburg extended far beyond American Jews. Half the U.S. Senate asked the president to change his plans; so did the American Legion; so did one of Reagan's favorite Christian leaders, Billy

Graham; so did his own wife. He was adamant. He would not embarrass his ally, Helmut Kohl, and Kohl insisted on the visit. So Air Force One took off for Germany, leaving behind a large group of Americans whose opinion of Reagan was now less than it had been.

Bitburg's embarrassment would have been much worse except for two things. Famed General Matthew Ridgway, the 82nd Airborne Division commander in World War II, volunteered to join the President at Bitburg, helping to take some of the focus off Reagan himself. There was also a ceremony immediately before at the Bergen-Belsen concentration camp, where Reagan paid homage to the 6 million Holocaust victims.

Standing amid the mass graves of thousands of victims, Reagan said, "here lie people—Jews—whose death was inflicted for no other reason than their very existence. . . . Humanity refuses to accept that freedom or the spirit of man can ever be extinguished. . . . Out of the ashes—hope, and from all the pain, promise. . . . Here they lie. Never to hope. Never to pray. Never to love. Never to heal. Never to laugh. Never to cry. *Never again!*"

It was a moving tribute, but it was overshadowed by what came a few hours later at Bitburg. The visit to the by-now-infamous cemetery was very abbreviated, with no speech, no ceremony—even a mere proxy handshake, General Ridgway with a German general, rather than Reagan and Kohl. Still, nothing could erase the painful sight of an American president standing by the graves of Nazi Waffen SS soldiers and suggesting by his presence and his participation in the laying of a wreath, that it was time to forget the Second World War—Hitler's war. Reagan looked quite glum. Perhaps he could still hear Elie Wiesel's reproach: "That place, Mr. President, is not your place."

Bitburg was bad enough, but a far worse result of losing the experienced advice of Deaver, Meese, and Baker was the Iran-Contra scandal, which unfolded in 1985 and 1986. The affair owed its origin partly to Reagan's anguish over the fate of a half-dozen American hostages kidnapped in Lebanon by the Shiite terrorist group Hezbollah (with close ties to Iran). He had sworn many times never to negotiate with kidnappers, but he was eager to try anything that might liberate these unfortunate people. Also, Robert McFarlane, Reagan's National Security Advisor (the third in line as they went by), believed that Iran could become, as it had been before 1979, a bulwark against Soviet influence in the Middle East.

The Iranian government of Ayatollah Khomeini had been declared a state sponsor of terrorism and, in the midst of a long, draining war with Iraq, was subject to an arms embargo by several Western nations. McFarlane thought that if the United States provided arms to moderate elements in Iran, and if they in turn could convince Hezbollah to release the hostages, both idealism and realism would be served. Reagan would achieve his humanitarian goal and Iranian moderates, grateful for the arms, would bring Iran back to its former pro-Western and anti-Soviet alignment.

Most Americans would have agreed that these were worthwhile aims, but there were complications. Reagan would have to "fudge" his pledge never to negotiate with hostage takers, and the U.S. government would have to break the arms embargo and anger its allies. Within Iran itself, the moderates—if there were any—would somehow have to overthrow the rule of the mullahs under Khomeini, and the kidnappers would have to refrain from simply seizing more hostages to replace any they set free.

The worst complication was that Colonel Oliver North, who became heavily involved in the operation, had two goals of his own, both highly illegal. Those he worked with, both Americans and foreigners, wanted to overcharge the Iranians for the weapons and pocket some of the profit. North planned to funnel the rest of the excess money secretly to the Nicaraguan contras, despite a congressional law against any such help.

When McFarlane presented his idea in July 1985, he found it easy to convince Reagan that "arms for hostages" would not violate the pledge against dealing with kidnappers. The arms would go to the Iranians, who would then obtain the release of hostages without any direct contact between the United States and Hezbollah. This fig leaf was enough for a president desperate to rescue helpless Americans.

Both Secretary of State Shultz and Secretary of Defense Weinberger argued strongly against the plan, worried that it would become public and damage American diplomacy and Reagan's reputation. Besides, they doubted it would work. However, the president was so stubbornly fixated on the hostage issue that only a threat of resignation by the two secretaries might have changed his mind. They never issued such a threat and subsided into ineffective grumbling against McFarlane's idea.

The first shipments of arms—TOW anti-tank missiles—went to Iran in August and September with Reagan's approval, and this bought the release of one hostage. All was done indirectly; the weapons were sent from Israel to Iran, with the United States replenishing the Israeli stockpile. The Iranians talked to Hezbollah, who then turned their hostage loose. The process was highly irregular, although not illegal, but soon darker things began to happen.

McFarlane was replaced as National Security Advisor in December by John Poindexter, who, in the words of journalist Lou Cannon, "was able with a clear conscience to ignore the Constitution and to violate the laws he was sworn to uphold."[2] Poindexter and CIA Director William Casey pushed the operation into high gear, with Oliver North in charge of all the details—including sending Iranian money illegally to the contras. The next year would see Iran-Contra flourish and then collapse, almost taking Reagan's presidency with it to destruction.

That disaster was still in the future, however, when Reagan began the greatest journey of his presidency, the relationship with Mikhail Gorbachev that would lead to the end of the Cold War. There had been a hint of change as early as 1983, when, oddly bracketed by regular denunciations of Reagan as a warmonger and "a Hitler," came a letter from Yuri Andropov offering to talk about easing tensions. The president sent an encouraging reply, eliciting another friendly note from the Soviet leader.

This potential thawing of the Cold War ended abruptly with the downing of KAL007 that September, but Andropov's successor Konstantin Chernenko, although ill during his entire year's reign, knew the USSR badly needed relief from its military burden and economic problems. He was prepared to resume the interrupted Geneva arms talks when he also died, having opened the way for Gorbachev.

The new Kremlin boss made little impression on Reagan at first, who was convinced that if Gorbachev "wasn't a confirmed ideologue he never would have been chosen." By midsummer, however, the president was willing to believe that Gorbachev might be good news provided he understood that "I really meant 'arms reductions' & I wasn't interested in any detente nonsense."[3] A summit meeting was arranged for November.

Besides being realistic about Soviet weaknesses, Gorbachev understood that the United States was in a much stronger position than a few years earlier, with a growing economy, a better-armed military, a popular reelected president, and a supportive NATO alliance. Reagan, in turn, understood that if Gorbachev "really wants an arms control agreement, it will only be because he wants to reduce the burden of defense spending that is stagnating the Soviet economy. This could contribute to his opposition to our SDI. He doesn't want to face the cost of competing with us."[4] That issue would "be a case of an irresistible force meeting an immovable object."[5]

Reagan arrived early at the Geneva villa that was summit headquarters and was waiting for his rival on November 19, when Gorbachev emerged from his limousine armored against the cold in hat, scarf, and thick overcoat. The taller Reagan, seeming taller still from the steps of the villa, smiling and confident in a tailored blue suit—no hat, no scarf, no coat—bounded down to greet the Soviet leader. With a broad smile of welcome, he grasped Gorbachev's elbow and slowly guided him up the steps as if to say, "need some help, old fellow?" One would hardly imagine that Gorbachev was the younger by twenty years.

It was the perfect image of how Ronald Reagan saw the world: his prosperous, confident, welcoming America facing an adversary that was shaky, uncertain, and walled off from encroaching discomfort, at last beginning to realize its own inferiority in the modern world of thriving democracies. Gorbachev knew that he had been "had"; he was careful to ask, "the next time we meet, will it be coats on or coats off?"[6]

When the meeting began, Gorbachev spoke of the need for peace and arms reduction, while Reagan was bluntly frank: "let me tell you why we mistrust you and are suspicious of you." He criticized the Soviets' expanding influence into the Caribbean, Africa, and Afghanistan. Of course the United States had its own system of allies surrounding the USSR, from Japan through Pakistan to Turkey to West Germany, but in Reagan's mind that was different, designed to protect freedom, not to erode it. He closed the session with his standing offer to share a missile-defense system with the Soviets. He had told his aides that "Gorbachev has a political problem" because he "doesn't know how to back down on SDI."[7]

The first few hours set the tone for the rest of the summit. Gorbachev kept coming back to SDI, complaining that it raised fears of an American first strike; Reagan kept insisting that SDI was purely defensive and would lessen nuclear fears, not exacerbate them. Both were willing to reduce their two giant piles of atomic weapons, but on Gorbachev's side only if the United States abandoned SDI, which Reagan refused. If the Soviet leader had hoped that the American president would give up SDI as the price of progress in arms reduction, he left disappointed. As Edmund Morris totted up the summit score, it was "Immovable Object 1, Irresistible Force 0."[8]

In a sense, both went away winners because the major decision at Geneva was for Gorbachev to visit the United States and Reagan to follow in Moscow. Obviously, those trips would be embarrassingly empty gestures unless there was intervening progress on the major Cold War issues. Neither leader was likely to allow such a negative outcome, which boded well for future negotiations. The European allies and the American Congress both applauded Reagan, the first because he had not negotiated away their U.S. atomic "umbrella" and the second because he had inched the two superpowers a bit further away from the nuclear abyss.

The other major foreign issue of the year, involving South Africa, turned out much less pleasantly for the president. Reagan's foreign policy gaze was fixed primarily on Europe and the Soviet Union, and he saw Africa only out of the corner of his eye. For the United States, the two most nagging African issues were, in the north, the threat of Libyan dictator Muammar Gaddafi, and in the south, a military struggle in Namibia between South Africa's white-ruled government and a local left-wing resistance movement. President Carter had worked to find a solution to the Namibian issue, but Reagan's early African policy focused instead on the north.

The new administration saw Gaddafi as a dangerous troublemaker and worked to strengthen Tunisia and Egypt as buffers to his regional ambitions and to isolate him diplomatically. There were even two brief military episodes. In the summer of 1981 the United States shot down two Libyan planes in the Mediterranean, and in 1986 American planes bombed Libya to retaliate for a Gaddafi-sponsored terrorist attack on Americans in Berlin.

Africans themselves were far more interested in the American attitude toward the Union of South Africa, where a white minority ruled a restless black majority through ruthless segregation and military repression. By 1981, international momentum was building for strong economic sanctions against South Africa, and in the United States there was growing pressure on corporations and other institutions to end investment and cut off contacts.

Reagan was reluctant, seeing the world as a battlefield between free nations and Soviet imperialism. South Africa was a strong ally in the Cold War, and an upheaval there might fasten Soviet influence upon the continent, especially as Communists and other Marxists were prominent in the African National Congress, the anti-apartheid movement. Instead, the president hoped that "constructive engagement" would gradually and peacefully change South Africa, but it was unlikely that constructive engagement could accomplish much without direct U.S. pressure on the South African government. No such pressure was forthcoming from Reagan, who regarded the regime as an unpalatable but necessary ally, much like Stalin's Soviet dictatorship had been during World War II.

By the end of Reagan's first term, opponents of apartheid abroad and at home were increasingly frustrated and bitter at his "coddling" of a racist regime. The peak of rhetorical outrage occurred in the fall of 1984, when black South African bishop Desmond Tutu spoke to the U.S. Congress, denouncing Reagan's policy as "immoral, evil, and totally un-Christian."

At the same time, some Republicans shifted their position; three dozen House conservatives abandoned constructive engagement, demanding stronger action. A bipartisan coalition produced the Anti-Apartheid Act of 1985, which passed Congress by large margins. Reagan faced a difficult choice: sign the bill although he personally opposed sanctions, or veto the bill and risk having it passed over his veto. Instead of either, he issued an executive order embodying most of the sanctions in the bill, and Congress reluctantly accepted this as a partial victory. However, from the mood of the country and of Congress (even in his own party), it was clear that tougher measures were coming, whether Reagan liked it or not.

Foreign policy briefly took a back seat in 1986 with the stunning televised explosion of the space shuttle *Challenger* on January 28. The disaster was the harder to accept because it was so unexpected. Never had even one astronaut been lost in flight; now, suddenly, an entire crew of seven was gone. It was one of those sharp and sudden blows that demand comment from a president, and Reagan's response was just right.

In a short telecast from the Oval Office, he praised the "seven heroes," name by individual name, who, in the words of the poet John Magee, had "slipped the surly bonds of Earth to touch the face of God." He joined the nation in mourning their loss and put the sad occasion in a context immediately understandable to all who knew their country's history.

"We've grown used to the idea of space," he said, "and perhaps we forget that we've only just begun. We're still pioneers. They . . . were pioneers." Speaking to millions of school children who had been shown the launch in class because one of the crew was a teacher, the president said, "it's all part of taking a chance and expanding man's horizons. The future doesn't belong to the fainthearted; it belongs to the brave."

Here, in a short few minutes, was one of the constant themes in Ronald Reagan's rhetoric—the connection of the present and the future with the American past. The image of the pioneers pushing their way across a beckoning but dangerous continent was tied to the vision of a boundless future in the vast unknown of outer space. It was, in Reagan's mind, all part of the great American venture, and he knew his words would find a welcome among his viewers.

Soon enough, Reagan was back to dealing with earthly problems. For him, the greatest, next to the Cold War, was the frustrating inability to strike back effectively against Islamic terrorists who carried out hundreds of attacks on Americans during his presidency, from kidnapping and individual murders to mass bombings. Several times he considered retaliating against terrorists in Lebanon but held back because there were no clear targets and there were likely to be heavy civilian casualties.

The one major action he undertook was against Libya, where Gaddafi bragged about supporting radical left-wing violence in Europe and anti-Israel and anti-Western terrorism in the Middle East. Reagan was also worried that Libya might become a beachhead for Soviet influence in North Africa. When Libyan agents bombed a West Berlin nightclub in April 1986, killing or wounding about eighty American service members, the president decided to respond. U.S. planes attacked Libyan military targets, destroying more than a dozen aircraft and several radar installations. Several bombs fell wide of their targets and killed fifteen civilians.

Although a large majority of Americans approved the air strike, the reaction was quite different abroad. The United Nations condemned the action as a violation of international law, as did the Arab League, the African Union, and the third-world nations of the Non-Aligned Movement. More importantly, the retaliatory bombing did not seem to stop, or even reduce, future terrorist acts.

If Reagan was frustrated trying to change Gaddafi's behavior abroad, he had much better luck at home changing the American judiciary. Often before he became president, Reagan had criticized "judicial activism" in the federal courts. He believed that liberal judges decided cases on the basis of their own political views rather than the clear meaning of the Constitution and the laws. To him, that destroyed the constitutional separation of powers; judges should interpret the law, not make the law. As president, he insisted that people recommended as federal judges should believe in the principle of "judicial restraint."

Two of Reagan's old California hands, Ed Meese and William French Smith, set up a well-organized process to find potential conservative judges, study their legal writing, and conduct personal interviews to learn as much as they could of a candidate's thinking about the Constitution. No pinpoint questions were asked about particular issues, but the generic process did produce people with solid conservative principles. It was also a more diverse group, by gender, ethnic background, and education, than those appointed by any previous Republican president.

Of the almost four hundred federal judges Reagan nominated—more than any other president—only a few had any trouble being confirmed by the Senate. Overall, they were high-quality selections. According to the American Bar Association's ratings, a higher percentage of Reagan's appointees were "well qualified" or "exceptionally well qualified" than the judges chosen by the four preceding presidents (Carter, Ford, Nixon, and Johnson).

They were also more conservative than any group of judges in fifty years, and for this reason liberals were in an almost constant state of outrage at the Reagan judiciary. When first elected, the president hoped that his persuasive powers could produce constitutional amendments restoring prayer in the schools and reversing the *Roe v. Wade* abortion-rights ruling. Once he realized this was a futile quest, he never made a serious political effort on these issues. Instead, conservatives relied on Reagan's judges, growing in number every year, to accomplish their goals.

This is why some pro-life leaders objected to the 1981 appointment of Sandra Day O'Connor to the Supreme Court; they detected in her past record signs that she might be "soft" on abortion. They were vastly pleased, however, when Reagan elevated Justice William Rehnquist to be Chief Justice and chose as his replacement Antonin Scalia, the first Italian American on the Supreme Court.

The addition of Scalia to the Court and Rehnquist's promotion to Chief Justice in September 1986, along with the nomination of the several hundred lower court judges in the 1980s, reassured conservatives that a judicial revolution was underway. Indeed it was, led by the "conservative activism" of Scalia and Rehnquist. However, it could not have happened without Republican control of the U.S. Senate, which was in danger as the November midterm election approached.

The transformation of the courts, while important, was a slow incremental process, but Reagan's greatest single achievement of 1986 was the Tax

Reform Act. He had begun a high-visibility personal push for tax reform even before his sweeping reelection victory in November 1984. He agreed completely with his predecessor, Jimmy Carter, that the federal income tax code was "a disgrace to the human race." If the public was cynical about government in general, it was especially so about the federal tax code, which was enormously complicated and seemed enormously unfair. Although the top tax rate was 50 percent, some very profitable corporations and very wealthy individuals paid almost nothing.

Reagan would have preferred simply cutting taxes, but federal budget deficits were so high that he conceded that any savings from lower rates had to be made up by eliminating deductions and tax breaks. This would have the added benefit of simplifying the thousands of pages of the Internal Revenue Code, into whose many crevices were tucked special favors for all sorts of businesses—insurance companies, defense contractors, real estate developers, the petroleum industry, and countless others.

In January 1984, he ordered the Treasury Department to develop a fairer, simpler tax code that did not increase the overall tax burden. In the slow, deliberate way Washington often works, it took over two years to write, revise, and debate the plan. Reagan, as usual, knew few of the details but cared deeply about the basic idea. At one point, he saved the bill in the House by personally convincing reluctant Republicans to vote for it. His chief allies were Congressman Jack Kemp and Senator Robert Packwood, while on the Democratic side Congressman Dan Rostenkowski and Senator Bill Bradley took the lead—a thoroughly bipartisan team.

The bill also crossed ideological lines. Liberal Democrats wanted to close tax loopholes and abolish many deductions for corporations and high-income families. Supply-side Republicans wanted lower tax rates to encourage investment and economic growth. Neither could win without agreeing to what the other side wanted, and with Reagan's rhetorical help and quiet lobbying, they succeeded.

The Tax Reform Act of 1986 gave a 100 percent tax cut to 6 million of the lowest-income families; as Reagan had suggested, they were made entirely exempt from the federal income tax. The bottom tax bracket was raised from 11 to 15 percent, but the personal exemption and standard deduction were increased, and the 15 percent bracket was expanded to include millions of families who had been paying higher rates. For the middle class, there was a higher home mortgage interest deduction as well as the larger personal exemption, and for high-income taxpayers the top rate was cut from 50 percent down to 28 percent, although in return many tax shelters for the wealthy were abolished.

Overall, the combination of the 1981 and 1986 bills moved the federal income tax system in a more "progressive" direction. Internal Revenue

Service figures show that the top 1 percent of taxpayers, who had contributed 18 percent of the total income tax burden in Reagan's first year, paid 28 percent of the total in his last year. On the other end, the bottom half of taxpayers saw their share of total tax collections fall from 8 to 6 percent, not even counting the 6 million lowest-income families who paid no tax at all under the new law.

Perhaps the most surprising aspect of the 1986 Act is that it raised taxes on business in order to cut taxes on individuals by a total of $9 billion. This is not something one usually expects from a Republican president, especially one like Reagan, who believed that economic prosperity depended upon American business being profitable enough to create new jobs and pay higher wages.

In all, the Tax Reform Act of 1986 is generally described as the most important tax change since the income tax began in 1913. It was a victory for the strange alliance of liberal and "supply-side" conservative policy makers over the horde of lobbyists who patrol the corridors of the Capitol. The fullest study of the bill's passage concluded that Reagan was "the most important player" because his strong backing "for an effort once considered the bastion of liberals carried tremendous symbolic significance."[9]

As if to prove that fortune is a fickle bestower of benefits, this domestic triumph was followed by the apparent failure of the second Reagan-Gorbachev summit in October 1986. The new Soviet leader had decreed a new foreign policy that year, based on diplomacy rather than military intimidation. More fundamentally, he announced an end to the confrontation between "socialism" (i.e., Communism) and capitalism that Marx and Lenin had declared an inevitable theme of history.

Despite the new mood, Soviet and American negotiators had made little headway since the Geneva summit in coming to an agreement on nuclear arms. As before, the sticking point was Reagan's insistence on the Strategic Defensive Initiative and Gorbachev's equal insistence on stopping it. Both sides hoped that a new October summit in Reykjavik, Iceland, could break the ice, so to speak.

Gorbachev brought a fistful of arms-control ideas. He accepted Reagan's previous suggestion of a 50 percent cut in nuclear missiles, but now included bombers and submarine-launched missiles. He added a total elimination of each side's intermediate- and short-range missiles in Europe. Trying his best to bring Reagan around to these massive nuclear cuts, which would leave Western Europe "under the gun" of the Soviet conventional superiority in troops, tanks, artillery, and planes, Gorbachev even offered a concession on SDI. He would not oppose U.S. research in laboratory experiments so long as there was no work beyond that.

U.S. negotiators were enthusiastic about these proposals, at least as a starting point. Reagan himself still clung to Star Wars as a way to make nuclear weapons obsolete, pointing out that the USSR had been carrying on SDI research for years. There was a vast difference, however, between the Soviets' ground-based missile defense and Reagan's hopes for a space-based system, which many even in his own administration insisted was a hopeless fantasy. He once again offered to share any technology that the United States developed, but Gorbachev simply did not believe him.

On the second day the negotiating teams drew closer and closer to a world-changing agreement: continuing the Anti-Ballistic Missile Treaty, eliminating all strategic nuclear weapons, removing all intermediate-range missiles in Europe, and—to assuage NATO fears—a huge cut in the Warsaw Pact conventional forces. But it all depended on Reagan abandoning the Strategic Defense Initiative. Reagan asked: if the Soviets were willing to eliminate nuclear weapons, why did they fear a defense against them? Gorbachev asked: if nuclear weapons were going to be eliminated, why did the United States need a defense against them?

Neither could answer the other's objection, and on this rock the summit foundered. As the two grim leaders marched out, Gorbachev plaintively said, "I don't know what else I could have done," to which a tight-lipped Reagan replied, "you could have said 'yes.'" Nevertheless, Gorbachev insisted that merely by being willing to discuss seriously the end of nuclear weapons, "this is the beginning of the end of the Cold War."[10]

As frustrating as it was, the summit was not Reagan's only October disappointment. As he had feared since the previous year, Congress was determined to enact powerful economic sanctions against South Africa, despite his threatened veto. Led by the Congressional Black Caucus, but with major Republican support, the Anti-Apartheid Act of 1986 passed both houses by a lopsided vote. The law forbade all American trade with or investment in South Africa, and even cut off air travel.

Reagan did veto the bill, complaining that harsh economic punishment would hurt most the very people it was designed to help: black workers in South Africa. He hoped that, at least, the members of his own party would support him, but many did not. By almost four-to-one margins in both houses, Congress overruled a presidential veto on a foreign-policy issue for the first time in nearly a century. Afterward, Reagan fell in line with good grace, warning the apartheid regime that the black majority "should not be kept waiting" for the creation of "a truly free society." He urged "South Africans of good will, black and white" to "seize the moment."

The third major event of that October had mixed results for Reagan. The good news was that a plan to solve the problem of illegal immigration passed Congress; the bad news was that the law did not work as its supporters had hoped. In the 1980s, as today, high levels of illegal immigration (largely from Mexico) became a major political issue. Businesses, especially agricultural employers, readily hired these undocumented immigrants as a source of low-wage labor.

A bipartisan attempt to solve the problem, the Simpson-Mazzoli bill, passed in October 1986 and received Reagan's signature a month later. In one of his regular radio broadcasts before he became president, he had wondered "about the illegal alien fuss. . . . Are those illegal tourists actually doing work our own people wont [sic] do?"[11] During the 1984 campaign, on the other hand, Reagan supported amnesty for illegal immigrants who had put down roots in the United States. Simpson-Mazzoli had three major provisions: improved border security to stop illegal crossings; penalties for employers who hired illegal workers; and an amnesty to legalize immigrants who had been in the United States since 1982, had no criminal record, and knew at least some English.

In the years after Reagan left the White House, it became obvious that the law had not worked; the border was still porous and employers could easily avoid penalties for hiring undocumented laborers. The only lasting result was to legalize some 3 million people who had entered the United States contrary to law. The flow of undocumented workers across the border continued and even increased; by early the next century there were more than 10 million immigrants living illegally in the United States.

If Reagan thought October was a "down" month, it was positively cheery compared to November. The midterm election results ended six years of Republican control in the Senate. It would have been a miracle if some Republican senators had not lost in 1986, especially those swept into office on the Reagan tide in 1980. Furthermore, the tendency of the president's party to lose seats in the off-year election of a second term had become a fixture of American political history: the "sixth-year curse." Reagan dutifully toured the country asking voters to strengthen his hold on Congress, but presidents can only rarely transfer their personal popularity to other candidates when the president is not on the ballot himself.

Even though Reagan remained personally popular, voters confirmed on election day that the Democrats were still the normal majority party in the United States, as they had been for fifty years. Republicans lost six of the seats they had newly won in 1980 and two more besides. The Senate went from 53–47 Republican to a 55–45 Democratic majority. Results for the House of Representatives were similar; Democrats solidified their majority, gaining five additional seats. They had a 6-million-vote margin (55 to 45 percent) in the nationwide congressional vote and held a majority of House seats in every one of the ten largest states.

The real bombshell fell just after the election, when the embarrassing news of Iran-Contra became public. By early 1986, the NSC duo of Poindexter and Oliver North, with CIA cooperation, was operating with Reagan's full approval to sell American weapons directly to Iran. By occasionally releasing a hostage and then seizing another, Hezbollah militants kept their Iranian sponsor supplied with American weapons for the war against Iraq. In the meantime, Chief of Staff Donald Regan was passively allowing the affair to careen recklessly along a path that was bound to end in a tangle of wrecked reputations and damaged diplomacy.

More TOW missiles were flown to Iran in February and May, and North tried to secure freedom for all the hostages at once. When that ploy failed, Reagan recorded his "heartbreaking disappointment."[12] He was even willing to try a military rescue, but no one could pin down the exact location, so he continued to approve sending the weapons. As the weeks went by, North and his associates increasingly operated without regard for even the tenuous guidance from Poindexter.

Hezbollah released another hostage in July but kidnapped two more in September and another the next month. No one has been able to explain why Reagan did not realize that his payoffs to the kidnappers were simply producing more kidnappings to replenish the "bank balance" of hostages each time one was released. Ironically, in late August he had signed a new antiterrorism law banning military sales to Iran, even as Poindexter, Casey, and North tried to keep the arms flowing as long as they could.

By the summer of 1986, it was no longer possible to hope that the Khomeini regime or a mythical "moderate" successor might again become a U.S. ally against the Soviet Union. Freeing an occasional hostage, making a profit for North's friends, and sending money to the contras were the remaining goals of the operation. Unfortunately for the perpetrators, others in the administration gradually became aware of their shenanigans. What made North's illegal diversion of money to the contras all the more foolish is that Congress had actually reversed the Boland amendment and approved military aid for the rebels, to begin in October.

There was one last spasm of missiles to Iran, and one more released hostage, before stories broke in the American media in November, revealing the entire operation. Congress was in an uproar, reporters were out for blood, and the voters were angry. Reagan briefed the congressional leadership and then spoke to the nation, stressing the strategic importance of Iran, minimizing the arms shipments, and claiming that there was no trade of "arms for hostages." Neither audience accepted his explanation.

In fact, a huge majority of Americans opposed sending arms to Iran for any purpose, whether strategic or for hostages. Barely one in seven believed the president's story. For the first time, Reagan's "nuclear weapon"—taking his case directly to the people—had proven a dud. His fundamental problem was that he accepted what his lying subordinates told him and passed those lies on to the public, undermining his own credibility.

A news conference later in November went no better. Again, because he had received false and incomplete information from those responsible, his answers to media questions were often erroneous. He would not admit that it was a mistake to allow the operation to proceed and, as politicians often do when backed into a corner, he blamed the media exposure for ruining his hostage-release plan.

Reagan was concerned enough to have Attorney General Meese launch an internal investigation, but meanwhile, Casey and Poindexter were telling lies to a congressional committee, and North was busily shredding stacks of incriminating documents. When Meese reported the truth, including North's largesse to the contras, the president was stunned, but he still inexplicably thought the colonel was a hero and cursed the media.

Nevertheless, Poindexter and North had to go, and Casey would have followed them had he not been felled by a fatal illness. Trying to recover his footing, Reagan appointed an investigating board including Republican Senator John Tower and former Democratic Senator Edmund Muskie, but nothing could save his approval rating from the greatest one-month collapse in the fifty-year history of opinion polling. Those around him actually began to worry about the possibility of impeachment.

The arms-for-hostages operation was foolish, diplomatically damaging, and violated Reagan's own policy of not negotiating with terrorists, but the diversion of money to the contras was worse. It was positively illegal, and if Reagan had approved it or even knew of it, his presidency would be finished either by resignation or by impeachment. No one knows for sure, even now, "what the president knew and when did he know it?" but it seems most likely that Reagan was not told of the plan for contra funding, or if he had been he soon forgot. This was not at all unusual for him. As far back as the governorship, if he was interested in a subject he could absorb detailed briefings; if he was not, he made no mental effort to retain even important information.

Throughout the winter of 1986–1987, the situation worsened. Congress, the media, and the public all wanted to know the truth, and Reagan wanted them to know the truth. He was convinced that shipping arms to Iran in return for Iranian help in getting Hezbollah to release hostages did not violate his "no negotiation" rule, but no one believed him. He was also convinced that he had not known of or approved the illegal funds for the contras, but most people were not sure whether to believe that either. It was a frustrating time for all.

By February 1987, however, the clouds began to clear. The Tower commission made its report, roundly criticizing Reagan's lax—almost nonexistent—management style but finding no evidence of his culpability in illegal activity. In the meantime, there was more house cleaning. Donald Regan gave way to Senator Howard Baker as Chief of Staff, and Poindexter was of course replaced as National Security Advisor.

In March, Reagan spoke to the nation, admitting full responsibility for the scandal and accepting both the complaints and the recommendations of the Tower commission. He was also able to report that he had installed a new team at the White House. On the central issue, however, he was still stubborn: "I told the American people I did not trade arms for hostages. My heart and my best intentions still tell me that's true, but the facts and the evidence tell me it is not." Or, as Chico Marx might have said, "who am I going to believe—me or my own eyes?"

After the speech, Reagan's presidency was at last on the mend. Poll ratings improved and public attention shifted from the dark shadow of Iran-Contra to the increasingly bright hopes of easing superpower tensions. Still, Iran-Contra lingered in the background. A three-judge panel chose Lawrence Walsh as special prosecutor to investigate everything. He devoted six years to the effort, spent over $40 million, and ultimately concluded that, while numerous people broke the law, there was no evidence that Reagan approved or knew of the illegal diversion of money to the contras. Had he known, it would have been an impeachable crime.

By the spring, it was a relief for the president to get back to the normal travails of office. With neither side of Capitol Hill in friendly hands after the 1986 election, he had totally lost control of the legislative agenda for the last two years of his term. One result was that his veto threat became less feared. In his first six years he vetoed thirty bills, of which six were passed over his veto, but only one of major consequence—the South Africa sanctions, which had broad bipartisan support.

After the Democratic gains in November 1986, Reagan was somewhat more reluctant to use the veto pen, rejecting only eight bills in his final two years. However, the only two vetoes of real importance—a water quality act and a public works program—were both overridden, with a number of Republicans abandoning the president to join the Democratic majority. Both of these rebuffs occurred in early 1987, when Iran-Contra had weakened Reagan's hold on public opinion, so that he could not appeal to the country over the head of Congress.

Reagan seized the chance to make positive news again when he went to Europe in May for the G7 economic summit. The meeting itself was low key; the real news was a presidential visit to Berlin for the most famous words of his career. Standing at the Brandenburg Gate with the Wall as his background, Reagan said that American presidents come to Berlin "because it's our duty to speak, in this place, of freedom" and of the insult to freedom symbolized by "this scar of a wall." He rejoiced to "find in Berlin a message of hope, . . . a message of triumph."

He contrasted the prosperity of the West with the poverty of the East: "in the Communist world, we see failure. . . . Even today, the Soviet Union still cannot feed itself." Drawing upon his conversations with Gorbachev, he was bold to hope that "the Soviets themselves may . . . be coming to understand the importance of freedom. . . . Are these the beginnings of profound changes in the Soviet state?" And then, the words that resonated round the world. "There is one sign the Soviets can make that . . . would advance dramatically the cause of freedom and peace. . . . Mr. Gorbachev, open this gate! Mr. Gorbachev, tear—down—this—wall!"

And the Wall came down. Not right away, of course, and hardly by his efforts alone. An edifice as vast as the Soviet empire, with seventy years of inertia propping it up, was not easily toppled, even by words as sharp and powerful as Reagan's at the Wall. But soon enough, his hammer-blow rhetoric at the Brandenburg Gate found its echo two years later in the actual hammers of jubilant Germans who, from both sides of the Wall, literally knocked it apart.

The easing of Cold War tensions helped Reagan's reputation recover from the catastrophe of Iran-Contra, and during his second term, it was abundantly clear that the twin economic disasters of recession and inflation had given way to a long-term economic expansion. A new disaster was building, however—a public health crisis in the form of the AIDS epidemic. Acquired Immune Deficiency Syndrome had barely been heard of in 1980, but it spread rapidly, chiefly through the urban homosexual communities and drug addicts by way of unprotected sex and reuse of contaminated needles. One of the most persistent criticisms of Reagan's presidential performance is that he seemed not to care about the AIDS crisis.

The facts reveal a more complicated picture. In the last year of Carter's presidency, the government spent barely $40 million on AIDS; in the last year of Reagan's, AIDS funding was $1.6 billion, nearly forty times as much. In 1983, his Secretary of Health and Human Services thanked the gay community for spreading information about AIDS; in 1985 and again in 1987, Reagan himself proclaimed the disease a top public-health priority. In 1988, he issued the first-ever ban on discrimination against federal employees with AIDS. A prominent gay writer on AIDS issues concluded that there was "little reason to believe that a different course of action by Reagan would have significantly altered the scientific state of knowledge" leading toward a cure or better treatment for AIDS victims.[13]

Why, then does Ronald Reagan still receive harsh criticism on this issue? There appear to be three reasons. First is his reluctance to take the lead, as president, in fighting this threat as he fought the economic threat and the Soviet danger. It was not until 1987, after much urging from the public health community and pressure from his wife, that he made a major public address on AIDS. By waiting a half-dozen years, Reagan forfeited a chance to be a leader on the issue, even though he understood that AIDS was a terrible plague, sympathized with its victims, denounced discrimination against them, and spent billions on AIDS research.

Neglecting to put the force of his popularity and the authority of his office behind an AIDS campaign, however, had nothing to do with the disease itself. He never led a personal crusade against cancer or heart disease either, and those killed far more people every year than AIDS. It was simply that he focused his presidential energy on a few overriding issues—reviving the economy, cutting taxes, curbing inflation, rebuilding the military, and ending the Cold War. Everything else—AIDS and several dozen other very important problems—were consigned to the vague background of his mental horizon.

The AIDS speech itself, delivered in May 1987, could have been much stronger. He emphasized that AIDS victims should not be stigmatized and that no one could contract the disease from casual contact, but he did not repeat Surgeon General Everett Koop's plea for widespread use of condoms. Furthermore, Reagan's call for mandatory AIDS testing for federal prison inmates aroused opposition from civil liberties advocates.

The second great criticism of Reagan was that his administration contained people who were vehemently hostile to homosexuality and who sometimes actually mocked the victims of AIDS. One said that homosexuals, having declared war on nature, were suffering nature's retribution. These hardline social conservatives waged a persistent battle against Koop's advocacy of condoms, which they saw as encouraging deviant behavior. By not firing them, or even rebuking them, Reagan paid a price by seeming to share their sentiments. He was always reluctant, as governor and president, to face up to unpleasant situations with subordinates, but in this case inaction damaged his own reputation.

His third strike, in the minds of critics, was failing to take up the recommendations of his own federal commission on AIDS, appointed after his 1987 speech. The commission's report in mid-1988 demanded a multibillion-dollar "war on AIDS," the classification of HIV infection as a disability on the same legal basis as any other, better care for AIDS victims, and many other steps. Reagan gave a vague nod of approval to the commission's work but did nothing much to carry out its ideas. This was no different from his neglect of many other national issues that were subordinate, in his mind, to the few great projects of his presidency, but in this instance tens of thousands of lives were at stake.

If Reagan put too little of his presidential influence into facing the AIDS crisis, he put a great deal into one of his major goals: a more conservative federal judiciary. Democratic control of the Senate after 1986 made this more difficult, however. When a new Supreme Court vacancy occurred in 1987, Edward Kennedy of Massachusetts and Joseph Biden of Delaware organized their new Senate majority to fight Reagan.

The president nominated Robert Bork, one of the select few judges the American Bar Association ever ranked as "exceptionally well qualified." Professional qualifications were not the issue for Democrats; Bork's legal opinions were. Liberals especially worried that he might be the deciding vote to reverse the *Roe v. Wade* abortion decision, which he considered the product of judicial tyranny over state authority, and his criticism of civil rights legislation seemed to them far outside the mainstream.

Kennedy, Biden, and the liberal groups outside Congress organized an impressive campaign, one that Robert Bronner, the most impartial scholar of the debate, described as an utterly ruthless distortion of Bork's legal views, including outright lies that he wanted a return to racial segregation in the schools. Bork's supporters were unprepared for the assault and had no real strategy to win his confirmation, nor did the nominee himself impress senators or the public favorably in his committee hearing. By the end of the process, polls showed that a majority of Americans agreed with Bork's opponents that his legal views were unacceptable.[14] He lost by 58–42 in the Senate, an initial major victory in what was to become a decades-long ideological war by both sides against judges of the "wrong" views.

Reagan was further embarrassed when his next choice, Douglas Ginzberg, was found to have used marijuana with his students while a law professor. He withdrew after ten days. Finally, the president sent up the name of Anthony Kennedy, a mainstream conservative with no record on abortion, and he was unanimously confirmed early in 1988. Kennedy, along with the earlier appointments of Scalia, O'Connor, and Chief Justice Rehnquist, formed a conservative bloc on the Court, especially in preferring state rather than federal solutions to many issues. In this they certainly pleased the man who chose them.

However, the four were not mere clones manufactured in some conservative law factory. Kennedy and O'Connor were friendlier to the legal rights of homosexuals than were Rehnquist and Scalia. They also upheld the central idea of *Roe v. Wade*, much to the anguish of pro-life conservatives. Those who kept score as decisions came down in future years ranked Kennedy and O'Connor as more moderate, while Scalia and Rehnquist were considered more consistently conservative.

When the 1986 Reykjavik conference broke up over the SDI issue, Reagan predicted that the Soviets would come back to the table, and they did. During 1987, Gorbachev made a serious concession by dropping his precondition that the United States limit itself to laboratory-only research on SDI. He did this both because he, like Reagan, needed to show the "home folks" some negotiating progress and because, with a shrewd understanding of American politics, he saw that Congress was unlikely to fund expansive SDI development no matter what Reagan wanted.

Once this impediment was removed, negotiators worked out the details of an historic agreement on short- and intermediate-range nuclear weapons. The result was, again, a Soviet concession to Reagan's original "zero-zero" proposals of several years earlier. All U.S. and Soviet missiles with a range up to 3,000 miles would be removed from Europe and destroyed. The numbers were very lopsided, with nearly 1,800 Soviet missiles marked for elimination versus half that many on the American side. Since all the U.S. missiles had only one warhead, while some of the USSR's had several, the "warhead count" was even more favorable for the United States.

In December 1987, the two leaders met in Washington to sign the Intermediate Nuclear Forces Treaty and agreed to work toward further reductions. Matching Reagan at his own game, Gorbachev "worked the crowd" on walks in downtown Washington and was hailed in the press. Conservatives, including some of Reagan's old allies, were distressed; one dismissed Reagan as "a useful idiot for Soviet propaganda." A usually friendly columnist accused the president of "intellectual disarmament" and said, "December 8 will be remembered as the day the Cold War was lost."[15] Of all the times Ronald Reagan had been underestimated in his public career, that prediction must surely have been the most embarrassingly wrong. The Cold War certainly *was* lost, but not by the United States. In two years, the Berlin Wall was down and Eastern Europe was free. In four years, the Soviet Union itself had disappeared from the map of the world.

Still, the treaty did need ratification by the U.S. Senate. When debate began in May of 1988, it was clear that a great majority favored approval—as did the American people generally—but opponents tried repeatedly to derail the treaty. North Carolina Republican Jesse Helms led the opposition, but even foreign-policy "realists" like Nixon and Kissinger, along with Alexander Haig and Casper Weinberger, Reagan's former secretaries of State and Defense, joined the critics.

The major complaint was that Reagan had signed a treaty that would "destroy NATO" and make Western Europe defenseless against the vast Soviet supremacy in conventional military power. The president could not convince his conservative critics, but treaty supporters heavily outnumbered them, and a bipartisan 93–5 vote ratified the pact just in time for Reagan to fly to Moscow and seal the deal with Gorbachev.

This was a turning point in the Atomic Age. Before Reagan, the nuclear arsenals of the United States and the USSR were constantly increasing. His abhorrence of atomic war, translated into action by the INF treaty, turned the nuclear curve downward. After the treaty, Reaganites sourly noted that the nuclear freeze movement, which condemned the president in his first term, gave him not a word of praise when in his second term he achieved by diplomacy more than they ever had by marching and shouting.

Ratified treaty in hand, Reagan held his last meeting with Gorbachev in Moscow at the end of May. By now they knew each other's personality and tactics well and were personal friends despite still-wide disagreement over issues like SDI. Outside the Kremlin, a reporter asked if Reagan still thought the Soviet Union was an "evil empire." The president said, "No," that was "another time, another era."[16] It was, as he told his biographer, "a grand historical moment"—the unofficial end of the Cold War.[17]

The other highlight of his visit was a speech to students at Moscow State University. One of the skills required of a successful actor is the ability to form an emotional connection with his audience. As president, Ronald Reagan kept this requirement always in mind. Especially when speaking overseas, he made sure to insert in each address a few flattering references to local historical and cultural figures. In Germany, for instance, he quoted Heine and Schiller; to the British Parliament, Gladstone and Churchill; to the United Nations, former UN ambassador Eleanor Roosevelt and former secretary general Dag Hammarsjold.

Now, addressing the assembled students and the wider audience of the Soviet people and their leaders in Moscow, Reagan called up memories of Dostoyevsky, Pasternak, and Gogol. The one-time enemy of the Evil Empire now brought "a message of peace and good will and hope for a growing friendship" and of "the possibilities of tomorrow."

His hearers might have winced as Reagan celebrated the transition from the industrial economy to the "economy of the mind," of silicon chips and DNA mapping and fiber optics—a revolution that had left their country far behind the West. The key to the world of the future, he said, quoting the founder of their university, was "freedom of thought," and he hailed "the power of economic freedom spreading around the world," even to that other great Communist state, China.

Reagan spoke at great length about the various expressions of freedom in America: religious liberty, jury trials, independent judges, unions and the right to strike, political demonstrations. To anchor the message in terms his audience would embrace, he quoted Pasternak's belief that what has "raised man above the beast is . . . the irresistible power of unarmed truth."

"Just a few years ago," Reagan marveled, "few would have imagined the progress our two nations have made." He went out of his way to praise Gorbachev several times, both for the internal changes taking place in the Soviet Union and for reducing superpower tensions. He closed by congratulating the students on "living in one of the most exciting, hopeful times in Soviet history," when the rigidness of the past was giving way to a boundless future.

All in all, it was one of Reagan's most inspiring speeches. More importantly, he was preaching to the choir, both in his immediate audience and in the Kremlin. Gorbachev understood very well that the Soviet Union had to change. It had to reform economically and politically—*perestroika* and *glasnost*—or sink to the status of a second-class state. The truth could be denied no longer; there were not two superpowers upon the Earth. There was only one, and it was led by Ronald Reagan.

Around the world, signs of easing tensions and the ebbing of Soviet influence began to appear. In Nicaragua, the Sandinista government and the contras agreed to a cease fire, and two years later, in the first free and competitive election since the 1920s, voters rejected Daniel Ortega's Marxist government. In Afghanistan, determined local resistance and massive U.S. military aid had finally forced the invading Soviet soldiers to leave. In Ethiopia, even 17,000 Cuban troops could not put down uprisings against the Communist government, and by 1991 it collapsed.

With his foreign policy succeeding and the economy still booming, Reagan gradually began to unwind his presidency. His one remaining concern was that the next president be someone to his liking—his loyal vice president for eight years, George H. W. Bush.

After Walter Mondale's crushing loss in 1984, Democrats cast about for a candidate who could escape the deadly "New Deal liberal" label (which Reagan himself had abandoned three decades before). There were several possibilities, but none survived the 1988 primary season, and Democrats wound up nominating a liberal anyway: Massachusetts Governor Michael Dukakis.

Bush had always been the front-runner for the Republican nomination in 1988 and, after a brief early stumble, was nominated with no opposition. He started the fall campaign behind Dukakis, but the turning point came when a Bush strategist assembled focus groups of Dukakis supporters and told them about some of the Massachusetts governor's positions. He had vetoed a bill requiring the Pledge of Allegiance in public schools, called himself a "card-carrying member" of the American Civil Liberties Union, and gave a weekend pass to a life-sentence murderer who then brutalized a Maryland couple. The focus groups were stunned: "My God, he's a liberal!" Half of them abandoned Dukakis on the spot.

After that, the election was over. It was simply a matter of telling the voters at large that Dukakis was really another McGovern, another Mondale, another liberal. Bush, who was not nearly the eager, outgoing campaigner Reagan had been, won a clear but narrower victory, beating Dukakis by 8 percent compared to the 18 percent margin of the 1984 landslide.

Even with the presidential loss, Democrats kept control of Congress and most state governments. Their 8 percent lead in the congressional vote showed that after two terms being frustrated by Reagan's popularity, Democrats remained the majority party in America. Reagan had eroded, but not erased, the legacy of Depression and New Deal. Still, the country was safely confided to a successor whose judgment he trusted.

As Reagan prepared to leave office, Iran-Contra was still delivering delayed blows to his managerial reputation. Two of his national security advisors were convicted, along with Oliver North, in 1989 and early 1990. The only consolation was that wrongdoing was broadly bipartisan. In the same two years the Democratic Speaker of the House, Jim Wright, had to resign because of ethics violations; Democratic Senator Alan Cranston was formally reprimanded for his own ethics failures; and one of Reagan's most sneering critics among the Washington elite, Clark Clifford, was indicted for illegal activity. Still, these misdeeds hardly rose to the level of the two-year-long multimillion-dollar manipulations of Iran-Contra.

As one might imagine, Reagan made no reference to this scandal when he spoke to the nation for the last time as President in January 1989. Instead, he said, the "two things that I'm proudest of" were the economic boom that created 19 million new jobs, and "the recovery of our morale" and America's leading role in the world.

He was modest about being called "The Great Communicator." Although he "communicated great things, they didn't spring full bloom from my brow, they came from the heart of a great nation." Yet he had no modesty about what the "Reagan Revolution" had accomplished, saying that "we meant to change a nation, and instead, we changed the world."

More than anything else, the president dwelt upon the thawing of the Cold War, "a satisfying new closeness with the Soviet Union." He praised Gorbachev as a different kind of Communist: "he knows some of the things wrong with his society and is trying to fix them. We wish him well." Although optimistic, Reagan was still cautious, repeating his constant mantra of "trust but verify."

Much had changed, at home and in the world, since Reagan's first political address to a national audience: "The Speech" for Barry Goldwater in 1964. In those twenty-five years, the Soviet empire, which had then seemed so threatening, had begun to crumble from within and would collapse entirely before 1989 was over. But one thing had not changed: Reagan's view of America. To the outgoing president, "she's still a beacon, still a magnet for all who must have freedom, for all the pilgrims from all the lost places who are hurtling through the darkness, toward home."

It was just this aspect of Reagan's rhetoric that most frustrated his critics on the left. Did the man simply not understand that shame, not pride, was the appropriate emotion for every thoughtful American? The very continent itself was stolen from the innocent Indians. Millions of Africans had been torn from their homes, held for two and a half centuries as mere property, and kept down by racism ever since. And what of all the other groups left out of Reagan's America—women, Hispanics, homosexuals, wage workers, and the poor in general? To many liberals, the true history of America deserved humble *mea culpas*, not Ronald Reagan's congratulatory optimism.

But wallowing in self-abnegation has never been popular among ordinary Americans. They much preferred to think of themselves and their country as Reagan did. They were proud of a nation willing to sacrifice hundreds of thousands of lives to eradicate slavery and hundreds of thousands more to save the Old World twice from conquest. They were proud of standing guard during four decades of Cold War against an "evil empire" that might even now be stumbling toward its grave. One could almost see them nodding agreement in their millions as Reagan ended his farewell talk with the words "all in all, not bad. Not bad at all." He left office with the highest approval ratings of any president since the beginning of opinion polls five decades before.

In Reagan's last hours in the Oval Office, his National Security Advisor, Colin Powell, gave the usual daily briefing. It was a short one: "the world is quiet today, Mr. President." That afternoon, on the plane to California—Reagan's final trip on Air Force One—the regular people were there one last time: the scheduler, the doctor, the photographer, the advance man, the traveling media. Just one was absent—the military officer with the "football," the nuclear codes to launch an American missile strike if atomic war broke out. He was with the new president now.

Reagan had often said that his Cold War strategy was simply, "we win; they lose." Amazingly, that is just what happened. After four decades of superpower tension, higher and higher piles of nuclear weapons, 100,000 American soldiers dead in Korea and Vietnam, and a last spasm of new pro-Soviet regimes in Afghanistan, Ethiopia, Angola, and Nicaragua—the Cold War was ending on Ronald Reagan's simple terms.

For years the wise men of academia and the diplomatic corps had invested their egos and reputations in continuing detente, "peaceful coexistence," and Mutual Assured Destruction, assuming an indefinite future of endless Cold War. Now they were left in the dust by Ronald Reagan's naïve vision of a world free of nuclear terror and free of Soviet Communism. "We win; they lose."

NOTES

1. Wiesel quoted in Morris, *Dutch*, 526.
2. Cannon, *President Reagan*, 555.
3. Brinkley, ed., *Reagan Diaries*, 317, 320, 337, 356.
4. Reagan quoted in Morris, *Dutch*, 554.
5. Brinkley, ed., *Reagan Diaries*, 365–366.
6. Kuhn, *Ronald Reagan in Private*, 168.
7. Reagan quoted in Morris, *Dutch*, 569.
8. Morris, *Dutch*, 574.
9. Alan S. Birnbaum and Jeffrey H. Murray, *Showdown at Gucci Gulch: Lawmakers, Lobbyists, and the Unlikely Triumph of Tax Reform* (Westminster, MD: Random House, 1987), 286.
10. Gorbachev quoted in Morris, *Dutch*, 599.
11. Skinner, ed., *Reagan in His Own Hand*, 302.
12. Brinkley, ed., *Reagan Diaries*, 415.
13. *Bay Area Reporter*, June 24, 2004.
14. Ethan Bronner, *Battle for Justice: How the Bork Nomination Shook America* (New York: W.W. Norton, 1989).
15. Richard Reeves, *President Reagan: The Triumph of Imagination* (New York: Simon & Schuster, 2005), 446.
16. *Los Angeles Times*, June 1, 1988.
17. Reagan quoted in Cannon, *President Reagan*, 705.

CHAPTER 9

RONALD REAGAN'S LEGACY

"He's no Ronald Reagan!" Like a witch doctor's malediction, these words can shrivel the hopes of any Republican who seeks national office today. Anyone who, as governor forced through the highest tax increase in his state's history, signed the nation's most liberal abortion bill, and increased state spending even more than his Democratic predecessor, would have no future in the Republican party.

By that standard, Ronald Reagan himself was no Ronald Reagan. And then, as president, he browbeat conservative congressmen and senators into voting for major tax hikes, never in eight years had a balanced budget, increased the national debt more than all previous presidents combined, and gave amnesty to millions of illegal aliens. How is this man in any sense the great American conservative champion?

And yet he is—and perhaps deserves to be. One of his attractions for those on the political right is his rhetoric. From the mid-1960s on, the Great Communicator preached optimism, patriotism, and firm anti-Communism. After the trauma of Bull Connor's bulldogs, Vietnam, and Watergate, many liberals found these sentiments embarrassing, but conservatives continued to value them just as liberals like FDR, Truman, Hubert Humphrey, and Kennedy once did.

In the days of Trafalgar, Britons spoke of the "Nelson touch," and a perfect example of the "Reagan touch," persisting beyond his presidency, is his address to the 1992 Republican national convention. Empires, he said, had once been "defined by land mass, subjugated peoples, and military might," but America, alone in all of history, is "an empire of ideals. . . . of democracy, of free men and free markets." He brushed aside the faint of faith—by which he meant liberal Democrats—who thought that America's

glory was a "brief flash of time; . . . a burst of greatness too bright and brilliant to sustain." Not so, he said. "We were meant to be masters of destiny,
not victims of fate."

Just two years later, Reagan was diagnosed with Alzheimer's disease, the
same affliction that had killed his mother. In a remarkable public letter, he
told Americans of his illness to encourage greater knowledge of Alzheimer's
and "a clearer understanding of the individuals and families who are
affected by it."

When he wrote, he still felt fine and expected to do "the things I have
always done . . . to share life's journey with my beloved Nancy and my
family" and to "enjoy the great outdoors," but he knew that the progression
of his disease would slowly steal these things from him. In this last great
challenge of his life, he clung still to his strong religious faith and simple
patriotism: "When the Lord calls me home, . . . I will leave with the greatest
love for this country of ours and eternal optimism for its future."

The letter closed with two simple sentences. "I now begin the journey
that will lead me into the sunset of my life. I know that for America there
will always be a bright dawn ahead." To the end, it was classic Reagan. He
could see all too well the shadow of his own mortality slowly blotting out
his remaining years, but America—America's light was eternal.

The most prominent theme in the writings about Reagan as president,
whether from scholars, journalists, insiders, or opponents, is the emphasis on "revolution." In fact, that is the exact title of one book; others
include *The Reagan Revolution, The Conservative Counter-Revolution,*
and *What I Saw at the Revolution.* How much impact did Reagan actually
have on the size of government? Was there a Reagan Revolution, or did
he, like many other would-be reformers, find the system too entrenched,
the bureaucrats too intractable, and the public too demanding, to allow
brave promises to become reality? The answer depends upon what is
being measured.

Conservatives would say that his one great economic failing was the
explosion of the national debt by $1.3 trillion in eight years, although
this pales beside the recent trillion-dollar deficits in a single year. It is
true that Democrats, in command of the U.S. House for both of Reagan's
terms, were not going to allow major reductions in federal spending, but
Reagan never even submitted a balanced budget. Neither did he ever
veto a budget, despite having sufficient Republicans in Congress to sustain vetoes.

His reputation as the Tax Cut King is well deserved, at least in part. The
25 percent income-tax reduction in 1981 saved American families billions
of dollars, and the Tax Reform Act of 1986 gave 6 million lower-income
families a permanent 100 percent tax cut. Less noticed, however, is that

between these two years there were substantial tax increases, which all together took away one-third of the more-publicized tax reductions.

Another way to judge the size of government is to count the total number of employees. President Reagan cut almost 30,000 people from a civilian payroll that totaled 1.1 million. A 3 percent reduction seems quite tame, hardly fitting the image of a man who vowed to take an axe to the root of the federal bureaucracy. Yet his predecessor, Jimmy Carter, added over 50,000 to the federal payroll in just four years, and his Republican successor, George H. W. Bush, added another 100,000 in his four years. The only presidents since 1950 who actually reduced federal civilian employment were Reagan himself and Bill Clinton.

A different measure of government power is the degree to which it controls the private decisions of individuals and businesses. An abbreviated way to calculate this is to count the number of pages in the Federal Register, which contains the text of every proposed government regulation. The size of the Register crept gradually upward in the 1950s and 1960s until Jimmy Carter became president in 1977. Then one law and regulation after another poured forth upon the land. There was an average of 75,000 pages of new regulations in each of the Carter years, double the rate of Nixon's presidency and four times that of Kennedy and Johnson.

Here is where the Reagan Revolution had its most direct impact. With a Republican majority in the Senate for six of Reagan's eight years, conservatives heading many cabinet departments, and a president determined to slow the growth of government, the result was dramatic. The Federal Register, which reached 87,000 pages in Carter's last year, shrank to 50,000 pages by 1988—still huge, but a clear change of direction.

The only misfortune for conservatives is that the march toward more bureaucracy resumed as soon as Reagan left office. Of all the presidents after World War II, he was the only one who did not issue more rules and regulations than his predecessor. To the liberal mind, much of this was a terrible retreat from the federal responsibility to protect health, curb dishonesty, and promote equality. Reagan's environmental record, for instance, is often "exhibit number one" for his critics. A secretary of the interior and an EPA director had to resign in disgrace, and enforcement of the Clean Air and Clean Water Acts was substantially slowed.

Finally, one may measure government by the amount of its spending. The federal budget falls into three large categories: mandatory spending, defense spending, and nondefense discretionary spending. The first category includes Social Security, Medicare, Medicaid, and interest on the national debt, all of which are fixed by law and not subject to annual budget debates. The second is self-explanatory; Congress debates and votes on the defense budget every year.

The third category is everything else that is subject to annual approval. This is the part of the budget over which Congress and the president fight most of their ideological battles and expend most of their time in the annual budget debates, and it is what most people and politicians mean when they speak of "government spending." This pot of money was what Reagan targeted in nearly three decades of public rhetoric since the 1950s, and this is where his hope of shrinking government would live or die.

In the two pre-Reagan decades, the presidents from Kennedy through Carter increased nondefense discretionary spending in "real" terms (factoring out inflation) by 78 percent. In the twenty years after Reagan, the two Bush presidents and Bill Clinton increased spending in real dollars by 86 percent. By contrast, nondefense discretionary spending in the Reagan years *fell* by 30 percent. In short, Reagan was the only president in a fifty-year period who was able, not merely to slow, but actually to reverse the rising tide of federal discretionary spending. Conservatives praise this achievement and treasure it in future memory. For liberals, it was a disgraceful abandonment of government's duty to meet public needs.

So, whether there really was a Reagan Revolution depends on how one judges the issue. If "big government" is measured by discretionary domestic spending, then Reagan temporarily reversed the growth of government in his eight years. He also reduced the number of bureaucrats and the number of regulations. However, none of these achievements (to conservatives) or deficiencies (to liberals) outlasted Reagan himself. The tax cuts, however, have been, for the most part, permanent. This has saved American families untold billions of dollars. On the other hand, because federal spending has risen faster than revenues, the ballooning national debt has also become permanent.

Reagan's goal of shrinking government may be, for conservatives, a forever unattainable dream. If the purpose of a representative republic is to reflect and respond to the wishes of the governed, then why does the federal government keep growing when poll takers report that there are twice as many conservatives as liberals in the American electorate? For several decades past, surveys of public opinion have shown that 40 percent of voters call themselves conservative, 40 percent are moderates, and only 20 percent say they are liberals. These figures have remained remarkably steady from the pre-Reagan years right through the "Age of Obama."

Political scientists say that these numbers are misleading; the American voter is "philosophically conservative" but "operationally liberal." For instance, majorities of the people will say that they prefer to cut federal spending rather than raise taxes, but they oppose cutting programs that benefit them. Unless the people at large change their minds about this, Reagan will have provided only a brief interruption in the long-term growth of federal power and spending.

When one looks beyond government to the entire American economy, Reagan's impact is more pronounced. Inflation in the 1970s was the highest of any decade in the twentieth century; the dollar was losing value by 14 percent every year. When Reagan left office in 1988, inflation had been cut to 4 percent. Even more impressive, the "wringing-out" of inflationary pressures (painful though it was to those who lived through the recession of 1982) and Reagan's legacy of relatively restrained spending and fiscal policies, have kept inflation low for nearly a generation.

Since the 1980s, prices have risen only 2.6 percent yearly, the smallest figure since the Great Depression. The American standard of living would be far worse than it is today had Reagan allowed the runaway inflation he inherited to continue unchecked. Almost as impressive, the economic growth that began under Reagan in 1982 lasted for almost one hundred months and created 21 million new jobs. If one discounts the brief recession of 1990, the "Reagan economy" grew almost continually for two decades.

Throughout Reagan's eight years, liberals issued almost daily accusations that he was callously indifferent to the plight of poor Americans, that saving taxpayer dollars meant more to him than salvaging the lives of the unfortunate. It might come as a surprise to learn that the share of the population living in poverty, which rose by 21 percent during Carter's four years, shrank by 9 percent during Reagan's tenure. For women, the poverty rate rose 22 percent under Carter and dropped 9 percent under Reagan. The rate of poverty among blacks grew 9 percent while Carter was president and dropped 10 percent in the Reagan years.

If one measures prosperity by income, the same conclusion emerges. Americans' per capita income rose by 1.7 percent in each year of Carter's presidency and 2.3 percent in each year of Reagan's—more than one-third faster. Overall, the average individual's income gained 19 percent in Reagan's eight years. The result was even more impressive for African Americans (a 21 percent increase) and women (a 27 percent increase), a much better result for both groups than in President Carter's administration. In the quarter-century since 1988, per capita income for all groups has risen much more slowly than it did during Reagan's tenure.

Public policy aside, conservatives also celebrate Reagan for reviving the fortunes of the Republican Party. For eighty years, poll takers have surveyed the partisan affiliation of American voters. Not surprisingly, the powerful impact of the Depression and Franklin Roosevelt's leadership in hard times and world war produced an electorate with more Democrats than Republicans for that entire period.

Only once in the three decades before Reagan did the Democrats have less than a 10 percent lead over Republicans. In the three decades since Reagan, only once did the Democrats have *more* than a 10 percent advantage. From 1950 through 1980, the average Democratic margin was 18 percent; since 1980 the average has been only 5 percent and occasionally the parties are tied. From 1950 to 1980, Democrats controlled the U.S. House of Representatives all but once, with an average majority of eighty seats; since 1980 the average Democratic majority has been only twenty-eight, and half the time there has actually been a Republican majority in the House.

Had Reagan's presidency actually made the Republican Party stronger, or had he merely enjoyed a personal popularity that did not bind voters more closely to his party? The figures above would seem quite definite. However, even before 1980, Republicans had been slowly gaining on the Democrats in the battle for voter loyalty. Barry Goldwater's catastrophic loss to Lyndon Johnson in 1964 had left the two-party system badly unbalanced. Sixty percent of voters identified with the Democratic Party; only 30 percent were Republicans.

Over the next decade and a half, the gap had gradually closed year by year, and by 1980 a two-to-one Democratic margin had been reduced to 14 percent. Perhaps the further narrowing of the partisan gap after 1988 was merely a continuation of the steady progress that had already been occurring ever since 1964, and Reagan's presidency was merely a coincidental companion of future Republican gains rather than their cause.

Reagan's greatest achievement by far, all conservatives would agree, is the successful—indeed, victorious—end of the Cold War. From the date of his demand at the Brandenburg Gate to "tear down this wall," it was barely a year before the INF treaty and the withdrawal of Soviet troops from Afghanistan marked the effective end of superpower enmity in 1988.

Before the end of 1989, Reagan's first year out of office, grassroots upheavals swept the Soviet satellites. From Poland through Germany, Czechoslovakia, and Hungary down to Romania and Bulgaria, the people spoke. They came into the streets by the hundreds, then by thousands and tens of thousands—workers, housewives, teachers, students. They stared an empire in the face and made it blink. It was a Rising of the Nations, the like of which had not been seen since Europe cast off the yoke of Bonaparte almost two centuries before.

The Wall came down, and not only in Berlin but all along the Iron Curtain. The barbed wire was rolled up, the machine guns removed, and the iron grip that had clutched all of Eastern Europe since 1945 was finally loosened. Before two more years had passed, the Soviet Union itself would be dissolved, the Communist party outlawed, and Gorbachev retired along with the nation he had led.

In his ancient funeral oration, Pericles said, "famous men have the whole world as their memorial." To his admirers, Ronald Reagan's memorial is Berlin free of its ugly wall, Eastern Europe free of Russian troops, and humanity free of its nuclear nightmare. If not quite Pericles's "whole world," they believe it is surely memorial enough.

Perhaps most striking, nowhere on the map of the globe today can the words "Soviet Union" be found. An empire that had sprawled across Eurasia from the Baltic to the Pacific vanished, crumpled up by its now free peoples and tossed into "the dustbin of history" just as Reagan had predicted.

Reagan's speech writer Peggy Noonan found in Stephen Vincent Benet's poem of John Brown, words that to her described the end of the Cold War:

> Sometimes there comes a crack in time itself. Sometimes an image that has stood so long it seems implanted as the polar star, is moved against an unfathomed force that suddenly will not have it any more. That force exists and moves, and when it moves it will employ a hard and actual stone to batter into bits an actual wall and change the actual scheme of things.[1]

For conservatives like Noonan, Ronald Reagan was that stone. His words and actions brought down not only an actual wall, but the empire that had built the wall. By refusing to accept four decades of Cold War and nuclear fear, he changed the actual scheme of things beyond all imagining. When Reagan died in 2004, his supporters saw the event as Edwin Markham did Lincoln's death in his poem, *Abraham Lincoln, Man of the People*: "as when a kingly cedar . . . goes down with a great shout upon the hills, and leaves a lonesome place against the sky."

Of course many thought otherwise about Reagan. In the words of one liberal critic, he spent his eight years "sleepwalking through history," not making history. Those who believe that government should expand its power, raise taxes, and increase spending to address the ills of the nation disagreed strongly with the picture drawn by Reagan's friends. To Tip O'Neill, the liberal Speaker of the House, Reagan was the worst president ever, and the AIDS activist Larry Kramer thought, "Reagan was just dreadful." Ronnie Dugger, publisher of the liberal *Texas Observer*, wrote an entire book, *On Reagan*, calling him a "hard-line right-wing ideologue" whose weapons were "selfishness and negativism."[2]

In addition to the general anti-Reagan critics, there are those who deny him any praise for the end of the Cold War and the disappearance of the Soviet Union. And how could they not? To give Reagan credit would be to admit that a witless actor's simpleminded view of the Cold War—"we win, they lose"—had, like the sword of Alexander, struck to the root of the thing while they stood baffled before the Gordian Knot of Mutual Assured Destruction, muttering the charmed words "detente" and "coexistence."

It is perfectly understandable. They had built their reputations on the assumption that the Soviet Union was here to stay. Hence, the only sensible, the only sane, policy was to avoid irritating the Russian Bear. Reagan took an axe to that theory and left it scattered in splinters and its acolytes bereft of a holy script.

Still, Mutual Assured Destruction *had* prevented a major war for over forty years since 1945, the longest period of peace between great powers in modern history. Reagan's great hope, SDI, *was* seen by the Soviets as a destabilizing and dangerous threat to peace. His tough rhetoric during the first term *did* anger the Kremlin and delay a thawing of the Cold War, according to Anatoly Dobrynin, Soviet ambassador to the United States.

Some said that Reagan was simply lucky. At a very fundamental level, there is some truth in this. If, growing up, he had been exactly the same person but black, he would never have had the opportunities that came his way in radio and Hollywood to guide him toward his political career. If he had been female, again he would have been denied the same chances starting out. He *was* lucky to be born white, male, and American. But millions had the same luck, and none of them became the man who reshaped the conservative movement, revived the American economy and the American spirit, slowed the growth of government, and pushed the tottering Soviet empire toward its final collapse.

Nancy Reagan had hoped that her husband would win the Nobel Peace Prize for negotiating the first treaty ever to eliminate an entire class of nuclear weapons and helping to end the Cold War. For a woman reputedly so coldly realistic, it was a remarkably naïve dream. The Peace Prize is awarded by a committee of the Norwegian Parliament, dominated in 1990, as for most of the postwar period, by the left-wing Labour (Socialist) Party.

Reagan's wife might well think that he was the primary force behind the events of 1988 and 1989. American conservatives agreed with her. So did many victims of the Gulag and leaders of the liberated nations of Eastern Europe. All their applause could not outweigh the belief of those who thought that Reagan deserved no more than a brief nod for these world-changing events. How could this nitwit have done something that for a half-century had eluded the best efforts of the best minds in world politics? The Peace Prize in 1990 went instead to a man for whom many American liberals and European Socialists had far more respect than they did for Ronald Reagan—Mikhail Gorbachev, General Secretary of the Communist Party of the Soviet Union.

And who can say that Gorbachev did not deserve it? Even if one claims that Ronald Reagan "won" the Cold War, it was Gorbachev who allowed his own country to lose it without a bloodbath. When the people of Eastern Europe rose up in 1989, Gorbachev told the grey-souled apparatchiks who ruled the satellite nations that this time, unlike Hungary in 1956 or Prague in 1968, there would be no tanks, no bayonets to save them.

After the demise of the "evil empire," it became fashionable to say that the Soviet Union had died of internal dry rot, not pressure from outside. Hence, its inevitable collapse had nothing to do with Reagan. This view of the USSR was not one that liberals expounded before 1989, however. When Reagan was claiming in the early 1980s that the last pages of Soviet history were "even now being written," the historian Arthur Schlesinger scoffed that it was wishful thinking to assume "the Soviet Union is on the verge of economic and social collapse." The famed Keynesian economist John Kenneth Galbraith actually said that the Soviet system was outdoing the economies of the West.[3] It was only in the late 1980s and after that Reagan's Cold War critics began to argue that the USSR died of old age and not because he gave it a push down the stairs.

This is not the view of leaders in the newly free nations of Eastern Europe. Lech Walesa, Poland's first post-Communist president, said that "Reagan is irreplaceable. Without him there would have been no victory [over Communism]." Mart Laar, Estonia's prime minister in the 1990s, expressed his own debt to Reagan: "Without this man, I would be somewhere in Siberia in chains. . . . Ronald Reagan was a man who changed world history."[4]

Many of the Soviet leaders themselves are convinced that Reagan was the one who administered the *coup de grâce*. Gorbachev's foreign policy spokesman, Gennady Gerasimov, said that Reagan was the "gravedigger of the Soviet Union and the spade that he used to prepare this grave was SDI." According to Foreign Secretary Eduard Shevardnadze, Reagan knew that the USSR was spending far more on the military than its creaky economy could afford, so "along comes Reagan and says: 'I am moving more chips on the table. You will have to match me if you want to stay in this race.'"[5] Genrikh Trofimenko, head of the Institute for the U.S.A. and Canada, bluntly admitted that "it was Ronald Reagan who won the Cold War and brought it to an end" by raising "the cost of potential victory for Moscow so high that it collapsed from the strain."[6]

Reagan's liberal critics will forever argue their point with American conservatives. It is more difficult for them to convince those who were actually on the ground in Eastern Europe like Walesa, in the Soviet government like Gerasimov, and in the Gulag, like Natan Sharansky. They will find it hardest of all, perhaps, to argue with the statues of Ronald Reagan that stand in the cities of liberated Eastern Europe and with the people who erected them, who, to this day, thank Reagan for their freedom. One pundit who has changed his mind is Garry Wills, who made great fun of the president in

Reagan's America, published in 1987. In the 2000 edition he now says "part of Reagan's legacy is what we do not see now. We see no Berlin Wall. He said, 'Tear down this wall,' and it was done. We see no Iron Curtain. In fact, we see no Soviet Union. He called it an Evil Empire, and it evaporated over-night."[7] An exaggeration, but one gets his point.

As one measure of how the world has been transformed, consider this story. In 1960, Nikita Khrushchev, ruler of the Soviet Union, came to New York for a United Nations meeting. In a long tirade denouncing America, his Cold War enemy, he raised his hand and banged his shoe on the table. It was his boast that Communism was the wave of the future; he used to threaten that "we will bury you."

In 1999, four decades after his father's anti-American outburst, Nikita's son Sergei Khrushchev raised *his* hand and took the oath of allegiance as an American citizen. Reagan had told the students at Moscow State University that "anyone, from any corner of the world, can come to live in America and become an American." Now, Sergei Khrushchev had proved his point. A different world, indeed.

Even Reagan's most fervent supporters cannot claim that he alone produced this change, but all except his most bitter critics agree that he had something large to do with it. Whether Ronald Reagan's presidency produced more good or more ill has been debated since his first taking office, and that argument will surely continue as it does for all presidents. But few would disagree that Reagan's impact, both at home and abroad, was profound.

Perhaps Reagan himself, as usual, summed it up best in his last address from the White House: "Once you begin a great movement, there's no telling where it'll end. We meant to change a nation," he said, "and instead, we changed a world." And, for better or worse, so he had.

Notes

1. Stephen Vincent Benet, *John Brown's Body* (New York: Rinehart, 1954), 53.
2. Kramer quoted in Deborah Hart Strober and Gerald S. Strober, ed., *Reagan: The Man and His Presidency* (Boston: Houghton Mifflin, 1998), 136; Ronnie Dugger, *On Reagan; The Man and His Presidency* (New York: McGraw-Hill, 1983), ix–x.
3. Schlesinger and Galbraith quoted in *Memorial Services in the Congress of the United States and Tributes in Eulogy of Ronald Reagan, Late a President of the United States* (Washington: U.S. Government Printing Office, 2005), 165.
4. Walesa and Laar quoted in *Libertas*, v. 30 no. 1 (Spring, 2009).
5. Gennady Gerasimov and Shevardnadze quoted in *Memorial Services*, 203, 299.
6. Trofimenko quoted in Paul Kengor, *The Crusader: Ronald Reagan and the Fall of Communism* (New York: Harper Collins, 2006), 301.
7. Wills, *Reagan's America: Innocents at Home* (New York: Penguin Books, 2d ed., 2000), xv.

DOCUMENTS

"A Time for Choosing"
October 27, 1964

This speech for Barry Goldwater's presidential race in 1964 introduced Reagan to a national audience and made him overnight a conservative sensation. It contained the major themes that marked his rhetoric from then on: the dangers of "big government" and Soviet Communism, and the idea of America as a beacon of liberty in a desperate world.

I have spent most of my life as a Democrat. I recently have seen fit to follow another course. I believe that the issues confronting us cross party lines. . . . No nation in history has ever survived a tax burden that reached a third of its national income. Today, 37 cents out of every dollar earned in this country is the tax collector's share, and yet. . . . we haven't balanced our budget 28 out of the last 34 years. . . . And we've just had announced that the dollar of 1939 will now purchase 45 cents in its total value. . . .

We're at war with the most dangerous enemy that has ever faced mankind in his long climb from the swamp to the stars, and. . . . it's time we ask ourselves if we still know the freedoms that were intended for us by the Founding Fathers. . . . If we lose freedom here, there's no place to escape to. This is the last stand on earth.

And this idea that government is beholden to the people, that it has no other source of power except the sovereign people, is still the newest and the most unique idea in all the long history of man's relation to man.

This is the issue of this election: Whether we believe in our capacity for self-government or whether we abandon the American revolution and confess that a little intellectual elite in a far-distant capitol can plan our lives for us better than we can plan them ourselves.

You and I are told increasingly we have to choose between a left or right. Well, I'd like to suggest there is no such thing as a left or right. There is only an up or down—man's old dream, the ultimate in individual freedom consistent with law and order, or down to the ant heap of totalitarianism. And regardless of their sincerity, . . . those who would trade our freedom for security have embarked on this downward course.

We have so many people who can't see a fat man standing beside a thin one without coming to the conclusion the fat man got that way by taking advantage of the thin one. So they're going to solve all the problems of human misery through government and government planning. Well, now, if government planning and welfare had the answer—and they've had almost 30 years of it. . . . Shouldn't they be telling us about the decline each year in the number of people needing help? . . . .

No government ever voluntarily reduces itself in size. So governments' programs, once launched, never disappear. Actually, a government bureau is the nearest thing to eternal life we'll ever see on this earth. . . .

Norman Thomas, six-times candidate for President on the Socialist Party ticket, said, "If Barry Goldwater became President, he would stop the advance of socialism in the United States." I think that's exactly what he will do. . . .

Our natural, unalienable rights are now considered to be a dispensation of government, and freedom has never been so fragile, so close to slipping from our grasp as it is at this moment. . . .

Those who would trade our freedom for the soup kitchen of the welfare state have told us they have a utopian solution of peace without victory. . . . They say if we'll only avoid any direct confrontation with the enemy, he'll forget his evil ways and learn to love us. All who oppose them are indicted as warmongers. . . .

We cannot buy our security, our freedom from the threat of the bomb by committing an immorality so great as saying to a billion human beings now enslaved behind the Iron Curtain, "Give up your dreams of freedom because to save our own skins, we're willing to make a deal with your slave masters." . . . There's only one guaranteed way you can have peace—and you can have it in the next second—surrender. . . .

Their policy of accommodation is appeasement, and it gives no choice between peace and war, only between fight or surrender. If we continue to accommodate, continue to back and retreat, eventually we have to face the final demand—the ultimatum. . . . And therein lies the road to war. . . .

If nothing in life is worth dying for, . . . should Moses have told the children of Israel to live in slavery under the pharaohs? Should Christ have refused the cross? Should the patriots at Concord Bridge have thrown down their guns and refused to fire the shot heard 'round the world?. . . .

Where, then is the road to peace. . . .

You and I have the courage to say to our enemies, "There is a price we will not pay." There is a point beyond which they must not advance. . . .

You and I have a rendezvous with destiny. We'll preserve for our children this, the last best hope of man on earth, or we'll sentence them to take the last step into a thousand years of darkness.

SOURCE

Ronald Reagan, *Greatest Speeches of Ronald Reagan* (West Palm Beach, FL: NewsMax.com, 2001).

DOCUMENT **2**

ACCEPTING REPUBLICAN PRESIDENTIAL NOMINATION JULY 17, 1980

Having won nomination easily while President Carter was struggling against Edward Kennedy's strong challenge, Reagan used this speech to denounce the incumbent's record of inflation at home and weakness abroad, and he promised to stand firm against Soviet pressure. He asked Americans to "recapture our destiny" and then closed with an unprecedented moment of prayer.

We face a disintegrating economy, a weakened defense and an energy policy based on the sharing of scarcity.

The major issue of this campaign is the direct political, personal and moral responsibility of Democratic Party leadership . . . for this unprecedented calamity. . . . They say that the United States has had its day in the sun; that our nation has passed its zenith . . . that the future will be one of sacrifice and few opportunities.

My fellow citizens, I utterly reject that view. . . .

[B]ack in 1976, Mr. Carter said, "Trust me." And a lot of people did. Now, many of those people are out of work. Many have seen their savings eaten away by inflation.

Isn't it once again time to renew our compact of freedom; to pledge to each other all that is best in our lives; all that gives meaning to them—for the sake of this, our beloved and blessed land?

Together, let us make this a new beginning. . . .

[O]ur federal government is overgrown and overweight. Indeed, it is time for our government to go on a diet. Therefore, my first act as chief executive will be to impose an immediate and thorough freeze on federal hiring. . . .

Any program that represents a waste of money . . . must have that waste eliminated or the program must go. . . . Everything that can be run more effectively by state and local government we shall turn over to state and local government. . . .

The American people are carrying the heaviest peacetime tax burden in our nation's history. . . . I have long advocated a 30 percent reduction in income tax rates. . . .

America's defense strength is at its lowest ebb in a generation, while the Soviet Union is vastly outspending us in both strategic and conventional arms.

Our European allies, looking nervously at the growing menace from the East, turn to us for leadership and fail to find it.

And, incredibly more than 50 of our fellow Americans have been held captive for over eight months by a dictatorial foreign power that holds us up to ridicule before the world. . . .

Who does not feel a growing sense of unease as our allies, facing repeated instances of an amateurish and confused administration, reluctantly conclude that America is unwilling or unable to fulfill its obligations as the leader of the free world? . . .

No American should vote until he or she has asked, is the United States stronger and more respected now than it was three-and-a-half years ago? Is the world today a safer place in which to live? . . .

Four times in my lifetime America has gone to war, bleeding the lives of its young men into the sands of beachheads, the fields of Europe and the jungles and rice paddies of Asia. We know only too well that war comes not when the forces of freedom are strong, but when they are weak. It is then that tyrants are tempted. . . .

Of all the objectives we seek, first and foremost is the establishment of lasting world peace. We must always stand ready to negotiate in good faith . . . the United States has an obligation to its citizens and to the people of the world never to let those who would destroy freedom dictate the future course of human life on this planet. I would regard my election as proof that we have renewed our resolve to preserve world peace and freedom.

It is impossible to capture in words the splendor of this vast continent which God has granted as our portion of this creation. There are no words to express the extraordinary strength and character of this breed of people we call Americans.

Tom Paine . . . wrote—during the darkest days of the American Revolution—"We have it in our power to begin the world over again."

The time is now, my fellow Americans, to recapture our destiny, to take it into our own hands. . . .

Can we doubt that only a Divine Providence placed this land, this island of freedom, here as a refuge for all those people in the world who yearn to breathe freely. . . .

I'll confess that I've been a little afraid to suggest what I'm going to suggest—I'm more afraid not to—that we begin our crusade joined together in a moment of silent prayer.

God bless America.

SOURCE

Greatest Speeches of Ronald Reagan.

REAGAN'S FIRST INAUGURAL ADDRESS
JANUARY 20, 1981

Reagan conjured up the Founders' faith in individual freedom, limited government, and the American future, warning that "government is not the solution to our problem; government is the problem." In a world full of dangers, the most powerful force on Earth was "the moral courage of free men and women." He also suggested that Inauguration Day should be a day of prayer.

The orderly transfer of authority as called for in the Constitution routinely takes place, as it has for almost two centuries, and few of us stop to think how unique we really are. In the eyes of many in the world, this every-4-year ceremony we accept as normal is nothing less than a miracle.

. . . We suffer from the longest and one of the worst sustained inflations in our national history. . . .

Idle industries have cast workers into unemployment, human misery, and personal indignity. Those who do work are denied a fair return for their labor by a tax system which penalizes successful achievement. . . .

For decades we have piled deficit upon deficit, mortgaging our future and our children's future for the temporary convenience of the present. . . . In this present crisis, government is not the solution to our problem; government is the problem. . . .

[T]his administration's objective will be a healthy, vigorous, growing economy that provides equal opportunities for all Americans with no barriers born of bigotry or discrimination. . . . Ending inflation means freeing all Americans from the terror of runaway living costs. All must share in the productive work of this "new beginning," and all must share in the bounty of a revived economy. . . .

Our government has no power except that granted it by the people. It is time to check and reverse the growth of government, which shows signs of having grown beyond the consent of the governed.

It is my intention to curb the size and influence of the Federal establishment and to demand recognition of the distinction between the powers granted to the Federal Government and those reserved to the States or to the people. . . .

Government can and must provide opportunity, not smother it; foster productivity, not stifle it. . . .

[O]ur present troubles parallel and are proportionate to the intervention and intrusion in our lives that result from unnecessary and excessive growth of government. It is time for us to realize that we're too great a nation to limit ourselves to small dreams. We're not, as some would have us believe, doomed to an inevitable decline. . . .

We have every right to dream heroic dreams. Those who say that we're in a time when there are not heroes . . . just don't know where to look . . . .

How can we love our country and not love our countrymen; and loving them, reach out a hand when they fall, heal them when they're sick, and provide opportunity to make them self-sufficient so they will be equal in fact and not just in theory?

Can we solve the problems confronting us? Well, the answer is an unequivocal and emphatic "yes." . . .

I will propose removing the roadblocks that have slowed our economy and reduced productivity. . . . It is time to reawaken this industrial giant, to get government back within its means, and to lighten our punitive tax burden. . . .

I believe we, the Americans of today, are ready to act worthy of ourselves, ready to do what must be done to ensure happiness and liberty for ourselves, our children, and our children's children. . . . We will again be the exemplar of freedom and a beacon of hope for those who do not now have freedom. . . .

As for the enemies of freedom, those who are potential adversaries, they will be reminded that peace is the highest aspiration of the American people. We will negotiate for it, sacrifice for it; we will not surrender for it, now or ever. . . .

Above all, we must realize that no arsenal or no weapon in the arsenals of the world is so formidable as the will and moral courage of free men and women. . . .

I'm told that tens of thousands of prayer meetings are being held on this day, and for that I'm deeply grateful. We are a nation under God, and I believe God intended for us to be free. It would be fitting and good, I think, if on each Inaugural Day in future years it should be declared a day of prayer.

The crisis we are facing today . . . does require . . . our best effort and our willingness to believe in ourselves and to believe in our capacity to perform great deeds, to believe that together with God's help we can and will resolve the problems which now confront us.

And after all, why shouldn't we believe that? We are Americans.

SOURCE

Public Papers of the Presidents of the United States: Ronald Reagan (Washington, DC: U.S. Government Printing Office, 15 vols., 1982–1991).

"WESTMINSTER ADDRESS" TO BRITISH PARLIAMENT JUNE 8, 1982

Paying tribute to Winston Churchill's fight against Nazi tyranny, Reagan called on Britain and its NATO partners to stand firm in opposition to Soviet tyranny. In predicting that Communism would wind up on the "ash heap of history," he mocked Leon Trotsky's use of the phrase in 1917 to predict the worldwide triumph of Communism.

———————

Speaking for all Americans, I want to say how very much at home we feel in your house. Every American would, because this is . . . one of democracy's shrines. Here the rights of free people and the processes of representation have been debated and refined. . . .

[F]rom here I will go to Bonn and then Berlin, where there stands a grim symbol of power untamed. The Berlin Wall, that dreadful gray gash across the city, is in its third decade. It is the fitting signature of the regime that built it. . . . From Stettin on the Baltic to Varna on the Black Sea, the regimes planted by totalitarianism have had more than 30 years to establish their legitimacy. But none—not one regime—has yet been able to risk free elections. Regimes planted by bayonets do not take root. . . .

There are threats now to our freedom, indeed to our very existence, that other generations could never even have imagined. There is first the threat of global war. . . .

At the same time there is a threat posed to human freedom by the enormous power of the modern state. . . .

Must civilization perish in a hail of fiery atoms? Must freedom wither in a quiet, deadening accommodation with totalitarian evil? . . . .

This is precisely our mission today: to preserve freedom as well as peace. It may not be easy to see; but I believe we live now at a turning point.

In an ironic sense Karl Marx was right. We are witnessing today a great revolutionary crisis. . . . But the crisis is happening not in the free, non-Marxist West, but in the home of Marxist-Leninism, the Soviet Union. It is the Soviet Union that runs against the tide of history by denying human freedom and human dignity to its citizens. It also is in deep economic difficulty. . . .

[O]ne of the simple but overwhelming facts of our time is this: Of all the millions of refugees we've seen in the modern world, their flight is always away from, not toward the Communist world. Today on the NATO line, our military forces face east to prevent a possible invasion. On the other side of the line, the Soviet forces also face east to prevent their people from leaving.

[T]otalitarian rule has caused in mankind an uprising of the intellect and will . . . rejection of the arbitrary power of the state, the refusal to subordinate the rights of the individual to the superstate, the realization that collectivism stifles all the best human impulses. . . .

Around the world today, the democratic revolution is gathering new strength. . . . In the Communist world as well, man's instinctive desire for freedom and self-determination surfaces again and again. To be sure, there are grim reminders of how brutally the police state attempts to snuff out this quest for self-rule—1953 in East Germany, 1956 in Hungary, 1968 in Czechoslovakia, 1981 in Poland. But the struggle continues in Poland. And we know that there are even those who strive and suffer for freedom within the confines of the Soviet Union itself. . . .

[F]reedom is not the sole prerogative of a lucky few, but the inalienable and universal right of all human beings. So states the United Nations Universal Declaration of Human Rights. . . .

The objective I propose is . . . to foster the infrastructure of democracy, the system of a free press, unions, political parties, universities, which allows a people to choose their own way to develop their own culture. . . .

At the same time, we invite the Soviet Union to consider with us how the competition of ideas and values—which it is committed to support—can be conducted on a peaceful and reciprocal basis. . . .

What I am describing now is a plan and a hope for the long term—the march of freedom and democracy which will leave Marxism-Leninism on the ash-heap of history as it has left other tyrannies which stifle the freedom and muzzle the self-expression of the people. . . .

During the dark days of the Second World War, when this island was incandescent with courage, Winston Churchill exclaimed about Britain's adversaries, "What kind of a people do they think we are?" Well, Britain's adversaries found out what extraordinary people the British are. But all the democracies paid a terrible price for allowing the dictators to underestimate us. We dare not make that mistake again. So, let us ask ourselves, "What kind of people do we think we are?" And let us answer, "Free people, worthy of freedom and determined not only to remain so but to help others gain their freedom as well."

SOURCE

Public Papers of the Presidents of the United States: Ronald Reagan.

THE "EVIL EMPIRE" SPEECH
MARCH 8, 1983

The "evil empire" paragraphs were a small part—although the most remembered—of Reagan's speech to evangelicals, which mostly dealt with religious faith and social issues. His blunt characterization of the Soviet empire was denounced not only by the USSR but also by many in Europe and the United States as needlessly provocative, but to Reagan it was only the simple truth.

––––––––––

[F]reedom prospers only where the blessings of God are avidly sought and humbly accepted. The American experiment in democracy rests on this insight. Its discovery was the great triumph of our Founding Fathers, voiced by William Penn when he said, "If we will not be governed by God, we must be governed by tyrants."

Explaining the inalienable rights of men, Jefferson said, "The God who gave us life, gave us liberty at the same time." . . .

Only through your work and prayers and those of millions of others can we hope to survive this perilous century and keep alive this experiment in liberty—this last, best hope of man. . . .

When our Founding Fathers passed the First Amendment, they sought to protect churches from government interference. They never intended to construct a wall of hostility between government and the concept of religious belief itself. . . .

Last year, I sent the Congress a constitutional amendment to restore prayer to public schools. Already this session, there's growing bipartisan support for the amendment, and I am calling on the Congress to act speedily to pass it and to let our children pray.

[A] Supreme Court decision literally wiped off the books of 50 States statutes protecting the rights of unborn children. Abortion on demand now takes the lives of up to one and a half million unborn children a year. Human life legislation ending this tragedy will some day pass the Congress, and you and I must never rest until it does. . . .

Now, I'm sure that you must get discouraged at times, but you've done better than you know, perhaps. There's a great spiritual awakening in America, a renewal of the traditional values that have been the bedrock of America's goodness and greatness. . . .

There is sin and evil in the world, and we're enjoined by Scripture and the Lord Jesus to oppose it with all our might. Our nation, too, has a legacy of evil with which it must deal. The glory of this land has been its capacity for transcending the moral evils of our past. For example, the long struggle of minority citizens for equal rights, once a source of disunity and civil war, is now a point of pride for all Americans. We must never go back. There is no room for racism, anti-Semitism, or other forms of ethnic and racial hatred in this country. . . .

America has kept alight the torch of freedom, but not just for ourselves but for millions of others around the world. . . .

[A]s good Marxist-Leninists, the Soviet leaders have openly and publicly declared that the only morality they recognize is that which will further their cause, which is world revolution. . . .

[T]he refusal of many influential people to accept this elementary fact of Soviet doctrine illustrates an historical reluctance to see totalitarian powers for what they are. . . . This doesn't mean we should isolate ourselves and refuse to seek an understanding with them. . . .

At the same time, however, they must be made to understand we will never . . . give away our freedom. We will never abandon our belief in God. And we will never stop searching for a genuine peace. But we can assure none of these things America stands for through the so-called nuclear freeze solutions proposed by some. . . .

A freeze would reward the Soviet Union for its enormous and unparalleled military buildup. It would prevent the essential and long overdue modernization of United States and allied defenses. . . .

[L]et us pray for the salvation of all of those who live in that totalitarian darkness. . . . But . . . while they preach the supremacy of the state, declare its omnipotence over individual man, and predict its eventual domination of all peoples on the Earth, they are the focus of evil in the modern world.

Beware the temptation of pride—the temptation of blithely declaring yourselves above it all and label both sides equally at fault, to ignore the facts of history and the aggressive impulses of an evil empire, to simply call the arms race a giant misunderstanding and thereby remove yourself from the struggle between right and wrong and good and evil. . . .

I believe that communism is another sad, bizarre chapter in human history whose last pages even now are being written. I believe this because the source of our strength in the quest for human freedom is not material, but spiritual. And because it knows no limitation, it must terrify and ultimately triumph over those who would enslave their fellow man. . . .

SOURCE

Public Papers of the Presidents of the United States: Ronald Reagan.

REMARKS ON THE 40TH ANNIVERSARY OF D-DAY
JUNE 6, 1984

Reagan was at his best in celebrating the patriotism of American heroes, and he showed this in his short, powerful evocation of the dangerous assault on the German positions perched on a cliff at Pointe du Hoc. Among the assembled veterans and other spectators, there were few dry eyes when he finished his praise of "the boys of Pointe du Hoc . . . the men who took the cliffs."

We're here to mark that day in history when the Allied peoples joined in battle to reclaim this continent to liberty. For four long years, much of Europe had been under a terrible shadow. Free nations had fallen, Jews cried out in the camps—millions cried out for liberation. Europe was enslaved, and the world prayed for its rescue. Here in Normandy the rescue began. Here the Allies stood and fought against tyranny in a giant undertaking unparalleled in human history.

We stand on a lonely, windswept point on the northern shore of France. . . . Behind me is a memorial that symbolizes the Ranger daggers that were thrust into the top of these cliffs. And before me are the men who put them there.

These are the boys of Pointe du Hoc. These are the men who took the cliffs. These are the champions who helped free a continent. These are the heroes who helped end a war. . . .

The men of Normandy had faith that what they were doing was right, faith that they fought for all humanity, faith that a just God would grant them mercy on this beachhead or on the next. . . . You were here to liberate, not to conquer, and so you and those others did not doubt your cause. And you were right not to doubt.

You all knew that some things are worth dying for. One's country is worth dying for, and democracy is worth dying for, because it's the most deeply honorable form of government ever devised by man. All of you loved liberty. All of you were willing to fight tyranny, and you knew the people of your countries were behind you.

Source

Public Papers of the Presidents of the United States: Ronald Reagan.

SPEECH ON THE IRAN-CONTRA CONTROVERSY
MARCH 4, 1987

Waiting until several months after the Iran-Contra scandal broke, so that he could tell "the whole truth," Reagan admitted that there had been an "arms for hostages" trade and that he had been too passive in managing subordinates. He promised to reform decision making and oversight in his administration. None of the Iran-Contra investigations charged Reagan with actual wrongdoing.

———————

The power of the Presidency is often thought to reside within this Oval Office. Yet it doesn't rest here; it rests in you, the American people, and in your trust. Your trust is what gives a President his powers of leadership and his personal strength, and it's what I want to talk to you about this evening.

For the past 3 months, I've been silent on the revelations about Iran. And you must have been thinking: "Well, why doesn't he tell us what's happening? . . . Others of you, I guess, were thinking: "What's he doing hiding out in the White House?" Well, the reason I haven't spoken to you before now is this: You deserve the truth. And as frustrating as the waiting has been, I felt it was improper to come to you with sketchy reports. . . .

I've paid a price for my silence in terms of your trust and confidence. But I've had to wait, as you have, for the complete story. . . . I appointed a special review board, the Tower board, which took on the chore of pulling the truth together for me and getting to the bottom of things. It has now issued its findings. . . .

As you know, it's well-stocked with criticisms, . . . but I was very relieved to read this sentence: ". . . the Board is convinced that the President does indeed want the full story to be told." And that will continue to be my pledge to you as the other investigations go forward. . . .

I've studied the Board's report. Its findings are honest, convincing, and highly critical; and I accept them. . . .

First, let me say I take full responsibility for my own actions and for those of my administration. As angry as I may be about activities undertaken without my knowledge, I am still accountable for those activities. As disappointed as I may be in some who served me, I'm still the one who must answer to the American people for this behavior. And as personally distasteful as I find secret bank accounts and diverted funds—well, as the Navy would say, this happened on my watch.

Let's start with the part that is the most controversial. A few months ago I told the American people I did not trade arms for hostages. My heart and my best intentions still tell me that's true, but the facts and the evidence tell me it is not. As the Tower board reported, what began as a strategic opening to Iran deteriorated, in its implementation, into trading arms for hostages. This runs counter to my own beliefs, to administration policy, and to the original strategy we had in mind. There are reasons why it happened, but no excuses. It was a mistake. . . .

I let my personal concern for the hostages spill over into the geo-political strategy of reaching out to Iran. I asked so many questions about the hostages' welfare that I didn't ask enough about the specifics of the total Iran plan.

Let me say to the hostage families: We have not given up. We never will. And I promise you we'll use every legitimate means to free your loved ones from captivity. . . .

Now, another major aspect of the Board's findings regards the transfer of funds to the Nicaraguan contras. . . . As I told the Tower board, I didn't know about any diversion of funds to the contras. But as President, I cannot escape responsibility. . . .

I endorse . . . the Tower board's recommendations. In fact, I'm going beyond its recommendations so as to put the house in even better order.

I'm taking action in three basic areas: personnel, national security policy, and the process for making sure that the system works. First, personnel—I've brought in an accomplished and highly respected new team here at the White House. They bring new blood, new energy, and new credibility and experience. . . .

Second, in the area of national security policy, I have ordered the NSC to begin a comprehensive review of all covert operations. I have also directed that any covert activity be in support of clear policy objectives and in compliance with American values. . . .

I am also determined to make the congressional oversight process work. Proper procedures for consultation with the Congress will be followed, not only in letter but in spirit. . . .

Now, what should happen when you make a mistake is this: You take your knocks, you learn your lessons, and then you move on. . . . [T]he business of our country and our people must proceed. . . . [B]y the time you reach my age, you've made plenty of mistakes. And if you've lived your life properly—so, you learn. You put things in perspective. You pull your energies together. You change. You go forward.

SOURCE

Public Papers of the Presidents of the United States: Ronald Reagan.

Speech at the Brandenburg Gate, Berlin
June 12, 1987

At the Brandenburg Gate, Reagan both praised Gorbachev for their mutual progress in better relations and challenged him to go further and "tear down this wall." In a tug-of-war with some of his advisors, the president had insisted on keeping those words in the speech. Three years later, Reagan came back and swung a hammer at the Wall as it was being gradually dismantled.

Twenty-four years ago, President John F. Kennedy visited Berlin, speaking to the people of this city and the world. . . . We come to Berlin, we American Presidents, because it's our duty to speak, in this place, of freedom. . . .

To those listening in East Berlin, a special word: Although I cannot be with you, I address my remarks to you just as surely as to those standing here before me. For I join you, as I join your fellow countrymen in the West, in this firm, this unalterable belief: Es gibt nur ein Berlin. [There is only one Berlin.]

Behind me stands a wall that encircles the free sectors of this city, part of a vast system of barriers that divides the entire continent of Europe. . . . Yet it is here in Berlin where the wall emerges most clearly—here, cutting across your city, where the news photo and the television screen have imprinted this brutal division of a continent upon the mind of the world.

[A]s long as this scar of a wall is permitted to stand, it is not the German question alone that remains open, but the question of freedom for all mankind. Yet I do not come here to lament. For I find in Berlin a message of hope, even in the shadow of this wall, a message of triumph. . . . Where four decades ago there was rubble, today in West Berlin there is the greatest industrial output of any city in Germany. . . .

In the 1950's, Khrushchev predicted: "We will bury you." But in the West today, we see a free world that has achieved a level of prosperity and well-being unprecedented in all human history. In the Communist world, we see failure.... [T]he Soviet Union still cannot feed itself. After these four decades, then, there stands before the entire world one great and inescapable conclusion: Freedom leads to prosperity. Freedom replaces the ancient hatreds among the nations with comity and peace. Freedom is the victor.

And now the Soviets themselves may, in a limited way, be coming to understand the importance of freedom. We hear much from Moscow about a new policy of reform and openness.... Are these the beginnings of profound changes in the Soviet state? Or are they token gestures, intended to raise false hopes in the West?... We welcome change and openness; for we believe that freedom and security go together, that the advance of human liberty can only strengthen the cause of world peace.

There is one sign the Soviets can make that would be unmistakable, that would advance dramatically the cause of freedom and peace. General Secretary Gorbachev, if you seek peace, if you seek prosperity for the Soviet Union and Eastern Europe, if you seek liberalization: Come here to this gate! Mr. Gorbachev, open this gate! Mr. Gorbachev, tear down this wall!

To be sure, we in the West must resist Soviet expansion. So we must maintain defenses of unassailable strength. Yet we seek peace; so we must strive to reduce arms on both sides....

East and West do not mistrust each other because we are armed; we are armed because we mistrust each other. And our differences are not about weapons but about liberty. When President Kennedy spoke at the City Hall those 24 years ago, freedom was encircled, Berlin was under siege. And today, despite all the pressures upon this city, Berlin stands secure in its liberty. And freedom itself is transforming the globe....

In Europe, only one nation and those it controls refuse to join the community of freedom. Yet ... the Soviet Union faces a choice: It must make fundamental changes, or it will become obsolete. Today thus represents a moment of hope. We in the West stand ready to cooperate with the East to promote true openness, to break down barriers that separate people, to create a safer, freer world....

As I looked out a moment ago from the Reichstag, that embodiment of German unity, I noticed words crudely spray-painted upon the wall, perhaps by a young Berliner, "This wall will fall. Beliefs become reality." Yes, across Europe, this wall will fall. For it cannot withstand faith; it cannot withstand truth. The wall cannot withstand freedom.

SOURCE

Public Papers of the Presidents of the United States: Ronald Reagan.

REMARKS AT MOSCOW STATE UNIVERSITY
MAY 31, 1988

To the students at Moscow State, Reagan praised Gorbachev's efforts at internal reform and ending the Cold War. He quoted several Russian writers in a salute to liberty, and he urged his audience to take a personal role in bringing the Soviet Union into a world of free nations.

I want to talk not just of the realities of today but of the possibilities of tomorrow. . . . In the new economy, human invention increasingly makes physical resources obsolete. We're breaking through the material conditions of existence to a world where man creates his own destiny. . . .

But progress is not foreordained. The key is freedom—freedom of thought, freedom of information, freedom of communication. The . . . father of this university, Mikhail Lomonosov, knew that. "It is common knowledge," he said, "that the achievements of science are considerable and rapid, particularly once the yoke of slavery is cast off and replaced by the freedom of philosophy. . . . "

We are seeing the power of economic freedom spreading around the world. . . . At the same time, the growth of democracy has become one of the most powerful political movements of our age. . . . Throughout the world, free markets are the model for growth. Democracy is the standard by which governments are measured.

We Americans make no secret of our belief in freedom. . . . Go to any American town, . . . and you'll see dozens of churches, representing many different beliefs—in many places, synagogues and mosques—and you'll see families of every conceivable nationality worshiping together. Go into any schoolroom, and there you will see children being taught the

Declaration of Independence, that they are endowed by their Creator with certain unalienable rights. . . . Go into any courtroom, and there will preside an independent judge, beholden to no government power. . . . March in any demonstration, and there are many of them; the people's right of assembly is guaranteed in the Constitution and protected by the police. Go into any union hall, where the members know their right to strike is protected by law. . . . But freedom is more even than this. Freedom is the right to question and change the established way of doing things. . . .

America is a nation made up of hundreds of nationalities. Our ties to you are more than ones of good feeling; they're ties of kinship. In America, you'll find Russians, Armenians, Ukrainians, peoples from Eastern Europe and Central Asia. . . .

I hope you know I go on about these things not simply to extol the virtues of my own country but to speak to the true greatness of the heart and soul of your land. . . . [O]ne of the most eloquent contemporary passages on human freedom . . . . comes . . . from one of the greatest writers of the 20th century, Boris Pasternak, in the novel "Dr. Zhivago." He writes: "what has for centuries raised man above the beast is not the cudgel, but an inward music—the irresistible power of unarmed truth."

Today the world looks expectantly to signs of change, steps toward greater freedom in the Soviet Union. We watch and we hope as we see positive changes taking place. . . .

But change would not mean rejection of the past. . . . [P]ositive change must be rooted in traditional values—in the land, in culture, in family and community—and it must take its life from the eternal things, from the source of all life, which is faith. Such change will lead to new understandings, new opportunities, to a broader future in which the tradition is not supplanted but finds its full flowering. That is the future beckoning to your generation. . . .

Just a few years ago, few would have imagined the progress our two nations have made together. . . . If this globe is to live in peace and prosper, if it is to embrace all the possibilities of the technological revolution, then nations must renounce, once and for all, the right to an expansionist foreign policy. . . .

[N]o mother would ever willingly sacrifice her sons for territorial gain, for economic advantage, for ideology. A people free to choose will always choose peace. . . .

Your generation is living in one of the most exciting, hopeful times in Soviet history. It is a time when the first breath of freedom stirs the air and the heart beats to the accelerated rhythm of hope, when the accumulated spiritual energies of a long silence yearn to break free. . . .

[W]e're hopeful that the promise of reform will be fulfilled. In this Moscow spring, this May 1988, we may be allowed that hope: that freedom . . . will blossom forth at last in the rich fertile soil of your people and culture. We may be allowed to hope that the marvelous sound of a new openness will keep rising through, ringing through, leading to a new world of reconciliation, friendship, and peace.

Source

Public Papers of the Presidents of the United States: Ronald Reagan.

DOCUMENT **10**

FAREWELL ADDRESS TO THE AMERICAN PEOPLE
JANUARY 11, 1989

Very few presidential farewell addresses are memorable, but Reagan's was.
Besides the usual bragging about achievements and warning of the dangers
of big government, there was the invocation of America's founding and its
boundless future that was a Reagan trademark. "America is freedom," he
said, "and freedom is special and rare."

This is the 34th time I'll speak to you from the Oval Office and the last.
We've been together 8 years now, and soon it'll be time for me to go.

[T]here were two great triumphs, two things that I'm proudest of. One is
the economic recovery, in which the people of America created—and
filled—19 million new jobs. The other is the recovery of our morale.
America is respected again in the world and looked to for leadership. . . .

Ours was the first revolution in the history of mankind that truly reversed
the course of government, and with three little words: "We the People" . . .
tell the government what to do; it doesn't tell us. . . .

I hope we have once again reminded people that man is not free unless
government is limited. . . .

Nothing is less free than pure communism—and yet we have, the past
few years, forged a satisfying new closeness with the Soviet Union. I've been
asked if this isn't a gamble, and my answer is no because we're basing our
actions not on words but deeds. . . .

We must keep up our guard, but we must also continue to work together
to lessen and eliminate tension and mistrust. My view is that President
Gorbachev is different from previous Soviet leaders. . . .

I've been asked if I have any regrets. Well, I do. The deficit is one. . . . I've thought a bit of the "shining city upon a hill." The phrase comes from John Winthrop, who wrote it to describe the America he imagined. And how stands the city on this winter night? More prosperous, more secure, and happier than it was 8 years ago. . . . And she's still a beacon, still a magnet for all who must have freedom, for all the pilgrims from all the lost places who are hurtling through the darkness, toward home. . . .

All in all, not bad—not bad at all.

Source

Public Papers of the Presidents of the United States: Ronald Reagan.

NOTE ON SOURCES

Due to considerations of length, the notes in *Ronald Reagan: Champion of Conservative America* are limited mostly to direct attribution of quotes. Listed below is a selection of key primary and secondary sources on the life, career, and rhetoric of Ronald Reagan that proved most helpful in the writing of this book. Anyone wishing to examine Reagan's life story can start with any of these books. A much fuller selection is available on the book's website.

Anderson, Martin. *Revolution: The Reagan Legacy.* New York: Harcourt, Brace, 1988.

Barrett, Lawrence. *Gambling with History: Ronald Reagan in the White House.* Garden City, NY: Doubleday, 1983.

Boyarsky, Bill. *The Rise of Ronald Reagan.* New York: Random House, 1968.

Bunch, William. *Tear Down This Myth: How the Reagan Legacy Has Distorted Our Politics and Haunts Our Future.* New York: Free Press, 2009.

Busch, Andrew. *Reagan's Victory: The Presidential Election of 1980 and the Rise of the Right.* Lawrence, KS: University of Kansas Press, 2005.

Cannon, Lou. *Governor Reagan: His Rise to Power.* New York: Public Affairs, 2003.

Cannon, Lou. *President Reagan: The Role of a Lifetime.* New York: Public Affairs, 2000.

Colacello, Bob. *Ronnie and Nancy: The Road to the White House.* New York: Warner Books, 2004.

Combs, Dick. *Inside the Soviet Alternate Universe.* University Park: Penn State University Press, 2008.

Dallek, Matthew. *The Right Moment: Ronald Reagan's First Victory and the Decisive Turning Point in American Politics.* New York: Free Press, 2000.

Dallek, Robert. *Ronald Reagan: The Politics of Symbolism.* Cambridge: Harvard University Press, 1999.

Davis, Patti. *The Way I See It: An Autobiography.* New York: Putnam, 1992.

Deaver, Michael. *A Different Drummer: My Thirty Years With Ronald Reagan.* New York: Harper Collins, 2001.

Diggins, John. *Ronald Reagan: Fate, Freedom, and the Making of History.* New York: W.W. Norton, 2008.

Drew, Elizabeth. *Portrait of an Election: The 1980 Presidential Campaign.* New York: Simon and Shuster, 1981.

Edwards, Anne. *Early Reagan: The Rise to Power.* New York: William Morrow, 1987.

Eliot, Mark. *Reagan, The Hollywood Years.* New York: Harmony Books, 2008.

Evans, Thomas W. *The Education of Ronald Reagan: The General Electric Years and the Untold Story of His Conversion to Conservatism.* New York: Columbia University Press, 2008.

Fischer, Beth. *The Reagan Reversal: Foreign Policy and the End of the Cold War.* Columbia, MO: University of Missouri Press, 1997.

Fitzgerald, Frances. *Way Out There in the Blue: Reagan, Star Wars, and the End of the Cold War.* New York: Simon & Schuster, 2000.

Garthoff, Raymond L. *The Great Transition: American-Soviet Relations and the End of the Cold War.* Washington, DC: Brookings Institution, 1994.

Germond, Jack W. and Jules Witcover. *Blue Smoke and Mirrors: How Reagan Won and Why Carter Lost the Election of 1980.* New York: Viking Press, 1981.

Goldman, Peter, *et al. The Quest for the Presidency, 1984.* New York: Bantam Books, 1985.

Haig, Alexander. *Caveat: Realism, Reagan, and Foreign Policy.* New York: Macmillan, 1984.

Hayward, Steven F. *The Age of Reagan: The Fall of the Old Liberal Order, 1964–1980.* Roseville, CA: Forum, 2001.

Hayward, Steven F. *The Age of Reagan: The Conservative Counter-Revolution, 1980–1989.* New York: Crown Forum, 2010.

Johnson, Haynes. *Sleepwalking through History: America in the Reagan Years.* New York: W.W. Norton, 1991.

Kengor, Paul. *The Crusader: Ronald Reagan and the Fall of Communism.* New York: Harper Collins, 2006.

Kengor, Paul and Peter Schweizer, ed. *The Reagan Presidency: Assessing the Man and His Legacy.* Lanham, MD: Rowman and Littlefield, 2005.

Lettow, Paul F. *Ronald Reagan and His Quest to Abolish Nuclear Weapons.* New York: Random House, 2005.

Matlock, Jack F. *Reagan and Gorbachev: How the Cold War Ended.* New York: Random House, 2004.

Meese, Ed. *With Reagan: The Inside Story.* Washington, DC: Regnery, 1992.

Moldea, Dan. *Dark Victory: Ronald Reagan, MCA, and the Mob.* New York: Viking, 1987.

Morris, Edmund. *Dutch: A Memoir of Ronald Reagan.* New York: Random House, 1999.

Reagan, Maureen. *First Father, First Daughter: A Memoir.* Boston: Little, Brown, 1989.

Reagan, Michael. *On the Outside Looking In.* New York: Zebra Books, 1988.

Reagan, Nancy. *My Turn, The Memoirs of Nancy Reagan.* New York: Random House, 1989.

Reagan, Ronald. *An American Life.* New York: Simon and Schuster, 1990.

Reagan, Ronald. *Where's the Rest of Me? Ronald Reagan Tells His Own Story.* New York: Dell Publishing Co., 1965.

Reeves, Richard. *President Reagan: The Triumph of Imagination.* New York: Simon & Schuster, 2005.

Regan, Donald T. *For the Record: From Wall Street to Washington.* New York: Harcourt Brace, 1988.

Schweitzer, Peter. *Reagan's War: The Epic Story of His Forty-Year Struggle and Final Triumph over Communism.* New York: Doubleday, 2002.

Shirley, Craig. *Rendezvous with Destiny: Ronald Reagan and the Campaign That Changed America.* Wilmington, DE: ISI Books, 2011.

Shultz, George. *Turmoil and Triumph: My Years as Secretary of State.* New York: Scribner's, 1993.

Stockman, David A. *The Triumph of Politics: How the Reagan Revolution Failed.* New York: Harper and Row, 1986.

Tygiel, Jules. *Ronald Reagan and the Triumph of American Conservatism.* New York: Pearson Longman, 2d. ed., 2006.

Vaughn, Stephen. *Ronald Reagan in Hollywood.* New York: Cambridge University Press, 1994.

Weinberger, Caspar. *Fighting for Peace: Seven Critical Years in the Pentagon.* New York: Warner Books, 1990.

Wilentz, Sean. *The Age of Reagan: A History, 1974–2008.* New York: Harper and Row, 2008.

Wills, Garry. *Reagan's America: Innocents at Home.* New York: Doubleday, 1987.

INDEX